Contents

This book is wholly dedicated to two 'life enhancers'.

To Julie, my wife, without whom, no book.
And to Thomas Bernard Robinson OBE, without whom . . .

Preface

This book has been adapted from *The Secrets of Effective Direct Mail* and has been updated, revised and restructured in the process.

The comprehensive original version contained almost everything I know about direct mail. Its purpose was to tell all about direct mail—not only the practical aspects but all those things that set it in position within the remarkable direct marketing spectrum as one of the greatest advertising and selling methods of all time.

This shorter version has a more down to earth mission. It aims to tell you not *everything* you should know about direct mail, but *what* you should know about direct mail in order to put together a highly effective and competent campaign or mailing. This is the basic hands-on advice you need when the decision is made: 'OK, let's do it. Let's send out a mailing.'

Nevertheless, if you view direct mail in isolation from the other effective and powerful direct marketing techniques, then you might, as they say, cut off your nose to spite your face. Or, perhaps more pleasantly put, lose out!

In 'Secrets' I took the opportunity to remind readers that much nonsense has been spoken and written about the 'simple act of selling'. Still more about advertising. And a whole myth has been built around the great god, Marketing.

While there is, of course, some fundamental truth and value in much of what is taught on these subjects, too few have yet started to worship the new alternative—Direct Marketing—and spread its gospel.

In the last few years, that which I describe as 'an alternative' has taken shape, formalised and grown so fast that many, who should know, confidently predict it will take over.

Direct marketing will certainly take over. The 'new alternative' is already perceived as the ultimate process. It improves and becomes more sophisticated as each day passes. It uses the latest technology to propel the selling process back decades, to the days when quality of relationship between the producer or purveyor and the customer was caring, individual and vital. It is both an art and a science; but above all else, it is the future.

One extra comment for women readers. Inevitably from time to time I have, for the sake of plain English or simple sentence construction, opted for the male gender. I trust my anticipation of your understanding over this will be justified. If not, my sincere apologies. Your compensation will be found amongst these pages where you will learn that women usually make much better direct marketers than men.

Acknowledgements

In the original 'Secrets' we gratefully acknowledged three people who deserve the same again here. They are:

Mike Adams, whose faith in 'Secrets' and the whole concept of The John Fraser-Robinson Direct Marketing Series has been rewarded by the sales: and to whom I owe a debt of thanks for many things over many years.

Tamsin Overstall, who researched the first book so carefully for me, discovered direct marketing into the bargain, and for all her hard work and trouble had her name wrongly spelt in the original work. Sorry, Tamsin!

And Julie Fraser-Robinson, about whom the original said that she 'listened, talked, discussed, argued, encouraged and added. And constantly cared and supported. A very generous wife.' She still does, and she still is.

'DOLLAR FOR DOLLAR, NO ADVERTISING MEDIUM WILL RETURN MORE TO YOUR BUSINESS THAN DIRECT MAIL'

(Murray Raphel)

1

Introducing the worst kept secret in the marketing world

It's no secret these days that direct mail has a lot going for it. Indeed, as a major (if not *the* major) player in the direct marketing arena, it is well worthy of your time and attention. However, before we narrow down to the focused topic of direct mail, we ought to give some thought to the crown of which it is the jewel: direct marketing.

THE SEVEN 'A'S OF DIRECT MARKETING ARE ALSO THE SEVEN 'AYES' OF DIRECT MARKETING

Each 'aye' offers a sound, powerful reason why you should choose the direct marketing approach to advertising.

1   It's *accountable*, down to the last penny. You can see what works and what doesn't; what is cost-effective and what isn't.
2   It has the *added value* of the advertising effect, included at no extra cost, on top of the bankable business it will do for you.
3   It is *answer-back* advertising. We deal in dialogues, not monologues. As a result, we make contacts and create relationships.
4   Direct marketing is *allegiance* advertising. We command loyalty by creating friends as well as customers. We understand individual service. We give promises and we keep them. How do you know? Because we *always* guarantee it.
5   Direct marketing is *automated* advertising. You can draw on

the latest technology to take you back to the days when service, recognition and individual attention were the watchwords of success. And—surprise!—they still are: the more so, because they're all too rare these days.

6   Direct marketing is *appropriate* advertising. It yields the potential of tight, close targeting. You gather, hold, review and appraise—all *before* you approach the customer or prospect.

7   And lastly, direct marketing is *action* advertising. It goes for the ultimate. It sells. What better action is there? By putting across attractive propositions, it inspires the prospects into action.

To develop these points, let me ask you seven questions. I'll make the whole process less arduous by giving you the answers too! Well, at least *my* answers.

1   Why spend your money on ordinary advertising when you can buy *accountable* advertising?

The fact is, that the advertising you will buy as part of your *direct* marketing process has, or should have, a clear sales objective: whether you seek to generate sales *per se* or stimulate leads for a salesforce to follow up, or whether you wish to build traffic for your retailers, agents, dealers or distributors to convert to sales— you can know precisely what the sales result is.

Quite naturally, if you are advertising to achieve complete sales you have two perfect yardsticks:

1   The *cost per reply*—that is, the cost of the advertising divided by the number of replies.

2   The *cost per sale*—that is, the cost of the advertising divided by the number of sales.

Both of these can be readily related to a budget or, better, to a marketing allowance per unit sale.

This is a discipline quite foreign to those who work in conventional advertising. Have Bounty ever explained, to whoever writes their storyboard, what it means to have that one extra shot requiring another two half-naked beauties sucking sensually on 'the product' as they wander, nymph-like along the white tropical sand. It is actually going to require sales of a further million or so packs. My economics, not theirs, I hasten to add!

In contrast, the direct marketing creative director knows about such economics. He or she knows that the more that is spent on the advertising, the more the target responses move up in proportion. Moreover, no self-respecting creative in direct marketing will be happy working on a cost per enquiry. The sale is not complete yet. And therefore the job is not done.

One of the major influences that lies within the creative area is the *quality* of reply. I make this point since it is a quite common misconception that the creative is the major contributor to the *quantity* of replies. This is not so. Although it is difficult to assign direct proportion to the typical value of the creative contribution, I would estimate it at between 25 and 35 per cent.

I find that, in terms of the cost per enquiry, creative is less influential in the overall mix of influences; whereas, in terms of the cost per sale, its relevance is much heightened.

No matter whether your advertising seeks to sell in total, or to generate an initial response for follow-up—and no matter whether you intend to convert to sale by salesforce or by one or other of the marketing media—you will find it is generally the creative that most significantly affects the ratio of enquiry to sale; in other words, the conversion rate.

The point of this becomes clear when you consider the method of calculating the cost per sale. And this I commend as the most appropriate short-term (or single campaign) measure of your accountable advertising.

$$\text{Cost per sale} = \frac{\text{Cost of advertising} + \text{Cost of conversion}}{\text{Number of ultimate sales*}}$$

* Ultimate sales are those that stick. After returns. After money-back guarantee claims. After any 'cooling-off' periods. In other words, when the money is safely and irrevocably in the bank.

It is vital that, as near as possible, a true 'cost of conversion' is entered: the true cost of your salesperson's time; the ten visits to get four sales that make your 40 per cent conversion rate; or whatever. Also, the full cost of mailing out brochures and samples to all 1400 enquirers, even though only 350 will become cash-in-the-bank customers, to achieve your 25 per cent conversion rate.

The creative approach is in clear focus. Creative that over-excites, over-sells or promises the undeliverable will result in a high response, but a low conversion. It will thereby increase the proportion of sales calls or post-enquiry conversion packs, as well as the amount of front-end advertising required to achieve your sales targets. If ever there was a commonsense argument for honesty in advertising, this must be it. The economics reinforce the ethics.

Is it any wonder that most direct response television seems to adopt creative requiring simple rostrum camera studio production? Anything more adventurous could add 35 per cent to the sales targets.

This accountability—the capability for certain knowledge as to the effects of your advertising, not by campaign, but by individual ad—forms part of my rationale. Indeed, a cornerstone.

2   Why spend your money on ordinary advertising when you can have *added-value* advertising?

The previous point takes care of the direct response part of direct response advertising. If you've got it right, it will already have paid for itself before you reap the added advantage of the pure advertising aspect.

In other words, as well as accountable advertising, it is also added-value advertising. After all, is it likely that those who responded are the only people who read, were influenced by, or simply noted, your ad? Indeed not. Many more will have read the copy. Many, many more will have scanned your pictures and caught your headline just as if it were an ordinary ad.

Direct marketing, including all aspects of direct response advertising, offers you accountable advertising with the added value of the 'free' advertising beyond the sales you achieve.

Powerful stuff.

3   Why spend your money on ordinary advertising when you can have *answer-back* advertising?

Direct marketing ads—whatever the media in which they appear—are designed to promote a dialogue. This means that they have clearly defined, but often quite different, tactical objectives to classical advertising. This is amply demonstrated by classical ads that incorporate, for instance, money-off coupons. I see a money-off coupon as a sales promotion device. It is clearly there to promote a single sale, quite often a trial of a new product or sampling of an existing product, in the hope that there is a long-term residual sales increase as a result of customer satisfaction with the product or service.

Yet often the existence of the coupon is, from the copy platform, largely or totally ignored. In most cases (and somewhat cynically, I suspect by accident) the graphics team get it right: the coupon stands out like a sore thumb.

Examine, if you will, how the desire to create answer-back advertising is different.

Monologue advertising has the simple objective of dealing with 'top of the mind' reactions from the consumer: corporate image; brand awareness; new product information; image advertising.

Dialogue advertising is very different. Equally simple, . . . but very different. It makes the advertiser approachable. It invites the reader to respond or participate, to visit, to ring up, or to drop a line.

This desire to create a dialogue radically affects creativity and choice of media. For example, direct response posters are a rarity. Careless copy, or tempting graphics may promote graffiti, but rarely any other sort of dialogue, for it is a fact that posters are limited in the information they can successfully impart. Although there have been exceptions, it is accepted they are not a good direct response medium.

Direct marketing media selection and creativity tends towards those that, for example, can offer a response card or coupon, or can provide a Freephone or 0800 number, and therefore lend themselves not only to offer the dialogue, but also to create the desire for it.

Monologues are a complete communication. They are a beginning and an end. Dialogues are potentially the beginnings of relationships, from which sales are a more certain result.

4   Why spend your money on ordinary advertising when you can have *allegiance* advertising?

It is very, very rare indeed for any direct marketer to be in business for a one time quick buck. It is a fundamental of direct marketing that there is the Ten-X factor of the existing customer.

It is my experience that, as a rule, it is at least ten times more cost-effective to repeat sell an existing customer than it is to seek out a new one.

That can be twice the order value at one-fifth the advertising cost, or perhaps five times the order value at twice the response— or any combination of levels. The strange thing is that, whatever the ratio of cost to effectiveness, it is quite extraordinary just how frequently the resulting figures show a ten times more cost-effective result.

And, as many direct marketers have learned, the more repeat sales that are made with customers, the more loyal, friendly and willing they become. Which is why the whole concept of RFM analysis is so important.

RFM stands for *recency*, *frequency* and *monetary value*. Even at the present time, I am aware that this topic is an entirely new subject within a subject. Yet the relevance and value of RFM is such that it must be covered.

Direct marketing experience, particularly with mail order,

indicates that RFM analysis can so greatly enhance targeting of both the audience and the message, that it can most dramatically improve cost-effectiveness.

Recency indicates the time when a customer last purchased. Frequency, as it more readily suggests, is the number of purchases across given time spans. And monetary value, the third indicator, is where we look at the total spend of the customer and the spend per sale, and patterns thereof.

From such analysis, customers can be clustered together into common types and the timing, sales value and nature of offer can be determined to find the most suitable future path. Moreover, the individual sales message, particularly in the case of telemarketing and direct mail, can be readily adapted in view of the historical experience.

None of this information is, after all, anything more than would be used, often subjectively or instinctively, by a good salesperson. But then I hold strong views that direct marketing is not, and never will be, anything more than the simple application of professional salesmanship; but in its purest sense—and often without a visiting salesperson. This is a point that will re-emerge later since direct marketing is also of quite exceptional power in the tactical support of a salesforce, not just for prospecting but in the development of a long-term customer relationship.

Strive as I do to find fresh ways of presenting ideas to audiences at presentations around the world, there is one that constantly defies improvement . . . and I hope will position the Ten-X factor in your mind.

LET'S CLIMB THE LOYALTY LADDER

The Loyalty Ladder is the original concept of a salesman called Ray Consada (I hope I have his name right!). It was picked up and worked on by Murray Raphel and Ray Considine and is published in their book *The Great Brain Robbery*. Let's first take a look at the diagram (Fig. 1.1) and then I'll talk you through it.

The thoughts developed by Murray and Ray explain that the

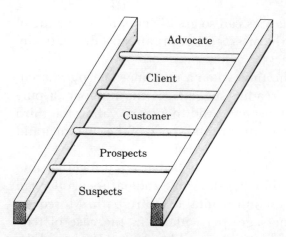

Figure 1.1   The Loyalty Ladder

world is made up of people who wander around blissfully unaware of your existence.

The Loyalty Ladder theory acknowledges that your advertising—direct response or other—raises the knowledge and interest level of significant numbers of *suspects* who therefore become *prospects*.

Once the prospects have identified themselves, the unchained might of your sales effort is directed at them. But who can challenge the unassailable wizardry of your sales team? Not many! So some of the prospects become *customers*.

It's a sad but accurate thought that so many at this point run around, leaping for joy, content that they have made a sale. What blind fools! The Ten-X factor confirms the increased ease with which a repeat sale will be forthcoming. And as success yields another sale, so too must we find a new league for the customer to belong to. And a more generous name to call them by. How about *clients*, says Murray—his distinction of a multi-purchase customer.

And lastly, inevitably, on the top of the pile are the *advocates*, so called because they're so enraptured and enchanted with their relationship with you that they pay you the quite extraordinary and invaluable compliment of getting involved with your advertising. They do it by *word of mouth*, which is not only the cheapest but, I suggest, also the most effective 'advertising' it is possible to buy—containing implicit and often actual endorsement of the product.

The snag, of course, is that you can't buy word of mouth. You have to earn it. The benefit is, that not only does word of mouth carry a built-in testimonial value, it also depends on the satisfactory and very cost-effective result of the Ten-X philosophy. This recognises that you have by now enjoyed a repeat-selling relationship with your customer, which should have been enormously profitable. Adequate compensation for the fact that no money on earth will buy word of mouth. You really have to earn it.

It is an indisputable process. A well-recognised feature of the sustained use of direct marketing is that it breeds an amazing level of loyalty from customers and thus truly deserves the description of 'allegiance advertising'.

5   Why spend your money on ordinary advertising when you can buy *automated* advertising?

Direct marketing flourishes in our hi-tech age. It lends itself so naturally to computers, laser printers, interactive electronic media and such things. This is happening in parallel with the fact that what is hi-tech one day is comparatively low-tech the next. Take the laser printer for example. Once, and not long ago, this was the fodder of only the rich and patient; it was mechanically Heath Robinson in its paper-handling technology and had a base price of £250 000 or so. And, what seems like only months later, is now more reliable with less down-time and is available in desktop form for less than £1000.

We only have to listen to the language of direct marketing to realise that it could only exist during, alongside or because of (I suspect it's equal doses of all three of those) the computer age. For example, database marketing, electronic media and telephone marketing too. Even an apparently innocent subject such as off-the-page advertising will undoubtedly reveal the value of computer-aided media selection and results' analysis. So much to do with direct marketing benefits from the processing and number-crunching capabilities of the computer.

But I beg you to remember that each record processed, or each number crunched, is at least a human being. But, far more important, it is also a potential or existing customer.

It's vital that you understand that automated advertising is a real and immensely deep well of opportunity for you. You must never regard it as dealing with cost saving or productivity, because, if you do, you'll shrivel, not grow. Then the most exciting sales opportunity to come along in the history of marketing will unceremoniously pass by your business.

It's a major mistake to view automated advertising as a way of maintaining today's standards for less money. In fact, I suggest you let automated advertising set tomorrow's objectives on yesterday's standards at today's prices.

LET ME EXPLAIN ABOUT 'MY BUSINESS'

Remember that old notion—the customer is king? It suggests, among other things, that success is assured if you dedicate yourself to customer service. I don't have a problem with this notion. In fact, I have always tried to live up to it. It's some of the places I go to where they haven't read the books!

The philosophy of 'customer is king' requires the virtues of something we all already know. We know because we like it when it happens to us. And it doesn't happen often enough.

We all like to be remembered. We all like to be cared for. We all like recognition. We love good service. And bask in personal attention.

And when you feel this happening, you have found what *you* can call 'My Business'.

Take my London hotel for example.

A few years ago, I took a suite in a hotel on Park Lane. I was attending the British Direct Marketing Awards. It wasn't a good night for me. It was a GREAT night. Probably a once-in-a-lifetime night.

I collected six or seven certificates, five trophies and the coveted Gold Award. For me, a real event since it made me the only person to have received the 'Gold' twice in the entire history of the event.

The odd bottle of champagne was seen to pass the table. But most of it stayed right there. Around 4 a.m. I staggered into my hotel. I was showered with greetings and congratulations. There and then it seemed that everyone on night duty was joining in.

When I checked out around lunchtime I made a point of thanking the manager for his kind handwritten note, which had been delivered on my breakfast tray.

Let a year go by. A year, I have to say, when I think I only used the hotel once between my 'Gold' night and today.

How do you think I felt when the front desk clerk greeted me with this:

'Mr Fraser-Robinson! We are so pleased to have you back with us again. We checked with your secretary, and she said it was Awards night. So we've given you the same suite as last year. It seemed so lucky for you.'

And more along those lines.

How did I feel? Wouldn't you make that 'my hotel'?

So what is this? Salesmanship? Professionalism? Excellence?

Yes, it is undoubtedly all of those things. It's also note-taking, record-keeping, and a great deal of belief in the very highest standards of relationships.

Have you noticed how people accolade professionals? You go to *the* grocer. You go to *the* supermarket. But you talk about '*my* accountant', '*my* solicitor'. Even the ones you don't like: '*my* bank manager.' You decide to 'own' these people because they are important to you. Or, rather, because they've made themselves important to you. Or even, influential in your life.

So I know I've made it when a client says 'JFR is my direct marketing man!'—I still have a job to do when they say 'I use JFR'. Personally, I 'use' a toilet.

My advice is to go for a 'my' position in the lives of your customers. No matter whether you're a (my) charity, a (my) jeweller or a (my) supermarket. They *owe* you when they *own* you, because you've made yourself theirs.

There's nothing particularly new in this thought. Pendulums swing. And this one is on its way back. Ask IBM. Or . . . . (can *you* write your name here?).

A PERSONAL PRINCIPLE

Before I move on to my next topic, I should like to place before you a personal business principle. Link this principle to direct marketing and you will have all the success you seek. Probably more.

THE OBJECT OF A BUSINESS IS NOT TO MAKE MONEY

THE OBJECT OF A BUSINESS IS TO SERVE ITS CUSTOMERS

THE *RESULT* IS TO MAKE MONEY

6   Why spend money on ordinary advertising when you can buy *appropriate* advertising?

It was a well-made joke at the time that agency folk in direct marketing have never worried about being in the junk mail business. After all, look how well the Burger Chains have done with junk food.

What makes such mail 'junk' to its recipients is the lack of appropriateness to them, their lifestyles and their work, interests or pastimes.

So try this one out for size.

The more a communication relates to us, the more interesting we find it. The more interesting we find something, the more likely we are to read it.

The more we read of something, the more likely we are to be persuaded by it. The more we are persuaded by something, the more likely we are to want to adopt it. The more we want to adopt something, the more we want to . . .

You're right . . . we want to buy it.

Did you ever buy anything from junk mail? Of course you didn't. The stuff you didn't buy from—that's junk. But the ones that hit home, well—they were quite interesting (remember those 'I did get *one* the other day that . . .' conversations?). Junk isn't interesting. And the reverse is true. If it's interesting, it isn't junk. It's appropriate to you. Or put it another way: the advertiser got the targeting right. As more and more direct marketing becomes database-driven, so it increases the opportunity to improve the appropriateness of the advertising—its relevance—to the recipient.

The more you know about a customer or prospect, the more you can understand. The more you understand about people, the more closely you can relate to them. And the more successful the potential of those relationships will be.

As this book moves nearer its specialist subject, so you will notice that direct mail—far from being junk mail any longer—can be, should be and must be relevant and appropriate, or it will fail. People will vote with their rubbish bins.

On the other hand, it does pay to examine why so much direct mail will go that way, and why so many people claim that they throw it away. Why do they say that? Are they reluctant to admit that they are influenced or, worse, convinced by it?

I don't think so. They say they throw it away because that's what they do. The fact is that direct mail—like most direct marketing media—is a low-response medium. Many more people will reject than respond. I have had clients overjoyed with a half of 1 per cent response. So it makes sense that you are likely to talk with, perhaps, up to 99 times more people who weren't interested enough, than the one who was. And you'll recall that, if it's not interesting, it's junk. There's not a lot in between.

Don't concern yourself with the fact that it's a very rare exception when you find more people who respond than those who don't. On the other hand, there's no reason why it shouldn't be a goal!

Direct marketing—information-based hi-tech advertising—

enables you to make your advertising more appropriate. And, consistently, no more so than with direct mail. That's one reason why an ad in a national daily will be successful in pulling an order from 1 in 2000, when direct mail can be expected to pull at 20 or 30 times higher. The indisputable fact that it can, and will, says a lot about the power of direct mail.

One strength of most direct marketing media and messages is that they so often provide you with the opportunity to be more appropriate. And, therefore, more effective.

7   Why spend your money on ordinary advertising when you can buy *action* advertising?

Direct marketing is about action—action in the form of sales, or action in the form of sales enquiries.

Direct marketing should therefore be provocative. It should provoke action. It must be powerful, persuasive and exciting enough to arouse desire in people. It is not just that they should be aware of you, but also to make you more prominent in their minds—to think well of you, or to recognise you. Those simple tasks fall into the role of ordinary advertising. Direct marketing must be stronger still.

And here's one reason why it is so strong.

UNDERSTAND THE POWER OF A PROPOSITION

Nearly all direct marketing ads include a proposition. After all, if you want to rouse someone to take the action you want, there is nothing like an attractive or acceptable proposition to do it.

We all need bones to chew on. But if you want response, then you must give me something to chew over, something to say 'Yes' to.

Make me an offer. If it's a good one, I'll accept.

Compare this concept with ordinary advertising and you'll see that most ordinary advertising is passive. It may still be persuasive—but passive. It may place the message in your head, but it isn't explicit enough. It arrogantly assumes that you'll react. But you don't of course, not usually.

Every advertising message should make an offer. It's the offer that suggests the action. And if the offer is conveyed thoughtfully, it will more than suggest action, it will close the sale.

Offer has, of course, two meanings. There is an offer, in the sense of a proposition. Take my advice: include one. But also, there is an offer in the sense of a 'special offer' available to you. And very potent it is too. We all like to receive a little extra: something for nothing; something to reward us for placing our business with you.

THE PENDULUM IS SWINGING NOW

Most advertisers have been using elements of the direct marketing process for years. Find me a business-to-business marketer who hasn't used direct mail; a charity that hasn't tried house-to-house distribution; a language course that hasn't tried loose inserts; or a newspaper without telesales. But direct marketing, (I suppose) being below-the-line, has historically been the province of the client.

It was the client who organised and controlled things. But now that has all changed. Today, more and more ads carry coupons (which incidentally does nothing towards turning an ad into a direct response ad: it only makes them ads with coupons).

What's happened is that more and more people are taking direct marketing seriously, since they've already done some of it and they know it works. They've got the figures, the costs, the results and the sales to prove it.

BUT WILL IT EVER MAKE THE MAJORITY OF ALL MARKETING?

Certainly. I've predicted that 65 or 75 per cent is likely. And not then as a total of people who opt in full to choose direct marketing as the only way they will distribute. I think by far the greatest majority will find uses for both.

And why not? There's plenty of room. It certainly doesn't have to be a one-or-the-other situation. There will always be a place for classical marketing and advertising. There will always be a place for direct marketing and direct response advertising. And there will always be a place for PR and sales promotion.

However, what is absolutely inevitable is that direct marketing *will* take over as the place where the majority of advertising money goes. More clients will look towards having a direct marketing agency, a classical advertising agency and a PR agency as standard. In that order . . . until the eventual fusion comes.

So I don't envisage this causing huge withdrawals from television or the national dailies. Rather that the use to which advertising is put—its objectives—will change.

COMPUTERISED CARING—EFFECTIVE USE OF 'ACTIVE DATABASE ATTACK' TO ENSURE POWERFUL AND FULFILLING CUSTOMER RELATIONSHIPS

At first thought, it probably sounds unlikely. Even the very words 'computerised caring' seem almost contradictory. And 'active database attack' doesn't sound very caring, does it?

For a moment, let's forget all thoughts of computers and consider these basic and proven concepts which add vital weight and emphasis to our beliefs and suggest a whole *raison d'être*.

1   The *nearer* you can get to *understanding and providing* what the buyer wants, *the more likely* you are to *make a sale*.
2   The *more* you get to *know* a customer's *needs* the more you can line up your commodities to provide a *second* sale thus leading to further *regular sales*.
3   The more in *parallel* to any single customer's *needs* you keep your commodity range—what you have to sell—the *longer* the relationship with that single customer is likely to be.

This is no smart theory. It's why all good salespeople 'work their book'. Often their 'little black book'.

Contacts, phone numbers, the age of their kids, birthdays—all sorts of useful information that the salesperson uses to keep in mind the buyer's situation.

This recognises something that all effective salespeople know. Sales are made through delivering material and emotional satisfaction.

What does this mean? It means simply that academics may be able to define marketing as the 'process of moving goods from the seller to the buyer' but that won't work with selling. I call it the 'simple act of selling'; a focus of the human interaction that is the bedrock of decision. The decision to purchase.

Selling is like a reverse prism through which one feeds the whole spectrum of purchasing influences and out of the other side shines the pure white light of success.

So you can divide and examine the elements of influence on a sale—by all means price, quality, reliability, service, delivery, etc. But you must not forget—whichever marketing process you use—that selling is mostly a social, human interaction. Even mail order selling.

Of equal importance to the achievement of sale, are the emotional qualities: confidence, truth, respect, etc.

Two salesmen met in a pub. One had just returned from a holiday in Spain. 'It was a great holiday,' he said, 'and all thanks to this.' He tossed a black plastic pocket book onto the table. On the front he had written one word: 'CONTACTS'.

The second salesman smiled. 'I love Spain too. In fact I own a villa there. And I do agree with you. It's all thanks to this.' He placed his notebook carefully alongside the other. Clearly he had enscribed on its front cover one word: 'FRIENDS'.

I hate the whole misnomer of the phrase 'business-to-business'. The fact is that one business does *not* buy from another. One business does *not* sell to another. *People* buy and sell.

I suggested earlier that the machinery of direct marketing— the qualities of automated advertising—enables it to shave decades off the way people buy and sell in today's environment.

By this I mean that the direct marketing store is close to the old corner store. It's personal and friendly—which is great, because I observe the world getting less personal and less friendly. This might seem strange when you think that although it is allegedly 'direct', it frequently involves not one single moment where two human beings—the seller and the buyer—actually meet.

We are selling at arm's length. Therefore, what I am talking about now is shortening the arm. This, too, involves the material and the emotional. When we look at the 'simple act of selling' and the resources available, we realise that if a third salesman—a direct marketing salesman—had joined the other two in the pub, he too could have placed a pocketbook on the table. And also on the cover of his book there would be enscribed one word. It would likewise be in large clear letters. It would say: 'DATABASE'.

WHAT IS A DATABASE?

In 1984, Henry Hoke commented in the US magazine *Direct Marketing*: . . . 'We're often asked, "What's the difference between marketing and direct marketing?" The shorthand answer is database, the existence of a database.'

What is database marketing and what is a marketing database?

I do like simple things. Simple statements. Simple concepts. Not just because they're easy to take in and remember, but because they are often so utterly provocative. They provoke thought, discussion, speculation, enhancement. They give freedom for individual expansion and exploration.

So now, my equally simple and completely adequate definition of a database.

You'll remember, of course, the days of lists: address lists; customer lists; prospect lists; broked lists; rented lists.

Well, what's a list? Answer: it's the whereabouts of people.

And what's a database? It's the *whereabouts and the whatabouts* of people.

I did say it was simple!

So what 'whatabouts' do you need to know about people? Exactly the same things that our salesmen friends wrote in their pocketbooks. Do not be fooled by the apparent simplicity of these statements. If you revert to my comment about 'arm's length', this is one of the best ways you can close the gap, or shorten the arm.

Along with the technological media advances that direct marketing makes its friends, the existence and role of a database is the axis around which the mighty hub of direct marketing revolves.

It is the information that drives your product programme. It is the information that inspires your company development. It is the information that attracts new customers and builds repeat sales. And that self same information determines the appropriateness, relevance and appeal of your proposition to the individual human beings who are your market. It is the memory bank that selects for you the most effective ways to communicate with people—the methods they prefer; the products they prefer; the timing they prefer. It is the facility that enables you to close the distance between you and your market. It is the means by which—today and in the future—you will, through harnessing technology, be able to have the mutually satisfactory, personal and cost-effective sales relationship with as many multiples of one as you wish. But always see and be seen that you treat each as THE ONE.

A database is what turns direct marketing into relationship marketing. It is today and tomorrow the single most important resource to a direct marketer apart from the existence of the product to be sold.

A marketing database is a resource that is as valuable to the life of a healthy company as food and water is to a healthy human being. If abused or unethically handled, it is also as dangerous as the most fateful, virulent virus you can imagine.

Use a long-term strategy—even behind short-term goals
Take it from me, even if you think you're after a quick buck, you

won't be. Direct marketing is a bug that gets you. Don't worry, you'll love it. But it'll get you sure as anything. There's nothing between the disillusioned (they thought it was easy) and the disciples (they thought it was worth the trouble). I find an increasing number of both. I have no sympathy with the disillusioned, which contains by far the largest number of over-opportunist, fast-buck merchants. The disciples are where you will find the rank and file of the professionals. Caring and thoughtful; constantly learning and improving; and fully appreciative that customers are forever. Forever is what you make it.

What I urge you to do here is examine very carefully and fix as accurately as possible a value on a customer. Once you have done it, communicate it. When you hear a casual or terse piece of payment-chasing in accounts, or a sloppy greeting from the switchboard, hit them with the facts. 'Do you realise each customer we get is worth £X over a typical seven-year period? Do you know how hard it is to replace a lost customer? And it costs £Y just to get them in the first place.' Well, maybe not quite like that! But let them know anyway.

When you establish the value of the full term of a sales relationship with a customer, you start to understand so much. The Ten-X factor, the Loyalty Ladder and My Business will become three facets of a new way of life for you.

And you will see why a marketing database is vital. You can't achieve the ultimate direct marketing relationship without them.

And you will see why . . .

- *Which?* and other publishers will give you a long, free subscription offer. It's heavy duty sampling (and habit-forming!).
- Charities take a loss on recruiting a new donor or member. The Ten-X factor works just as well—often better for them. One charity I know will get almost a 40 per cent response from certain donor mailings, and has for over 20 years. Their list is several hundred thousand strong!
- People offer you jewellery sets at £9.95; 27-piece luggage sets

for £29.95; three books for 99 pence. Or, an office beverage vending machine free as long as you buy the ingredients and supplies from the given supplier.

- You can buy one type of insurance, and get another—or a first period of cover free or at a vastly reduced price. And the popular derivative of that, employment and sickness or re-dundancy cover free with finance plans or loans.

All of these offers are there because someone in the organisation has sat down and established the value of the customer or organisation over the full or long term. This can come from carefully considered projections, and what is called 'regression analysis'—looking back at the where, when, why, what and how often sales can be achieved. Remember RFM analysis? All to do with recency, frequency and monetary value.

WHAT IS THE FASTEST WAY TO PROFIT FROM DIRECT MARKETING?

Let me tell you.

This does not involve you in any further expense or effort. You are holding the answer. You are discovering—and are going to have revealed to you—the secrets of direct marketing's most powerful single weapon. The method that will become—almost certainly—the most cost-effective for you. In two words, direct mail.

2

Secrets you should think about

Direct mail has a few things that need some thought before you dash out to order your envelopes, start hunting down the lists and gear up the sales or order-handling team to deal with the response.

What type of response do you want, for example? So let's start our journey to the creation of a mailing with some thought about some of these aspects.

First . . .

MAILINGS ARE GETTING SMALLER . . . ARE YOURS?

Gosh! Times have changed. We used to grub around just about everywhere trying to find more lists to add to a mailing. Quantity was the name of the game. Now, with increased information, increased sophistication and increased awareness of the side effects of badly targeted mail on its recipients, the trend is usually and quite correctly in the exact opposite direction. Indeed, the future will see more and more effort to reduce mailing totals and so response rates should go higher and higher. Not just because of increasingly sophisticated sales techniques, but more because technology and database marketing will give us an increasingly complete picture of those to whom we are writing, and what they want to buy from us.

One thing we already know. Targeting the audience is not

enough; you must also target the message. Moreover, as the software, systems and database capabilities improve we're all working to achieve the full benefits of exactly those psychographic, demographic and other data which increase our view of the individual—our customer.

The unknown here—the foggy areas that will gradually clear as time passes—have to do, in part, with the cost of all this.

In the past, the discipline has followed a reverse pattern. Once you've got your pack, find as many names as you can, get the price in the post down. And maximise.

But as well as cost, as the segments get smaller, we must consider the practicality. There will come a point where such tight segmentation and narrow targeting may change the medium selected. The telephone, for example. And what of the interactive electronic media. Well, they are up and running, albeit with varying degrees of modesty and take-up.

Another change that must stretch the intellectuals of the direct marketing industry is the quantification of, and the use of our communications to the vast majority—that is, those who received but did not respond.

To date, what do we know? The answer is, 'Not a lot'. Some say, 'why do you care?' And we care for this reason: because they are the vast majority, the vast majority of the advertising spend is being cast at them. Advertisers will become increasingly demanding and will not rest content for much longer with the simple argument that since direct marketers were achieving their volume and profit targets from those who do respond, the advertising effect on those who didn't respond is free.

Sure. Free. But what's it worth? We already know that direct mail gets readership levels way beyond press. We know it gets recall way beyond television. We understand that it provides an intensity of sales message absorption beyond most things—often even a face-to-face sales call.

But what's it worth? Advertisers spending the vast majority of their money on these, the vast majority of people, will rightly demand answers, and the industry must provide them.

HOW CAN YOU UNDERSTAND YOUR AUDIENCE?

Creatives know that you can't get inside people's heads until you get inside their lives. That's why so many of us sit around, chisel in hand like constipated sculptors, trying to imagine what a typical prospect looks like or *feels* like.

> No professional in the direct response business can create a winning package when he doesn't know *everything* there is to know about the human being he's writing to.

These words, by an American freelance copywriter in the late 1970s, are utter bilge, of course. But it is one of those fine sentences that, while being rich in rubbish, is also true in sentiment.

That entire concept is more achievable in today's database world. But, I ask you, *'everything'* there is to know!!

However, it certainly will help, before we can decide that we understand enough about our audience (and that we can presume to set about telling them how our proposition will improve or enhance their lives), to know how and why they have been selected to receive it.

I offer a plea here, that you should involve the creative team—at least the copywriter—in as much preparation as possible. The more they understand, and indeed contribute, to elements such as list selection, discussion on incentive choices and reviews of previous results the better. And their involvement will always be better than hand-me-down memos and the seventh copy of a contact report. For this will contribute to the overall understanding, not only of what they have to do, but to whom they have to do it. And, therefore, how they will do it.

HOW TO FIND THE BEST KIND OF DIRECT MARKETING AGENCY

Easy! Look for a one-man band! It goes downhill from there. That's naturally going to mean that he or she will have to be schizophrenic super-heroes. Superman or Wonderwoman in full regalia, knickers outside tights, the perfect account director/manager/executive AND the world-beating creative genius. And that's only one half of their life. Next, the media Clerk Kent and then the production/traffic/print/laser/computer genius beavering away in the back room, proving that he or she is undoubtedly superhuman really.

Gosh! All that and specialising in your business too. Of course, it sounds fine in theory. It is a theory! In practice, more people can add greater talent, greater knowledge, greater specialisation and more capacity. But what goes in the global understanding—the brain being the globe— of what it's all about, is the sheer fusion and integration of the marketing plan in *every* aspect.

What happens is that the fusion dissipates as the communications chain gets longer on both sides—no matter how many meetings or memos or how much participation and involvement the systems and procedures of the agency and client permit.

Stop any top-of-the-business direct marketing people and they'll have to agree, if they're honest. If they're running a big agency, of course, they'll no doubt argue the point, and you may have to strap them to a lie detector. So, in my very personal view, you need to balance it out. Look carefully at the structure and nature of the skills available on the client side and go for as near as possible the perfect dovetail.

> *Understanding what constitutes the audience,*
> *is a major fact of understanding what*
> *will make them buy.*

This is an undeniable fact, and is simple common sense. But making it happen is about the gathering, analysing and digesting of information. And then we are faced with its interpretation and with the way that interpretation affects the implementation. Then, and only then, can the communication effectively take place.

The days are long gone, of course, when we had to resort to an all-embracing single message to a whole market.

That happened back in the fifties. Advertisers found—surprise, surprise—that if you identified the message in some way with the readers, they liked it. And therefore the response went up.

So, simple printing plate changes saw the emergence of attempts to link with the particular segments (lists they were then!) that make up the mailing.

> Dear Doctor
>   Dear Dentist
>   Dear Teacher
>   Dear Gardener
>   Dear Motorist

Fine. A little later the next step emerged. What happens if we actually change or vary the message to suit the segment? Eureka! Bath water everywhere! Letters had whole first paragraphs that identified with and adjusted main benefit statements to the doctor, dentist, teacher, gardener and motorist.

You know what happened. Responses went up.

Meanwhile, over in the business-to-business market they'd been fooling people for years. Given the much higher value of the sales—and therefore the money available—they'd been sending out automatically typed letters. These were not produced by electronic equipment, of course. It was electromechanical. The list was held on a sort of 'pianola' roll of paper that only played one tune.

That was expensive. So a second best was also available. This involved running the main body of the text on litho or facsimile printing machines and then 'matching in' the name, address, date and personal salutation. The world became more and more full of clever clogs who examined their mail in the morning by turning the letters over to see where the indentations of the typewriter stopped. If you ran your hands over the back of the top and it felt like Braille until about one-third down, you knew it was a mailing. Drat!

The business mailers looked back over their shoulders to see what was happening on the consumer side.

The curtain parted to reveal a huge box with winking lights. The computer had arrived. Direct mail and direct marketing were about to hit warp speed. Hyperspace was on its way.

That was the late sixties! Hyperspace is still on its way. It's just that someone keeps moving it further back.

Back? You might think that a strange choice of word. *Back?*

But back we go. As sure as sure can be. Hyperspace exists with the perfection of one-to-one communication. Just the buyer and the seller. Not one to a million (the fifties). Not one to a hundred thousand (the sixties). Not one to ten thousand (the seventies). Not one to a thousand (the eighties). But one to one. Back to the corner store again. And back even beyond that.

As we considered together earlier, what makes the difference is information . . . knowing the customers or prospects. Understanding their needs, desires and aspirations. Do they need a house? Well, they have a small one, perhaps they'd like a bigger one? How many children do they have? How old are they? How much money do they have to spend? Would they rather have a good holiday each year with the kids? Or acquire things, like a second car or a new kitchen?

What kind of people are they? What do they read? What videos do they rent? What sort of clothes—sizes, colours, styles—do they like? What do they like to eat and drink?

How often do they go to the bank? How often do they use their credit cards? Where do they use them? WHO ARE THEY?

It's like the old village doctor mentality. You know or you can find out these things. You may never repeat them. You may only use them for the good of the patients: in understanding them; in treating them; in improving your interaction with them.

However, we have to be careful not to infringe the rights of an individual to choose who is involved in their lives. We must protect and even advance this right.

The need to gather information in order to communicate better is one thing. The need to accept the full responsibilities of such a trust is another. They are, and must stay, inseparable.

Psychographics, demographics, geographics and lifestyle discriminators—all these things are indeed useful to communicate better, and more appropriately. And that is equally good for both sides of the fence. These data allow us to understand our audience, and enable us to be less and less junk and more and more relevant and interesting. The ultimate is that recipients, impressed by the compelling accuracy of our interpretation of their actions—the way we understand them as people, and thereby the way we approach them and what we say to them— may cease even to consider for a moment that we have intruded into their lives, or consider that we might breach their right to privacy.

In our quest to segment, introduce database manipulation techniques and improve cost-effectiveness, we must all play the village doctor. And remember that even doctors can prescribe the wrong medicine. The consumer has the right to throw it away, no matter how it makes us feel.

There can be no doubt that an audience that is well understood—or even just feels well understood—responds better. While the whole thing remains controlled, honest and ethical, the trip to hyperspace and the planet Wuntowun is in no danger of abort . . . or even self-destruct.

So let's just pull all that together.

It is vital, to get the message across in the most effective way possible, that all those involved—advertisers, agencies, bureaux, whoever—know as much as possible about the database they own and the many different human beings it represents. The more information that can be gathered and shared, the more 'briefed' the advertiser's creative team will be. And, therefore, the more appropriate and intelligent the resulting message will be. Overbriefing—the provision of too much information—is a luxury all creative people would prefer to the crime of 'you know the sort of thing', or worse, 'like the last time—but different!'.

Another major benefit you will appreciate in understanding your audience is how best to create direct mail for them, and how best to deploy some of the unique qualities of direct mail. Actually they are not in themselves all unique—but the fact that direct mail offers these benefits all together every time you use it is certainly unique. And powerful. I think particularly here of four of its qualities. The fact that it can be so selective, creative, personal and flexible. Let's take those qualities one by one.

DIRECT MAIL IS *SELECTIVE*

How many ways can you make it selective? About as many ways as the people on your list! That's a bit glib! Let's have a look at what this quality is all about, and how selectivity works.

Most people talk about selectivity as a general quality that direct mail possesses to select groups of individuals in, or out for that matter, of the broader target market.

So let's look first at this thought.

There are basically two sorts of media:

1   Those that *select* the market.
2   Those *selected by* the market.

Thus, for example, photographers will read amateur photographic magazines. Company directors will read *The Director*. What has actually happened here is that the media owner has identified a market and then set about building up a readership.

Direct mail charges through the middle and enables us to mail company directors of photographers! But that's an incidental for the moment.

Then there are those media which, in some respects, it can be argued, select their markets. But I prefer to think of this the other way round: the consumer decides. This has to do with range of choice, but also the style of the media. We choose the radio station we want to listen to; we choose the TV channel we want; and, I think, we choose the newspapers we read.

Those are the extremes, of course; the black and white. There is plenty of grey.

This could involve the available lists of specific types of people, perhaps by purchasing history—something you have subscribed to, given to, or bought from. Or it could be something you have qualified as, or visited or whatever.

However, as in the very simple way we saw earlier, direct mail enables you to select the message for the market: a doctor's message for doctors; a photographer's message for photographers; and so on.

Structural engineers. Book buyers. Record buyers. Car owners. Dog owners. People into horoscopes. Health foods. Take your pick. You can be very selective too. Record buyers by type of music. Car owners by type or make of car. Dog owners by type of dog.

In fact, you can also select the message you would like to go to each and every list—by geographics, or . . . the choices are apparently endless. Select by sex . . . or job title. But unlike the other media, with direct mail you can go right on selecting and fine tuning. Doctors in West Yorkshire—no problem. Photographers in Brighton—no problem.

On and on . . . doctors over the age of 40 in West Yorkshire; photographers with their own processing in Brighton.

Still no problem.

Meanwhile the other media have long succumbed. *Pulse Magazine* goes to doctors in the UK, and that's that.

But direct mail hasn't finished yet. We can be selective in other ways still. All those inside a given catchment area of your store. YES. All those outside the same area. YES. We'll send them a catalogue! How about all those around your competitors' stores?

You only want the odd numbered houses? OK, well if that's what you want. Still no problem. As silly as it sounds, selecting only those with names not numbers has done quite well before now. Sales areas; TV areas; counties; towns; suburbs; single or computer-selected clusters of enumeration districts—you can have practically anything geographic you like.

Businesses; consumers; heads of businesses; heads of households (if anyone still owns up to such a title!); purchasing directors; sales managers; etc. etc. . . . .

Still no problem for the mighty direct mail. It's so selective you can even select who *doesn't* see it.

DIRECT MAIL IS *CREATIVE*

Here I'd like you to take a look, not at the creative process itself, but more at how that process can be exploited, and the benefit creativity brings to direct mail. The selling edge we get with direct mail is obvious if we use the creative differences wisely and thoughtfully to bind everything together.

You'll see how that thoughtful binding is used to do these things:

- to grab more *attention*
- to create more *interest*
- to stimulate more *desire*
- to provoke more *action*.

Let's look at the four 'S'-ential differences.

'S'-ential no. 1

Here is direct mail's Singular Selling Strength: *it's solo.*

By using selectivity you've managed to get yourself in front of the individual sales prospect with whom you want to communicate. And so the great news is that once you get there, you have that prospect's sole attention.

What a perfect opportunity. No salesperson could ask for more at this stage. No others around battling for attention. *You are it!*

So, in order to ensure that you don't waste your golden moment, you need to have something clear in your head. It's *cost* a *lot* of *money* to get there. Direct mail is expensive. All that selectivity is at a price. You are paying to have the wastage cut away in great handfuls. But more, you are paying for the un-bridled power, too—not to mention the wages of the postal staff who transported and finally delivered your message for you. Hence, my advice here might seem strange. I urge you to develop a relaxed—not careless or sloppy—but *relaxed* attitude of 'in for a penny, in for a pound'.

This takes courage at first. But as you come to know the medium and know how it pays back, this courage will surely turn to confidence.

To help you think it through, let me point out that the base cost—the origination, the planning, the time spent, the lists, the materials, printing and the postage—will be expensive anyway.

Thus, to do the selling job professionally, thoroughly and in every way as best you can, won't add much more to your costs. Think of it like this:

	Cost	Potential effect
Worst job	100	100
Best job	120	150

So do the job properly. Remembering, at the end of the day, you always have the certain knowledge of measured, controllable cost-effectiveness. This is a luxury that conventional marketing rarely affords and classical advertising hardly ever.

I think I would ask you to interpret my advice two ways . . .

1   *At the creative outset go for the affordable best*   If your affordable best doesn't work, nothing less will. Once you've established the pulling power of your affordable best, then review the whole project, *not* with a view to making it cheaper, but with an objective of making it work better.

In this review process—once the power of your work is proven—be sure that:

2   *Savings aren't made at the cost of sales*   If in doubt, test it. This is not a suggestion that you should irresponsibly throw money at a project. If you are a 'bargain basement' advertiser and you suddenly mail to customers on the most wonderful die-stamped, thermographed hand-made 200 gsm paper, it's not going to have any positive benefit for you. Probably the opposite. They'll think you've flipped! Or they will sense that

you've been taken over by Fortnum and Mason and are no longer for them!

Spend prudently but don't penny pinch, because the penny you are pinching is quite possibly giving all the other pennies less chance to do their job. And you're spending—or sending—them anyway.

So remember. You're alone with your potential customer. Don't lose the sale because you didn't spend that last bit that would enable you to do the job effectively—that is, to get that sale.

'S'-ential no. 2

Direct mail tells the *Sales Story Sensibly* because it's *structured*.

One of the great, great advantages that direct mail has over other media is that you can enjoy the freedom of an almost infinite number of different formats, many with successful track records of pulling response for other people.

This brings you choice. To make that choice you need to look not only at the practicalities of the job but also at the opportunity to tell your creative story—your sales pitch—in the way *you* want. Consider each format from this view. Here's an example of each . . .

THE PRACTICAL

If you need to get a cheque or paperwork back it will normally pay you, both in response and speed of that response, to choose a format that offers a post-paid return addressed envelope. FACT!

THE OPPORTUNIST

Even if you do have 11 000 clear plastic A4 size 'envelopes' in the stores, you should mail this package in good quality white C4 envelopes because it gives a truer picture of the company. But more important, you don't want these never-approached-before-prospects to be frightened off by what the plastic envelope reveals to them before you have lost your chance to gain their attention and arouse their interest.

CHOOSING A FORMAT FOR YOUR MAILING

The word I used a few paragraphs back was 'infinite'. And so it is. However, given your objectives and economics, and looking at the best way to achieve them, it should be possible to make some basic decisions, such as to rule in or rule out certain possibilities.

First, we need to look at the basic communications opportunity. Do you have a clean sweep at, or are you using or taking advantage of, some other event? Or do you need to get in touch with your audience?

The clean sweep

If you have a clean sweep, you have the widest choice. That can be good news or bad news. The more you have to choose from, the harder it can be to decide on the right one or ones.

Let's run through a few of my most popular formats—those that I know work consistently well—and check out a few visual and verbal examples. This is nothing—I mean *nothing*—like a definitive list; it is just a quick canter through some favourites.

The basic pack formula   Standing the test of time, the ever logical, ever present, ever successful letter, leaflet, response device formula is a sound starting place. It's not quite that simple of course, because you will need an outer envelope, and possibly a return envelope too. In lead generation you could well often leave out a formal leaflet, using perhaps an illustrated letter in its place.

On the other hand, you could equally consider bolstering the interest level a little with a die-cut, pull tab, or 'lift to reveal' device. Whatever! The point is that in my experience the direct mail equivalent of the staff of life is the outer envelope, letter, leaflet, response device and (if required) a reply envelope. More will appear about the role and function of these pieces separately when we take a more detailed look at creative.

ADDITIONAL ITEMS YOU CAN ADD . . .

Let's take a look at some.

Extra leaflets Be clear about the function of these but don't worry too much about 'cluttering' up the envelope. Multi-enclosure packs can work well in many situations, but nothing works well if it confuses, wastes time, or is dull. If you have clear functions for pieces then it can help the reader to identify the function with the copy and art.

- Quotes from newspapers can print and fold like mini-newspapers.
- Stories can be told in handwriting underneath or even on the back of photos.
- Announcements, 'Hurry, Hurry' and Stop Press items imply news, urgency or last-minute thoughts; as do telex or telegram style art—or a dummy release marked 'Embargo'.

Endorsements These can be anything from a fake (printed reproduction) rubber stamp (suggesting the institutional, such as a local authority or tourist office), a specially positioned label or sticker (such as a kite mark or Design Council logo) attached to a separate full size or mini-reproduction of the letter from the endorser.

Do ensure you have approvals from endorsing individuals or organisations, or indeed from any third party you might want to use as a case history or testimonial. Most people are flattered to be asked and are willing to help, and many like to see their names in print.

Involvement pieces These work well in both consumer and business mail. They can be used to highlight and even make choice easier to select. They can use the elements of surprise, curiosity or intrigue for real or just for emphasis. These include a myriad of permutations, including prize draws, sweepstakes, games, stamps, competitions, etc.

Useful or interest features   These will build retention of sales information and keep your name in front of prospects. They are particularly valuable when you have no control over the timing. For example, while working for Hertz on a mailing which sold instant availability of replacement vehicles in case of breakdown, I asked the chap when he wanted to mail. 'Two days before they break down,' he said helpfully.

REMEMBER, THE THIRD DIMENSION

Something that few other media offer is the opportunity to use the three-dimensional example. Samples, gifts or gimmicks abound and can create quite a stir. They can also distract rather than add to the sales message—so I do urge careful consideration and testing wherever possible.

So very, very often they add tremendous cost, and to very little effect. Two particular three-dimensional examples come to mind.

The first was the record player, in a whole new sense! My friend, Mike Adams, also received this pack, and keeps it among his treasured samples, guarding it with his life.

Innocent enough—but with the added intrigue of a slightly lumpy envelope (never a bad one, that—remember how you used to shake, squeeze and poke the presents round the Christmas tree!)—it arrived in a regular DL envelope. It consisted of a piece of board about A4 in size which, when folded into thirds, formed a triangular shape and made a small record player. And to prove it—as the simple instructions explained—there was a plastic 'record' on the top of the base and a stylus in the fold-over from the top. All that was needed was my finger—and a reasonably constant rotating speed! I placed the end of my finger into the recessed space and started to turn it. With great delight I listened as a wavering but nonetheless quite distinct voice started to sell me these mini-record players for my next 'record results' mailing.

Fantastic! I dashed from my office down to creative. The department came to a standstill. And the standstill spread like a bush fire. I calculated later that the record player had become just that—it broke all records for people playing in the office. I dread to think of the cost of the lost man hours. We calculated it to somewhere between 20 and 25 hours.

I've met a lot of people who received this mailing. When I mention it even after all these years, everyone in the 'trade' remembers it. But sadly I haven't met one person who responded, let alone bought.

The second, after many, many years, was abandoned. Yet, like the record player, is fondly recalled by all those who were on its mailing list. The advertiser, John Dickinson and Co., the makers of Croxley paper and envelopes, used to dispatch a small posy of fresh primroses to selected customers every spring. It was a charming and perfectly underplayed customer relations exercise. We looked forward to it each year. Whether they were all gathered from the fields around the mill or not—who cared! As far as our business and many others like us were concerned, we didn't notice when the first cuckoo was reported in *The Times*, when the lambs started leaping, or when the bluebells covered the woodlands like a poet's carpet. Spring wasn't spring until that little box of primroses arrived.

At which point, may I ask you to stop reading for a moment and write a list of all the other advertising media of which you are aware that offer you this kind of recall, this kind of loyalty and affection building. This kind of *sheer selling power*.

It won't be a very long list!

So what's the point? Let's get back to relevance. And look at it from there.

The record player was relevant. It couldn't be more so. But, in the cold light of day, affectionate as I feel for it all this time later, I couldn't honestly have put it up to a client. It was costly. It was silly. It was badly planned. If they had included a reply card and enabled me to enquire about the prices rather than quoting them,

I still might not have bought in the end, but at least they would have got a lead. And when following up—with the record player as their opener—they might at least have scored with something else, another product.

And Dickinson's primroses? In pure direct response terms, this is difficult to assess. In customer relations terms, for this customer—100 per cent. I can't say I ever gave them an order just because of the primroses, but now—even eight, nine or ten years after they stopped—I still think of them as a caring company. And even if I don't see the reps these days, they'll always get a friendly welcome from me. What price that after all this time?

As long ago as the primroses—maybe longer—a case history appeared in a post office booklet promoting direct mail.

It featured a mailing for a vehicle contract hire company. The mailing consisted of a pop-up 3D replica of one of their vehicles. Sellotaped to the top was a coin. 'Use this to give us a ring' invited the message on the side of the van.

At exactly the same time, and probably why I remember it now, I was involved with one of their competitors. The campaign was a series of three straightforward sales letters and an enquiry card folded into a window envelope.

We were pulling over three times the response of the 'pop-up' truck at quite literally less than one-tenth of the cost. That makes thirty times more effective use of the advertising money!

The pop-up truck advertiser was over the moon. According to the story, he had secured more than (and remember, this is a *long* time ago!) £1 000 000 of turnover. I know for a fact the campaign I worked on achieved nothing like that. But then we were concentrating on 400 prospects in Manchester. They had mailed over 20 000—fifty times as many. The moral here is clear. Three-dimensional advertising is available with direct mail and, looking back, is particularly effective in business-to-business mail. My own past is littered with 3D mailings. But never, I think, where the same result could be achieved for less, or where there wasn't some real relevance of the gimmick to the objective or product.

I've mailed fresh (but muddy) carrots to promote incentives;

spent bullet cases; old, and useless, foreign bank notes; bottles of whisky (miniatures!); enclosed gold labels in the shape— stunningly realistic—of krugerrands. I've also mailed pink feathers, red roses, backgammon sets. You name it. But each was because it had an *easily linked*, *tangible*, *relevant* association with the objective of the mailing.

3D is powerful. And costly. Used intelligently, it can be very cost-effective. Ask the MP who dispatched buckets of cow dung to his colleagues on the opposite side of the House. And Reader's Digest who attached a five-pence piece to their packs.

RSVP

Almost any event, exhibition, seminar or reception will benefit from an invitation. My experience suggests that the more an invitation looks like an invitation, the better it works. So start from an ideal of a gold-bordered heavy card, hand filled in with my name in a classic Royal Blue ink!

If it's an invitation to the local Spar to test the new all-in-one Yugoslavian loo-cleaner, aperitif and aphid spray, that's going to be a little over the top.

So again a balance of corporate and event positioning and tone will no doubt sign your path for you. As will production details, the data, media and, inevitably, cost.

Never resist the urge to enclose a good letter with the invitation. And do think about the practicalities of the event. The ease and convenience, the timing, the parking arrangements, the refreshments, and so on! The more attractive, informative and useful, convenient and enjoyable the event sounds, the better.

I became very aware with my conference series that people attend for a whole gamut of reasons. From a day out and a good lunch to an expenses paid trip to the other end of the country.

It was quite startling to see how, when we were in Scotland, at least one-third of delegates came from London, and vice versa!

When we printed the full lunch menu and mentioned the free wine, up went the response!

AND THEN THERE'S THE 'FREE RIDE' . . .

On many occasions you will not have a 'clean sweep'. You'll find you have an opportunity, as we say, to 'free ride' along with some other communication. You'll be looking at a range of formats that tie in with the objectives or production circumstances that prevail from the individual opportunity. Thus you might think about 'one-piece' mailers, and the more straightforward inserts or 'bill-stuffers' or even the 'pack within a pack'.

One-piece-mailers and mechanised origami

A vast range of increasingly ambitious and clever devices is available now. Most are formed from up to metre length runs of paper printed from the reel. On-line finishing enables very varied perforating, folding and gluing to achieve anything from a multi-folded all-in-one, to a pack that 'bursts' on opening to reveal a separate letter, leaflet, response slip and return envelope.

Such devices can include rub-off, scratch 'n 'sniff, sticky stamps and a range of other items—all at very economical rates when compared with 'proper' pack prices.

Despite their economies, they have not taken over the world! There is no doubt that the recipient often treats these formats less respectfully and with a lower perceived value than an individual solus mailing. In much the same way as house-to-house distribution most often has a lower perceived value. Thus, as I have found quite frequently, but with some spectacular contrary experiences, an identical pack differing only in its delivery method, and not being therefore in an addressed envelope, can pull as little as between one-tenth and one-fifth its direct mailed equivalent.

It must also be said, returning to one-piece mailers, that some of them are too clever by half, and practically require a degree in origami before the recipient can gain the full benefit of the proposition. Therefore, one must also consider the complexity of the message you require to put across as an important factor in your choice of format.

It is interesting to see that—as the ingenuity of the manufacturers increases (in terms of the different shapes, sizes, and formats that can be developed)—so too they are increasingly available with quite a degree of single and multiple personalisations, mainly through the ink-jet process.

I started out on this topic of formats by saying that one of the 'S'-entials delivered by format is that it tells the sales story sensibly because from the format should come the structure to make it happen.

I suggested that before choosing the format—but particularly in relation to additional items—you should have a clear idea of the role and function of each piece.

I had previously indicated my own preference—given a clean sweep—for probably the most popular combination that can be used as a complete package, or at least a starting point from which you can add other items as the sales story extends or expands.

LETTER—LEAFLET—RESPONSE PIECE

One of the reasons that this time-honoured pack is so effective is that readers are familiar with it. They accept it. They find it fits in with the normal way of doing things. And it's so comfortable and easy to follow.

- They expect the *letter* to INTRODUCE AND SET THE SCENE, A BIT LIKE A GOOD SALESPERSON DOES.
- They expect the *leaflet* to ADOPT A LESS PERSONAL STANCE AND PROVIDE MORE DETAILED INFORMATION AND PICTURES.
- They expect the *response piece* to GATHER ANY NECESSARY DETAILS AND CARRY THEIR ORDER OR ENQUIRY BACK TO YOU.

This suits them. And believe me, more than nine times out of ten, it should suit you too. So, when you're looking for formats, considering some of the one-piece devices, or negotiating with other departments, aim for a solution which, wherever possible, gets you as near to this winning format as can be.

S'-ential no. 3

Direct mail is *sense-you-all*. It gives you smell, sight and sound to play with.

I received a rather tasteless (thank heavens!) Christmas card a few years ago. On the front was a light brown printed square, garlanded in a classic holly and berries design.

'SMELL THIS,' read the front page. Of course, I did.

Recoiling from a truly vile odour, I opened the card to find a cartoon reindeer smiling. 'IT'S GENUINE REINDEER DROPPINGS,' it said. 'MERRY CHRISTMAS. NOW WASH YOUR HANDS.'

It's amazing what they can do these days.

And so, as you may have guessed, we arrive at what I believe printers refer to as 'micro-encapsulations'. You and I shall demean ourselves and call it 'Scratch and Sniff'.

To start with, avoid reindeer muck at all costs.

As an interesting counterpart to that, I was fascinated to hear of the 'mailing' (it was actually delivered by courier service) used by an airline to launch their new route into Brussels from the UK. Novelty abounded—but no more so than to the top travel agents in Brussels, key prospects to sell their regular executive business service. The ingenious marketing team arranged to deliver a copy of that morning's newspaper with the lead story replaced with a specially written 'story' covering their new service, along with suitable pictures. The paper was delivered with a piping hot cup of coffee, two warm croissants, and a note of explanation. This was one sure way to get the message read. And what a great opener for the telephone follow-up.

A local coffee supplier mailed out businesses in West Sussex to sell the concept of fresh coffee in place of machine vending. They enclosed a generous handful of coffee beans. 'Smell these when you sit down with your next cup of disappointment,' they invited, 'and then decide which you'd rather have.' They backed this up with some convincing cost arguments and followed through with a fascinating water analysis offer, explaining that they would individually blend, roast and grind the coffee to your exact preference, and to match the water in your area, just as any good restaurant would insist. Once the analysis was completed, and your blend chosen, you could accept a week's supply free. Try to get your staff back to 'cups of disappointment' after that!

And then there is sound. Be careful with this one. For years, I've used good and bad examples in my conferences. One favourite 'baddy' is a mailing which consisted of a sturdy square envelope labelled with my office address on the outside. To this day, I don't know who sent it. Inside there was a 7in. single record. The sleeve bears only their telephone numbers. And the record label the same.

That was it. Nothing else.

For a bit of fun, whichever country I've been in, I've asked audiences to assess the wisdom of this—undoubtedly ad agency inspired gem—by raising their hands if they had a record player in their office. Across the last five years only two people raised their hands. One sold jukeboxes in Oslo; the other was a marketing manager at EMI Records in London.

Yet with cassette tapes—or even videos these days—you can be much safer. Especially in the consumer field. I would nevertheless counsel you to try the much cheaper alternative of a simple pack with the cassette or video as the offer, which has the added advantage of enticing response and thereby building you a list of luke-warm prospects, as well as focusing these relatively expensive items where they will do the most good.

THEN THERE'S A TOUCHING MOMENT . . .

Yes, there's no reason why you can't let your prospects actually touch too. Fabric, wallpaper, colour selection samples. Any number of options are yours to play with, to experiment and find what works best. They often work well, but the one sense that in my opinion works best is common sense.

'S'-ential no. 4
The last of my 'S'-entials recognises that direct mail Sends a Sales Star—and he's a *spaceman*.

Space is a luxury in most advertising media. Particularly in the press. The more you buy, the more it costs. While to some extent that is also true for direct mail, it is less so.

● *The first postal weight step goes up to 60 grams in the UK, and in many other places, 50 grams.*

You can get a vast amount of selling done inside 50 or 60 grams weight.

We're on to a fairly difficult subject here. It's not difficult for me, as I've proved this theory time after time, mailing after mailing, year in, year out. It's as true now as it was 10 years ago, and I have every confidence and every reason to believe it will still be so in 10 years' time.

Nearly everyone in direct marketing accepts it, lives by it. All the books—yes, ALL the books, confirm it. Yet for some reason people—that is, advertising people, marketing people, particularly non-direct marketing copywriters—still find it hard to accept, or maybe just hard to achieve.

But here we go, anyway.

LONGER COPY SELLS MORE

It's a really important point. And whereas I'm always conscious that generalisations can be huge pitfalls, I am going to repeat it one more time.

LONGER COPY SELLS MORE

In direct marketing, you will always be found out because of the ability to test and because of the ability to determine absolute cost-effectiveness.

Yet, if you go to a direct marketing conference and listen to speakers (and heavens, I've done it enough times—something like 400 or so in the last 10 years!) you'll notice one thing that almost all speakers have in common. They don't suggest an idea or two that might work—they *tell* you. And they tell you because they know.

The grandpappy of direct marketing, David Ogilvy, was quoted delivering the following message for the heads of ad agencies who hadn't started (or perhaps heard of!) direct market-ing. Here's what he said.

> Insist that all your people are trained in your direct response department. If you
> don't have one yet, make arrangements with a firm of direct marketing specialists
> to train your people. Make it a rule in your Agency that no copy is ever presented
> to Clients before it has been vetted by a direct response expert. The direct
> response expert *knows* what sells, the rest can only *guess*.

To many, hearing this display of what comes over as certain knowledge, it must seem intransigent, or inflexible, or even just downright arrogant. I can understand that, because for him, like me, it comes born of irrefutable, incontrovertible experience. Not one experience, but hundreds of experiences. Repeatedly tested and re-tested.

Of course we all accept that, if you flip a coin and 10, 20, or, seemingly impossibly, 30 times and the coin comes down on the same side, you start to question the flipper, the coin, and then your sanity. But this is not a game of chance. If it is a game at all, it is a game of experiences. And you know, at the end of the day, that if you're still not convinced you can always test. But do be certain—when you test—that you test *good* long copy against *good* short copy.

HOW LONG DOES IT TAKE TO MAKE A SALE?

This seems a valid question in this context, but what's the answer? Some wonderful cliche like 'As long as it takes'? *Yes*, actually.

But imagine yourself holding a classic four-page direct mar-keters letter. It's well paced. It's easy to read. It has a simple but effective layout. And the typography, basic as it is—with much of it typewritten—is next to perfect. Got the picture? You should have. This kind of letter is to be found in about 50 per cent of all consumer mailings . . . and nearer 95 per cent of all the successful ones!

How long will it take to read it? Five minutes perhaps? Well, certainly if it's jam-packed to bursting. But more typically, I would suggest somewhere between three and four minutes. Now let's add a product leaflet and order slip. Two envelopes—an inner for reply and an outer to get us there. One small 'Special Gift Announcement' flyer. And three sticky stamps.

What do you add that lot up to?

Let's pretend it's going your way and the reader is so wrapped up in it all that—most unusually—he or she decides to take in every word you write. Let's pretend! In which case, I estimate that we're looking at a total running time of maybe 10 to 13 minutes.

That may seem a great deal of time to a classical advertising copywriter who's used to holding the attention in 30 second bursts or for the odd minute or two. But, forget the advertising world. How does it measure up to a salesperson?

Not enough! That's how it measures up! But the world is a far more cruel place than that.

Only the most exceptional cases will invest a full 15 minutes or so of their time with you. And rarely will you, in practice, ask for it. The direct marketing creatives work their spells in bite-size chunks. And can often achieve the more simple objectives in as little as two or three minutes.

No salesperson could achieve under such conditions. Yet to direct marketers, it's a way of life. And when we run over from three minutes to five or six, people call that long copy.

Long? Long? I can't quite see it that way.

But it *looks* long.

Bad layout.

But it *feels* long.

Bad writing.

But it *goes on* so long.

Bad rationale.

But . . . but it's . . . it's absolute rubbish.

That's different!

Bad targeting. Bad timing. Bad offer. Bad pitch. Bad luck!

Let's think about some other little pieces of evidence and pop them in alongside my thought that direct marketing copy is only long in advertising terms. In selling terms, it's quite ridiculously short. And anyway, who's timing it?

Think positive. Forget for a moment the numbers falling by the wayside. Concentrate on those who were intrigued by your envelope message. They had that intrigue built to an irresistible level by the headline of your letter. They wanted the special offer in the picture alongside, and have decided to explore a little further. That's your green light to proceed. But fix it in your mind that you're now in a *stronger* position. You have made them *want* to read.

Now it's a balancing act. You've got to keep that momentum, expand it if possible, and start to create the desire to respond or to buy. Now *you* are in control. You'll only lose them if . . .

1 They're not *that* interested.
2 You say something they disagree with or disapprove of.
3 You fail to hold them.
4 You confuse or make them work too hard in the circumstances.
5 You're not fun, pleasant or good company to be with.

Don't look up. If you see that there are more people giving up than staying you'll get disheartened. You mustn't let that dent your confidence. Keep on. There's a hard nucleus who are absolutely riveted by you. And I can tell from their eyes, two or three have already decided in your favour. They're going to respond. They're reading now because it's confirming their inclination to accept. Keep going. Keep going. You're really going to win through. Give them all you've got. Every reason to accept.

Whew! Nearly done. Let them know there's not too much more to come. Repeat the offer. Summarise and round up with all the main goodies. Now tell them what they have to do next. Give them the offer one more time. Hand them the reply slip. Tell them about the reply envelope. You're very nearly there.

Reassure them one more time. Well done, you got the offer in again. That was brilliant! OK, thank them. Shake hands. Say goodbye. Right. Now get out. Let them think about it.

Fantastic! Just one more thing to do. Use that PS to poke your head round the door, smile, and give them the offer again one last time.

It's over. Well done. Your first successful direct mail sales call. A thousand people out there. Maybe more. And you got 15 or 20 to respond. What do you need me for? Congratulations.

Oh, by the way. Elapsed time 3 minutes, 42 seconds. It didn't seem that long to them. You must have a smooth tongue!

DIRECT MAIL IS *PERSONAL*

I would like to be clear on this point. I do not mean personalised. It certainly can be personalised with the recipient's name and address or other information. But, in this instance, I mean *personal*.

This, in context, is an extension of the points we have just made—particularly about length of copy where we explained a number of times that copy needed to be 'easy to read'.

It has also already started to emerge that a letter is a very effective, powerful and persuasive medium for communication. There are, as we have already learned, particular qualities that are at home in letters.

Indeed, if direct mail has a sneaky, underhand advantage over the other media it is undoubtedly this: it takes full advantage of what a letter is perceived to be by those who receive it. This is the unique regard in which it is held by us all.

Letters are friendly little things

Letters have a pleasant, almost disarming lack of formality without being pretentious, precocious or presumptive. They are also polite. They wait until you're ready for them. They don't shout over you like the radio and television. They're not inherently silly like posters and, more and more, press advertising.

They 'talk'—yes, that is the right word, for they are normally very conversational—in an easy way. Most are lively and fun to read. Some are stimulating; some are newsworthy; some are quite valuable; and some are very moving.

Letters are intimate. For example, you read them to yourself. And if you decide to let someone else see your letter, then you do. Unusual for advertising that. Some of this intimacy has to do with the way they—as letters—are perceived. Some of it has to do with the fact that they are undoubtedly the only advertising message that starts 'Dear' and ends 'Yours'. A final pledge of faith, sincerity or truth.

Letters are undoubtedly the single most effective piece of paper you can create for a sales message—unless, that is, they are very foolishly or insensitively written. Otherwise they will command attention, demand to be read.

THE SALESPERSON IN AN ENVELOPE . . .

Lots of people seem to choose the analogy that the letter is like the salesperson in an envelope. And it's a fair description.

The letter is the one that sets the scene and relates the subject of the mailing to the reader. It explains what it's all about. And what the reader needs to do.

And, of course, letters—well these sort of letters—are NEVER bad news. People know that, because they've never had one with *bad* news yet.

. . . AND LETTERS ARE SAFE

Letters are safe. Unlike a human salesperson they can be ignored, put down, or curled up into a ball and thrown on the fire.

Unlike a human salesperson, if a letter confronts you, you can't lose.

You don't feel as though you've offended anyone. You never feel guilty, or threatened or intimidated. Yes, with a letter the advantage stays with you.

Yet, you know what it's like when—and we all dread this moment—the salesperson's got you. You've been saying 'yes' for the last 20 minutes. They haven't sold you anything, they've 'made' you talk yourself into it. How *do* they do that? To get out of it you can't come up with a single sensible argument. They've dealt with the lot. You know you have to buy. But you're not going to. Because you just don't want to!

Face to face—on the phone—in your home, at their office, branch or shop, you now feel slightly guilty and embarrassed. You're the one who is uneasy. That's why you're shifting from foot to foot and looking around and hoping maybe a fire will break out.

And what of the phone? What do most people feel when the average (not the best—the typical) telephone salesperson gets to work? Defensive? On guard, and therefore threatened?

People write articles about how to hang up on telephone salespeople. They bandy techniques of how to dispense with people quickly and painlessly. They resent the often awkward and intrusive timing.

Over the top? Unfair? Maybe. For example, some say that few people like direct mail. True again. But how many actively dislike it? In one survey 70 per cent of retailers said they'd actually rather receive new product information via the mail than from reps. That is also the view of the majority of doctors. And apparently, only 6 per cent of direct mail is thrown away unopened.

At least a part of the answer is the cosiness of direct mail. With mail, the prospect is always in control. It's passive. Persuasive, certainly in most cases, but not threatening, intrusive or intimidating. And you are always, silently, alone with the reader.

Such things sound like cliches. And maybe they are. But, if you're not convinced by this emotional reasoning check out another. In 20 years and more in the business, I have not met one true direct marketing professional whose comments differ. Certainly not any without an axe to grind.

So direct mail letters may be—well, are—personal. But they never go too far. They can only succeed because you've decided to let them.

And because of all these qualities—the intimacy, the lack of threat, no fear of confrontation—they somehow become even more convincing. You're not on your guard; thus, it follows that because they are so friendly, they talk more like friends.

Conversational in language and tone. Very me-to-you. And if that's not personal, what is?

Personal or personalised

What is the distinction?

It's substantial. All direct mail should be personal. Some should be personalised.

First, let's look at the difference.

It is definable, but we don't need to define it. We all already know. When you look at some media—even when they beguile you—you know you're sharing them with other people. Direct mail has a position—which is part of its character—that is all its own.

Personal is descriptive of nature, tone and style. The approach is personal. The message is personal. And the ways in which that message is communicated—most especially in a letter—are personal; more personal, perhaps, than any other advertising medium can be.

Posters, TV ads, even press ads, direct response or others, cannot possibly share the intimacy of direct mail. Letters were designed for one-to-one communication.

And what of personalisation?

A different matter altogether.

Personalisation can never make a mailing. Few, if any, mailings have succeeded simply because they were personalised. It can, at best, only make a mediocre mailing better—but by no means always.

Personalisation is still a thing to test. If a personalised approach is a by-product of some other process, or some other objective you are trying to achieve (such as sending out a statement, bonus notice, reminder or similar), and you can obtain the benefit of it for little or no extra cost, then use it. For I've only rarely known it to pull less replies.

DIRECT MAIL IS *FLEXIBLE*

What kind of direct mail would you like yours to be?

Direct mail adapts to you and your market. You can readily adjust it, tailor-make it to your business, your capacity, the size, geography and capability of your salesforce.

- If you want more orders or more leads, you send out more mail. Easy.
- If you want less, or of higher quality, you tinker with it and it reacts. Easy.
- You want the replies to come in at a certain rate? Fine. If you know what response you're going to get, then just release it in appropriate quantities. Easy.
- And if you don't know the response, just pop a few out first and find out. Easy.
- You want to do something—such as select a bunch of people, but quickly? Easy.
- You want to stop it at short notice without penalties? Easy.
- You only want to stop it in a particular sales territory because they are overstretched, or you don't have any sales person covering? Easy.
- You want to change the timing, leave six particular people out, vary your message to 25 per cent of your market, make one offer to some, another offer to others? Easy.

Is there any other advertising medium which, at anything like the same price, can deliver such extraordinary flexibility and react so precisely to your needs?

In a word, NO.

THINGS TO KNOW ABOUT SELLING MAIL ORDER

So you've decided to go the whole hog! You want a complete sale. No problem. Indeed, I hope you'll already have picked up quite a lot of helpful ideas, thoughts and experiences.

You'll know, for example, that few people go for a one-off sale. You'll have thought about this. You'll be excited at the thought of the Ten-X factor for repeat sales and this will temper your profit targets for the short term. You will appreciate that if you are going to start a long and satisfactory and happy relationship with great profit potential for your business you have to take it seriously. Invest to test.

You will know that what you are going to do is something people do, and have done to them, every day. You're going to sell. They're going to buy. You are aware that while you will sell to them at a distance you must speak to them as if you were face-to-face.

You must remember that mail order wasn't dubbed 'convenience shopping' just for the fun of it. You have to be convenient and simple to buy from.

You must have the courage of your convictions, to tell the *whole* sales story—down to the last nut and bolt. You must be warm and reassuring. Include not just every benefit and feature—the sizzle and the steak—but in addition to all these you must add the case histories and testimonials and guarantees that will convince. You must be honest, and only make claims and promises you can deliver, or you will lose money hand over fist.

You must become obsessed not just with the desires you wish to stimulate, but also with the problems, pressure and uncertainties you can cause. How do I pay? How can I find out whether it does this or that? Why can't they do blue? Will it fit on the shelf? Where will the money come from? Do they pack carefully? Am I medium or large? Will they change it? Is my money safe? What if I fail the medical? Do they *care*?

A nagging doubt in any one of these comfort zones will lose you a sale.

You will realise that while many so-called experts consider mail order to be a 'numbers' game, it is not. It is a *people business*.

That is one of those gloriously dismissable cliches. But cliches become cliches because they are used a lot. Mostly that's because of the truth that lies behind them. So when you're selling at arm's length and striving—as I put it earlier—to shorten the arm, there is no better method than a straightforward and open display of utter humanness. That can't fail to make your communication personal. It also has a disarming frankness, and, if you can achieve it, a convincing charm.

Selling by mail order is a truly fascinating business. Using direct mail in the process only serves to add to the fascination. But I beg you not to dabble with it. If you're going to do it, do it properly. Take it seriously. Get it right. It will repay you hand-somely. Equally, if you flirt with it, you will find it is the fruit machine that's been tuned never to pay out. And each time you pull the handle, the results will be so teasingly near, so eminently achievable next time with slight improvements—or changes—that you'll 'pop the next coin in'! Ultimately it will cost you a fortune.

MAILBOX

ACKNOWLEDGE ORDERS AND ENQUIRIES

Many mail order companies choose not to go to the cost of acknowledging orders unless the price is high, or there's a stock or shipping problem.

Often this exercise, as well as being beneficial to customer relations, can break even, or better make a profit. How? Include another offer! List renters the world over will pay a premium for 'hot' names. This is as hot as you can get. Also it's a good time for a member-get-member (MGM) approach!

GENERATING LEADS FOR YOUR SALESFORCE

When I said don't flirt with mail order, I did not mean you shouldn't use direct mail or direct marketing for other things. Indeed, even some of the most dedicated mail order companies are only using mail order as a part of their total business mix. Nonetheless, the two principal uses of direct mail remain those of mail order and lead generation.

A third use, which follows close behind these, is traffic generation—that is, the use of direct mail to increase store traffic. It is successful at retail or wholesale levels—but is more evident in the retail arena. It is, in application, not so very different to lead generation. The most significant difference being, rather obviously, that the main objective will be to propose a store visit rather than the return of a product or service enquiry. However, its mechanics are quite similar. If you are considering a choice between a store visit or an enquiry, my advice is don't! Most times if you are proposing a store visit, it will pay you to offer the alternative of 'sending for details'—and it rarely does any harm to offer those thinking of returning an enquiry card the alternative of calling on you.

In the same way with lead generation, one will often benefit from offering the prospect the ability to ring a given number rather than return a card. Certainly those who are particularly keen, or in a hurry, will welcome this avenue. Both, naturally, are to be encouraged.

Why is direct mail so popular for lead generation?
The simple answer is: cost-effectiveness. Using a salesperson for what is called 'cold calling' is a very costly business.

Let's look at an example.

The first thing we need to recognise is just how costly a salesforce is. Research carried out some years ago confirmed this. I do not make this point to castigate salespeople as expensive or overpaid, but simply to explain that if we can refocus their particular skills on what they do best, then we shall get a better return on our investment.

The research I refer to analysed the way that salespeople spend their time. A dangerous notion! But anyway, it arrived at the conclusion presented in Table 2.1.

Table 2.1   Analysis of salespersons' time

Event	%
In touch with office	18
Waiting	17
Breaks	10
Travel	30
Miscellaneous	8
Selling	17
	100

The figures in the table are not important as specifics. Whether you or your sales team spend 17 or 14 or 25 per cent of sales time in front of prospects and clients, doesn't matter for the purpose of this explanation. The only thing we need to mark is that these people are only at the skill-end—getting in, selling and taking orders—for the minority of their time. What makes them expensive is that their most valuable skill is only at work for a small part of their time—most often substantially less than a quarter. It follows, therefore, that what I have described as 'refocusing' their skills at work—that is, getting them in front of buyers, selling—has to be worth doing. Subject to cost. Thus a process whereby you can achieve massive sales performance increases has to be worth examining in more detail. And that's what we'll do . . .

It always rains all day Monday . . . and Friday afternoons

The weather obliges because it knows this is peak 'cold-calling' time! So an intrepid warrior of the salesforce sets out to conquer the unknown, trying to get past receptionists who've heard it all before, secretaries who have been trained not to let salespeople in, notices that proclaim 'REPS ON THURSDAYS AND BY APPOINTMENT ONLY'. Disconsolately he leaves a hopeless trail of business cards and brochures behind, until he stumbles on the one potential buyer who is prepared to give him some time. Prepared, indeed, to see him.

In comparative terms, if we liken this to the Loyalty Ladder described in Chapter 1, this meeting moves a suspect to a prospect. Albeit, because he has managed to face the suspect his chances of making a sale are improved.

So, in the development of a warm 'prospect' our hero might have made, say five prospective calls, to get to see one on whom he can actually start to weave his spell.

Let's consider the costs of this process. We've had five wasted calls, and one successful one. The wasted calls will, of course, be short since he didn't actually get to see the decision maker. Let's assume the wasted calls have run up costs—salaries and other overheads included—of £50 each. For the successful call, our warrior will spend more time with the suspect, moving up the interest level, turning the suspect into a prospect, and he'll have more brochures to hand, use his sales aids, possibly try to get the prospect to see a demonstration, visit an installation, accept a trial offer. Whatever. We'll allow £75 for this visit. So it looks like this:

Five 'wasted' calls at £50	£250
One successful call at £75	£75
Total	£325

What happens next is what we call 'the conversion cycle'. The process of recalling on the prospect to close the sale.

Again, these are far more likely to be longer visits. Often the 'prospect' will start to reveal more information, introduce other people, and be prepared to talk in detail. And negotiations start. It is quite usual for this process to average two to three further visits. For the purpose of this example, I intend to average that out at two and a half visits, all at the figure of £75 that I allowed before.

Costs so far	£325.00
Add: 2.5 further calls at £75	£187.50
Total	£512.50

That's a lot of money. Yours may be more. Maybe less. You must do this sum yourself to see how it looks for you.

Next, you can take a look at how it works when you use direct mail to do the 'cold calling', refocusing the sales team on the conversion cycle. This will achieve an additional advantage for you. But we'll ignore that for my first demonstration.

I'm going to use a mailing that will cost £500 per thousand. That's to say, we might have mailed 8000 prospects and it cost us £4000.

Our mailing pulls a response of 2 per cent which means 160 enquiries will have cost us £25 each. The salesforce go pounding after the business. They find it's not exactly a bed of roses. Contrary to what all the 'experts' said at the sales conference, not all of these people actually want to buy. Some of them, would you believe, only want a brochure! Let's say that, through sheer hard work, diligence, and genius of course, the salesforce average a one-in-three conversion to sale.

In other words, since we had a direct mail cost per reply (enquiry) of £25, we can reckon that we have a direct mail cost per sale of £75. But that's not all, we still have the sales calls to pay for. These will nearly always be the longer type. They will nearly always be the type that include plenty of free product literature, a demonstration . . . or whatever. In other words, the £75 call not the £50 one. So let's add those in.

> Cost of mailing per sale
>   (Three leads required at £25)   £75
>   Now we have to call on the three
>   (Three calls at £75)   £225
> Total   £300

So you can see that against the cold-calling process we have already scored a tiny advantage—in fact, the direct mail method is about 8.5 per cent cheaper. Hardly worth all the fuss!

But we haven't really considered the major advantage yet.

Direct mail nearly always delivers a substantially better quality prospect than the cold-calling method. And it delivers this élite level of prospect for two important reasons that have a major influence on the conversion cycle. They make it shorter, more effective and easier to achieve a sale. The reasons are understandable when you think about them . . .

1   *The prospect has taken the initiative*
    You haven't been knocking on the door brow-beating receptionists, secretaries and the like, leaving innocent bodies strewn in your wake as you try to convince everyone that they really should see you. You haven't called, called again, and called again until finally, just 'cos you've got a winning smile and they're sorry for you or flattered that they merit three calls, they convince someone to give you a minute or two. Which you, cunning fox that you are, get up to seven or eight.
    What's happened is that this innocent, harmless, persuasive little number in an envelope has presented itself before the prospects. In their home or on their 'home' territory, they have made up their own minds in their own time—even if you did slide a few temptations in—that they want to get to know more. So you know, on one level or another, for whatever reason, they are interested in what you have to say or sell. So they've asked *you* to contact *them*. Naturally you will get more attention, a more interested and sympathetic hearing. They have demonstrated their interest.

2   *They know the basic facts before they express their interest*
    Very few people will send back a reply card asking for your 36-page colour brochure about 'water filtration equipment for fresh-water fast-moving streams and rivers at under £100000 unless, first, they've got such a river; second, it needs filtering; third, they have some influence over, or interest in, whether it gets filtered; and fourth, there's either £100K lying in a budget somewhere—or they think it's possible to get.
    Very few people will ask you for full details in response to 'Accept your FREE FABRIC SAMPLES and a copy of 'HOW TO RE-UPHOLSTER A THREE-PIECE SUITE IN JUST THREE WEEKENDS FOR UNDER £200—INCLUDING ALL MATERIALS AND TOOLS'

unless they have furniture that requires repair, some way of collecting £200 (or the £17 a month you'll offer!) and the time and the inclination, or a friend or son-in-law, to do the work.

In either case, I suggest our cold-calling super-hero could make not six, but sixty calls to find such a pearl among the swine—or needle in a haystack.

In most cases where the initiative has come from the prospect rather than from you, it's an easier sale. For 'easier' read 'more likely to succeed'. And with less effort.

Hence it is not uncommon to see a comparable conversion cycle trimmed—to get back to the example—from three more visits to a mere one or two.

Let's place that scenario into our figures.

If you remember, we'd allowed for a cost per prospect identification and first call of £300 against the cold calling £325. So . . .

Cost of three leads at £25	£75.00
Cost of three sales calls at £75	£225.00
Cost of one and half calls at £75	£112.50
Total	£412.50

So, in this example we've a cost per sale of £412.50 when we use direct mail against £512.50 for cold calling. Cold calling costs a further £100!

This, in my experience, is a very modest example. I've often seen this work out and prove through experience to be £200 to £300 more. Often substantially more. I urge you to work it out with your own figures. And when you do, remember the all-important by-product—a valuable list of hot prospects for future use.

THERE ARE ONLY THREE KINDS OF CUSTOMER IN THE LAND

The good news here is that direct mail is a great sales promoter for all of them.

Here are the three kinds of customer:

- EXISTING CUSTOMERS
- LAPSED CUSTOMERS
- PROSPECTIVE CUSTOMERS

Your tasks are clear. And direct mail is all set to help.

It can turn suspects into prospects and—sometimes with and sometimes without your help—it can turn prospects into customers. It can go back to your lapsed customers and get them back into the fold with another sale.

And it can go to work on your existing customers either to repeat sell or with customer care and loyalty programmes. Most favour a blend of the two.

No one has a problem working out which is the best of the lists. The old Ten-X factor puts the customer list streaks ahead. For second place there's often a tussle. Lapsed versus prospects.

And yet you'd be surprised how many throw away their list of lapsed customers. In the States there used to be a dealer who went round buying the old metal address plates and filing cabinets of record cards for scrap when companies went into liquidation. The receiver, looking at the scrap value, would virtually pay the dealer to take them away. He took them to the competitor companies who cheerfully parted with up to a dollar a name, yielding the smarty-pants dealer often up to 1000 per cent profit.

So this is the by-product I referred to earlier. A name. Not any old name, but someone who, at a given time and for a given reason, has 'put up a hand'—that is to say, placed an enquiry with you—and thereby effectively said to you 'OK. Here I am. Come and get me. I'm interested in what you have to sell. I can probably afford it. And I want to know more.' Or even, put another way, 'I/we could use your stuff. Tell us about it.'

The number of times you will come across a list of people who have expressed an interest in what you have to sell AND, effectively, have shown a willingness to do business with you, is pretty rare. I suggest you take good care of every enquiry placed with you. Preferably go one step further.

Respecting the prospect

From my own personal experience I never cease to be—not amazed—disappointed and despairing of the number of people who fail to recognise the value, or the cost, of a name. This failure manifests itself in two distinct ways. The first is apathy. Here I speak about the vast numbers of advertisers whose ads carry coupons, but who:

(a) either just don't bother to respond
     or:
(b) shove the latest brochure in a big brown envelope with a compliment slip and a photocopied list of dealers or stockists. (Stockists in many cases is a misnomer. If it's a new product, the odds that you will actually find one in stock are tiny. This is, I pray, a solely British phenomenon.)
     and then:
(c) file the names away in an old shoe box. (Of course, the cost of putting these onto a computer is astronomical.)

So what is the value of a name? It is a prospective customer's name. Well, you can look at it two ways as I see it. First, you can place a value on it in terms of what it has cost you to get. Or you can look at it in terms of its *potential* value to you as a new business contact. Let's look at that—because, depending on your product or service, it's quite possible this could be highly valuable. Maybe not the first time, but think of it in comparison to all the other lists you might be tempted to rent or even buy outright. What has this one got going for you?

1 These people are at least prepared to talk about doing business with you.
2 They've made that decision, not on a whim, but after your ad or mailing, or whatever, has given them some basic information on the product(s) or service(s) you offer.
3 The fact they've expressed such interest suggests:
    (a) they are in the market for some
    (b) they think they can afford it

(c)   they're prepared to think about it now—and, therefore, maybe again in the future.

4 Even if they decide not to accept this first proposition from you—it will be much easier to sell something else to someone who knows a bit about you, and who you've already impressed.

Don't over-step the mark

Moving back to the more general topic of lead generation, I would like to pull back a thought, underlining that there should be a quite distinct definition of the role of your direct mail and the role of your salesperson or device.

Generating an enquiry is about priming the prospect for the sale. Benefits achieve this, *not* features. Your job is to get the salesperson in front of a warm prospect. Someone who is interested and wants to buy. The salesperson's job is to get the sale. They are distinctly different objectives and will be achieved by different methods. You need very much to experiment to find the right balance of quantity and quality.

How to make fulfilment achieve exactly that

Fulfilment is the term used to describe the action of responding to a response—fulfilling a request for information or, indeed, fulfilling an order.

For the next few pages we shall concentrate on the fulfilment of requests for more information, or fulfilment as the second stage of a two-stage sale.

First, some advice for those who have nothing, or apparently nothing, for a product! I think particularly of finance companies, building societies, insurance companies and to some extent charities with membership or subscription renewals.

Those kinds of people whose 'product' is not in a box, is not three dimensional, will not grace the home or office, will not be seen or felt or used regularly—but is still very often quite pricey or a major outlay. They equally often send out, as the result of an order never mind an enquiry, the most appalling, flimsy and often incomprehensible set of worthless-looking scraps.

They've gone to enormous trouble and spent often sizeable sums of money to get a customer on the books. They've convinced some poor mortal to part with £15 a month for the next 20 years and what the new customer receives is a computer printed piece of 'systems' paper telling them, very often, lots of negative things. What effect does this have on the recipient who has just parted with an amount that will ultimately stack up to a spend—at £15 a month for 20 years—of £3600?

MAILBOX

GETTING FULFILMENT PACKAGES TAKEN MORE SERIOUSLY

Here's an idea that works extremely well—and will hardly set you back anything. No need to test it! Just do it. Depending on the quantities you're dealing with, it can be achieved for no more than the cost of having a rubber stamp made. Or some labels printed. Or even just a small piece of artwork to add to your existing envelope message.

What you're going to achieve is an instant lift in the prospect's eyes. You'll be better than just another old mailing. People will pant to get inside! You can obviously put a little creative thought into how you do it. But these are the basic magic words that will achieve this extra effect on those who've requested details from you.

'Here is the information you requested.'

With many financial products and services there is a mandatory cooling-off period. Or, at least, an opportunity for the buyer to reconsider. It is, therefore, imperative in my view, that three things should happen:

1   The 'product pack' should confirm the wisdom of the deci-sion. Not just to buy—but to buy from you. In other words, it should re-sell.

2   The 'product pack' should evoke confidence, but also look and feel worth the investment. It really does cost so very little in

relative terms to make a policy or savings plan or loan document look important and worth the money.

3   The 'product pack' should in some way be made useful and encourage the relationship. The best way to do that— encourage the relationship—is to start the next sale.

Now, back to fulfilling requests for information or fulfilling the second stage of a two-stage sell.

Most of what is said elsewhere—tactically, strategically, creatively—applies to fulfilment packages. They are, after all, only a mailing of a different sort. And the first, often overlooked, difference is that they are more important. Because, as we have come to recognise, they come after you have spent good advertising money stimulating the interest, and because they go to red-hot prospects. People who have taken action to demonstrate their interest in you by making contact with you. This is your big chance to make a sale or to set one up for the future.

You must take as much time, trouble and effort over the fulfilment—in many ways more—than you did over the original advertising.

Here are the steps you should take:

1   *Think about what* THEY *want*
Yes, they want more information. But what else? Inspiration? Reassurance? Advice? Help?

Within the confines of what you paid you must give them all of those things. But you must not stop there. You must offer them more. By phone. By mail. By visit. Or at a nearby outlet.

You must be felt to be caring, interested, understanding, and above all, approachable.

2   *Think about what* YOU *want*
. . . But from the recipients' point of view. It's no good just placing a confusing mass of information in front of them. Think about how to present it in a clear, logical, convincing way. Use your accompanying letter to lead people not just through the sales story but, quite literally, through the materials you are sending.

Also, think about what you want in terms of their next response, and sell that idea to them. Make a proposition. Describe the action you want from them and justify it. Give them reasons to do it. And in terms of taking the action you want, achieve these four ideals:

- Make the action attractive
- Make the action sensible
- Make the action clear
- Make the action simple.

And whatever else you do, don't forget to start by thanking them for contacting you!

In summary, your thinking is required on items that occur before, during and after your mailings. But even before you start the thinking process, perhaps you had better read what comes next, as this is all about some things you should know.

3

Secrets you should know

Fuzzy objectives—not knowing precisely what you want—have no place in direct marketing, let alone in direct mail. Once you have decided what you want out of it, then you can create a brief for the project. This chapter also combines some ideas to help you with timing, to prepare for your replies and to understand the communications task ahead of you. These are the topics you will discover in this chapter. Let us start by considering the objectives.

DEFINING CLEAR OBJECTIVES

First, we need to decide whether you are seeking sales leads, referred sales leads, a completed sale—or what?

Will the leads be followed up by salespeople? If so, how good are they? If there is no salesforce, will you use a fulfilment package? As you will see this will make a substantial difference to the strategy, tactics and economics of the job in hand.

FIVE POPULAR DIRECT MARKETING OBJECTIVES

1 *To sell:* One stage
              Two stage
2 *To generate leads*
3 *To generate traffic*
4 *To modify a relationship with the ultimate aim 'To sell'*

But what else is missing? It's a classical advertising objective:

5   *To inform*

There are other methods of informing. Direct mail is an expensive way to pass information, although it is extremely effective. These are the five classic reasons for the use of direct marketing, and there are a hundred reasons within each of the five!

Lead or sale?

This is going to influence the amount you say, and what you cover. It will also influence the basic objective of your creative approach.

There is no problem if you want a sale; you have to tell every aspect of the story. Include every single benefit you can think of— and I mean EVERY SINGLE benefit. And all the features you can muster—lock, stock and barrel. You only stop when you run out.

Going for a lead is a very different story, not just in how you tell, but in what you tell. Many people set about devising lead generating ads or mailings, misunderstanding the true objective. And if you haven't been down this logic path before, it can come as a bit of a shock to you.

There's no point in beating about the bush! So let's out with it
. . .

> *You will not achieve the optimum response by trying to sell the product or service.*

Hmm. Let's think about that.

If you sell the product or service effectively, you've gone too far. People will call you, saying 'I want one, I want one.'

There won't be many of them—not nearly enough to pay for the mailing. Well, if there are—fire the salesforce! You should be in mail order.

What we're trying to do here is get a *lead*. The salesforce have the job of converting to sale or telesales. Or the next mailing. Or whatever. But if you want a *lead*, you want a LEAD.

So the first and prime objective of the mailing is NOT to sell the product or service.

The objective is to sell the use of the enquiry card

The objective is to sell the use—the return—of the enquiry card *because* of the product or service.

If there's even a tiny thought in your head that's saying 'Come on, John, that's splitting hairs, just messing with words', abandon it.

This is crucial stuff. And if you don't believe me, tell me why no one gets it right. Well, almost no one. Quite often you'll find that a simple, good letter, a reply card and an outer envelope is as much as you'll need.

Most people tell too much. They go beyond the benefits into the features.

Did *you* ever send out a mailing consisting of a letter, a product leaflet and a reply card? You did? Fine, and where in the product leaflet was the product specification? On the back? In the centre spread? In a feature panel?

Anywhere is wrong. In lead generation we look to communicate the benefits, not the features. Since we want ENQUIRIES back, we leave our prospect panting for more. If you arouse curiosity (or interest) and satisfy it at the same time, you have a completed cycle.

If you arouse curiosity and interest and provide the *means* to satisfy at the same time, then you are channelling the readers towards the action you want. They send back the enquiry cards to start the process of satisfying that curiosity. That interest.

What's more, your salesforce are happy because they've got lots to talk about rather than just re-hash what the enquirer already knows.

If this sounds disappointingly basic, that's because it is. It is also vital. And it is fundamental to achieving the maximum response.

But there's a little more to come yet. We need to look at . . .

GETTING THE RIGHT BALANCE OF QUANTITY AND QUALITY

This is often a delicate balance to find. And that balance is nearly always different for every company. It depends on the nature, type and size of your salesforce, or whatever conversion process you employ.

For example, if you have a small, highly qualified and, therefore, perhaps expensive salesforce, you'll need a smaller quantity of high-quality leads. If, on the other hand, you have a large dynamic and thrusting sales team, you'll need higher quantity and lower qualities. Even the remuneration package needs to be taken into account. High commission, low basic will give one set of economic dynamics; high basic, low or no commission another.

How to ensure your mail has a compelling message

Understanding the audience is naturally a major requirement of the brief. And compelling messages are the essential task of the creative team. Compelling messages are always the end result of a compelling brief—a brief which more than gives the details, it *enthuses*.

I've spent so long working from briefs rather than working on them that I thought I'd catch up on some reading. I mean, I know what a brief is. I've seen hundreds of them, giving all the details, all the background from which we start to create.

They describe the product and tell you about the competition. They give you all manner of detail about the lists, any other media involved, the objectives, and all that stuff about the client's logo, product positioning, what to test, and follow-up procedures. There's masses of it!

So I read through the creative bits and pieces in other people's books, because the list I've popped in above is short of at least one vital element.

Money.

How much is there? How much do we have to play with? Ridiculous. Other people's books; all those Americans—Nash,

Caples, Rapp and Collins, Raphel—they must all mention money. They're Americans!

Well, yes, they do. This thing called creative budget. But that's no help, is it?

Yes, yes, of course; creative need to know how much they've got, to allocate correctly between copy, graphics, photography, finished art, etc. But that's not what I'm thinking about.

How much is there to spend? Not just on creative, but on the whole mailing.

As you will see later when we look at the costings, economics and maths, you can play some 'what if' games. But you must have a starting point. Creative, in 'playing' with different ideas, offers, personalisation techniques—the whole artist's pallet that they have at their disposal—will need to consider 'what if' they suggest this or that. But, this or that—new offers, new gifts, die cuts, shapes, special gumming or perforations—will affect not just their costs, but the overall production costs too. How will these, in turn, affect response? Up or down? And the quality? At the end of the day, it will inevitably come down to professional judgement. But, it must be educated and, from the financial aspect, well informed.

So, apart from a thorough brief economically speaking, how else can we ensure that we get the whole team off to a good start? How about this?

JFR'S BRIEFING DOCUMENT

1   THE OBJECTIVES
    1.1   *Sales objectives*
        ● The precise targets
          – Quantity %
          – Quality %
          – Cost per . . .
    1.2   *Business objectives*
        ● The relevance of the sales objectives to the business as a whole
    1.3   *Timing required*

2   THE PRODUCT/SERVICE
   2.1   *What is it?*
      - What does it do, how does it work, how much does it cost, etc.?
      - Is it complete, or any on-going or after sales elements?
   2.2   *Is it any good?*
      - What's wrong with it (weaknesses)?
      - What's right with it (strengths)?
   2.3   *Who says so? . . .*
      - And how do they know?
      - Can we quote them?
   2.4   *Is it unique?*
      - Or merely different? . . .
      - Specifically, how?
   2.5   *Any guarantees . . .*
      - Or other added customer/service benefits?
   2.6   *Is it mail order—or how is it to be sold?*

3   THE MARKET
   3.1   *How big is it?*
      - Market shares?
      - Where do you 'sit' in the market?
   3.2   *What does a buyer 'look' like?*
      - Research and sources
      - Geographics/demographics/psychographics/RFM
   3.3   *Who makes decisions and . . .*
      - How many involved?
      - Any third parties or other considerations?
   3.4   *Previous and latest experiences*
      - Samples
      - Any customer correspondence
      - Case histories
   3.5   *Selections/segmentations/lists*
      - Exploitable affinity or intermediary links or involvement

- Relevant endorsements
- Other activities
  - PR
  - Advertising
  - Sales promotion

3.6 *The competition*
- Run through same list as above where possible

4 THE MEDIA
4.1 *Why direct mail? . . .*
4.2 *And why not others?*
4.3 *How is audience data held?*
- Customer or file record layout
- Processing requirements
- Processing times
- Processing constraints, restrictions

4.4 *Any other media factors*
- Codes of practice
- Restrictions

5 THE BUDGET
5.1 *Total*
- Any specific allocations

5.2 *How budget is calculated*
- Mathematics of sale
- Dynamics of financial success/failure
- Break-even point

5.3 *Highest cost/risk factors*
- Of mailing
- Of project

6 CREATIVE
6.1 *Corporate*
- Positioning/image requirements
- Brand/product positioning and image requirement

6.2 *Product/service*
- Benefit/feature analysis

- Offer/proposition rationale
- In-house or other products or services or resources available as enhancements
  - Old stock/suppliers, etc.
  - Ancillary or consumable items

6.3 *Review of previous creative work*
- And results

6.4 *Systems/response handling/legal*
- Procedures
- Timing

6.5 *Specific test requirements*
- Statistical data/viability
- Variants identified
- Outline matrix

6.6 *Information gathering*
- Any data for future activity
- Repeat sales

6.7 *Buyer attitude statement*
- Before
- After

7 FOLLOW-UP PROCEDURES
7.1 *Methods/systems*
7.2 *Dispatch or follow-up times*
7.3 *Capacity/constraints*
- Manpower
- Resources

8 RESULTS ANALYSIS
8.1 *Who and how?*
8.2 *Reporting and review disciplines*
- Short term—when?
- Long term—when?

9 EFFECTS ON FUTURE
9.1 *In event of . . .*
- Success
- Failure

9.2   *Development/growth potential*
9.3   *Any 'if it works . . .' factors*

Given a comprehensive document like this—but most important—with a full, if long, meeting to discuss it, there is obviously no reason why your message shouldn't get through in a clear, articulate, informed and effective manner.

A word of advice: make sure you have the briefing meeting with the documents already written. Don't be tempted to use it as a confirming document. Or worse still, don't even think about trying to prepare it as the meeting proceeds. This will be a meeting of quite a few people, quite a few disciplines, and quite a few strong points of view. It should be for discussions, not strategic decisions.

MAILBOX

REPEAT MAILINGS OFTEN OUTPULL THE FIRST

When did you ever see a TV ad that only appeared once? Did you ever hear a radio commercial just the one time? When was the last time you saw a poster one-off on the underground?

I know direct mail is so powerful that it very often achieves its goals in one go. But that's like bringing your trawler into port because its full, when you're sure there are more fish out there. Go back for more!

There's nothing to stop you. In fact, even if you've got existing artwork with offer closing dates, you can still use it without too much expense by adding flashes which proclaim: OFFER EXTENDED—PLEASE APPLY BY (*new date*).

HOW TO MAIL WITH PRECISION TIMING

You can't! Not with finite precision. But you can do the best you can. And, of course, the postal service has a role to play in that. Consumer mail is best *received* (not mailed) on Friday or Saturday. Next best is Thursday. My advice, aim for Friday.

Business-to-business is best received on a Wednesday.

MAILBOX

NO PRESENT LIKE THE TIME

For some reason that I have never been able to fathom out, the 'Spring Window' is generally better than the 'Autumn Window'. It must be the sunshine in prospect and the recession of SAD—Seasonal Affective Disorder.

Topicality can make or break a mailing. 'Breakers' are anything from an election to the threat of a postal strike or a run of good summer weather. Whether the things break or just dent will depend, oddly enough, less on the strength of the breaker, and more on the resilience of the strong wall that is you, your product and your proposition. And the margin over break even at which you're operating.

If you are out trawling for names below or around break even—just as a charity might well be, for instance—a breaker will live up to its name. So when your director general is found to be up to something naughty with one of the Kenyan missionaries, who it transpires is the same sex and there's a small question mark over a missing £200000—and *The People* are asking where does the drug-crazed son of an insignificant Tory MP, the previous lover (of either!), fit in to all this—you've got a breaker on your hands!

Here's how to handle it. Lie down. Roll over. Raise your legs and hands in the air. Feign death. Eventually the carrion PR types will sort it all out for you!

But, if you're out there fishing in deep waters—away beyond break even—making 'very nice, thank you' returns, then you can probably stand most breakers. You may experience quiet periods during and after the breaker. Your main fear is a tidal wave.

That's probably anything from *The Sun* deciding it didn't understand your mailing, to the *Daily Express* and Esther Rantzen getting together on a BBC2 special to get nice, real, but broken people to boo a lot on a live show and blame you.

Then, there's the 'maker'. That's when Neil Kinnock, Cliff Richard and Sue Lawley join the Archbishop of Canterbury's fight to have you banned.

Am I joking? You decide.

Makers are, for example, good press or other media coverage prior to or at the time of mailing. There's just no substitute for being in the right place at the right time. And a PR agency can fix that for you! It's a standing joke in the business that as your mailing goes out you pray for rain. That's probably why there's so much mail order in Britain!

Tuesday and Thursday are next best. Monday and Friday are worst. Saturday for most businesses becomes Monday!

It will help you to have a basic understanding of the postal timings for the main delivery services in Britain—first and second class and Mailsort. The 'you get what you pay for' rule prevails— so the more precise you want the timing to be, the more the cost goes up. But you can get quantity discounts using Mailsort 1 or 2, which are the same delivery standards as normal first or second class.

Mail for all seasons

You need to know and understand a little more for direct marketing about seasonality—its relationship to your product, and its effect on your sales—than you do for classical advertising.

The little more you do need to know is this. In direct marketing we experience two response 'windows'. These are two periods when responses will be markedly better than the rest. They are (give or take the odd week!) the second week of January until the first week of June. And the second week of September until the second week of November. Of course, they are not dead cut-offs. And you must overlay this experience against your own and any seasonal aspect to the products.

WHAT DOES A RESPONSE LOOK LIKE?

This is not as stupid a question as it looks! For your response comes in three waves. The first two can be pretty depressing until you think them through.

Wave number two is the returns, gone-aways, nixies—or whichever of these you want to call them. They should be encouraged. After all the fewer of them on your list the better—so you should actually work at getting them back.

There are two things that can be done to encourage returns.

1   Provide the means for information up-dating and addition at *every* opportunity.
2   Ensure that there is some kind of return address on the outer envelope or carrier, thus encouraging the postal authorities to let you have the undeliverables in as many instances as possible.

These amendments or deletions should be dealt with just as quickly as possible. Also, you can 'hitch hike' for new addresses or forthcoming address details. You've seen the credit card companies and so on using the backs of their bangtails, the overleaf of their order, the bound-in insert of their magazine.

Returns can also come back because they were 'undeliverable'. This occurs for a number of reasons.

1   Sloppy input.
2   Handwritten and insufficiently validated input information leading to incorrect addresses.
3   The rats lied.

Another is an extension of 'the rats lied'. It has become a quite widely used ploy—put about by Citizens Advice Bureaux and the like. When you write 'not known at this address' on a mailing and send it back, your level of mailings tend to diminish quite quickly.

I tried this one with my bank manager. But he rang up!

Seriously, there are two great knocks that hit the inexperienced direct mail user right below the confidence belt at one of the weakest moments. That's the time lag between the mailing going out and the replies coming in. A sort of post-natal depression.

As I said, the returns are the second, but you'll get the funnies first. There's one I recall from the seven years or so that I was running my conference series 'The Secrets of Effective Direct Mail'. I built up, as you can imagine, quite a good client list of delegates. Preaching the Ten-X factor, I was always careful (and gratified by the results) to mail these out, trawling for referrals.

And it never ceased to amaze me how many people would come a second, or even a third, time. Now that's loyalty!

Anyway, after the first year, two particular previous delegates took great delight in responding to my invitations. The first would simply scrunch up the mailed items, flatten them, and force them into the reply paid envelope. He or she never identified themselves, which was a shame. Had they done so, I could have taken them off the list. Then I would have stopped irritating them. And they would have stopped irritating me. We'd both have been happy.

The other wanted me to get out more and enjoy myself. Every time I mailed him (and I assume it was a him), he would simply enclose a leaflet for a night club in London into my reply paid envelope and pop it in the post. Nice of him. But since, and I quote the headline, 'Sophisticated Nights for Gay Guys', was not my scene, I was never inclined to accept.

One charity I worked on used to get a 'disgusted' reply fairly regularly from the 'rightful Queen of England'. Unfortunately, she assumed we knew where she lived—somewhere in Preston—and so we couldn't remove her. She probably decided in the end we were going for a 'By Appointment'.

The first reply to the first mailing I was involved with for Bradford and Bingley Building Society was opened with great ceremony. We were all praying for an application for at least the top product that the mailing contained. Far from it! The reply envelope contained one ordinary domestic colour snap of a delectable young lady adorned only in 'naughty' white underwear. Her pose was only marginally less tantalising to the society's marketing men than the challenge of tracking her through the database, given only a postmark and time of posting!!

Yes, the funnies come first. People vent their feelings in many ways. Some are funny. Some are obscene. Sensitive people may prefer not to open your mail for you. Next come the genuine returns—what the trade calls the 'nixies'. These all have one thing in common. They're ten times larger coming back than when they went out. Or so it seems! They sit in a corner of the office, taking up space, and they can become a mountain. Strangely, when you count them, they shrink back to their normal size.

You should plan for nixies. They must be dealt with as soon as it is economically and logistically possible to do so. They will clean your list. Or the lists you rent. Some brokers and suppliers will even give you a postage refund if the quantity exceeds a pre-set percentage.

And what about those who respond?
What of them? What should your attitude be? In a word, WORSHIP.

The big problem with direct marketing is often its biggest attraction. Its accountability. People see that as a way of controlling—no, too often reducing—costs. How can they get away with the minimum acceptable level of service at the minimum level of cost? My philosophy was stated earlier. I'll repeat it.

THE OBJECT OF A BUSINESS IS NOT TO MAKE MONEY
THE OBJECT IS TO SERVE ITS CUSTOMERS
THE RESULT IS TO MAKE MONEY

An example. I often find myself at conference seminars and workshops extolling the virtues of speed—more precisely, using first-class business reply or freepost to get the orders or enquiries back. My advice is to let people know that you want to do business with them. Use first class. It has obvious extra benefits. In lead generation it reduces the time between the enquiry and the follow-up. For a few pence you can cut the follow-up time by 20 to 30 per cent. Ask any salesperson what is the most important thing about following up an enquiry and you'll be told, without a moment's hesitation, to follow up quickly. So, benefit to prospects—when they want to know, they want to know. The more interested they are, the more frustrated they get at delays, and the more likely they are to look around.

Similarly with mail order buyers. They can sit at home and wait. Or they can jump in their car and get it today. That's the choice. The longer the delay, the more likely the prospective buyer is to return the goods. And pick one up in town in the meantime.

Let them enquire first class. Let them buy first class. 'Ahh. We've tested that. It makes no difference', people tell me.

And you know, it never will make a difference if you don't count opinion; if you only look at the number of replies you get—not the ones you didn't get. And you constantly cost the short-term delivery of a promise, not the long-term satisfaction of a customer.

Our job, as direct marketers, is not just to serve the customer, but to serve the customer better. We all spend a lot of money getting enquiries and orders. The cost differential between

---

MAILBOX

PROJECT YOURSELF CONSISTENTLY

Project yourself consistently in line with your adopted corporate style. But think practically about the expense of doing it.

One well-known company had made yellow their colour. But a particular yellow. It never worked too well out of four colour—so they usually ran it as an expensive fifth 'self' colour. Their letters were mainly black and blue—plus, of course, the yellow. When the agency pointed out that this was putting up the cost to no real effect (proved by testing) the client said it had to be done. When the agency pointed out that the logo ran in black in the press, they were fired! You decide who was right.

A large insurance broker mailed out to generate enquiries from the very wealthy for a single premium investment of £20000 plus. The letter was printed to photocopy standards on the kind of paper they used to use for school toilet rolls in the 'good' old days! Their everyday heading was lavishly thermographed on heavyweight quality laid stock. The managing director had decreed that the time to spend money on clients was 'when they were spending money on us'. Stupid idiot! It looked as if he needed your £20000 to set up his business, or to pay last month's bills.

Let's be quite clear about this. Your readers cannot see, feel or experience you or your business. The only evidence—from which they will position you—is the mailing they hold. They should get a clear correct image when they see, feel and experience your mailing. Build your position to better or different than it is, and you will be found out. Fail to project the full quality and substance of it and you won't get an enquiry, let alone a sale.

servicing those adequately and servicing them well, often boils down to pennies.

Regularly, *Direct Response* magazine carries out a survey to see how well response handling measures up. The results are a disgrace to the marketing business. And believe me, as a result, someone else, somewhere, is picking up an order.

A colleague of mine carried out some research in Germany for a kitchen manufacturer. It was established that a purchase decision normally extends over about 18 months—that's to say, from the moment the prospects start thinking about a new kitchen, to the time they buy. Fascinated by this snippet, I instigated a coupon-clipping exercise in the UK to establish how long it takes to get the information you've asked for; how many people assume that simply sending out a product information pack is enough; how many realise that once may not be enough; and how many are prepared to rent their enquirers to other people.

The results are presented in Table 3.1, and as a professional marketer I find them embarrassing.

Table 3.1   Results of research into 'couponed' advertising

		%
1	*Response*	
	Actually responded in any way to a coupon enquiry	63
	(Can you believe that 37% of coupon advertisers didn't actually respond at all?)	
	Responded within seven days	32
	Responded with a considered and professional selling pack	34
	Rented list to other appropriate advertiser	4
2	*Follow-up*	
	Time delay of follow-up call (total 43%)	
	1 to 7 days	12
	7 to 14 days	22
	14+ days	9
		43
	Followed up more than once	12

Look at these results—and I rest my case. Your best will never be enough, unless you're prepared to put up with it. And if you are, you're on your way out.

MAILBOX

DO YOU WANT ALL THOSE REPLIES?

It's a balancing act. Quality v quantity. Let's just remember the context of quality: will the enquiry convert to a sale, or will the sale stick and not result in a cancellation or money-back claim?

Making the reply tempting will have a strong effect in both situations. Making it easy will too—but it will have more effect in lead generation, unless the mail order purchase is long and tedious, such as most motor insurance examples. But one company succeeded in filling in the application for the prospective buyer and cut down their work by possibly ten or more minutes, producing a massive increase in conversions.

The opposite is also true, but a dangerous tactic to tinker with. That's to say, you can decrease the number of replies and increase the quality of them by making it *harder* to reply.

As a general principle, I do advise you to regard this one as a last resort. So much of the profit or loss lies in the middle ground. Later, I shall explain how the recipients of direct mail fall into three and only three types—those on whom your mailing is either *wanted*, *wasted* or *working*. What I describe here as the 'middle ground' is precisely those we identified as the ones on whom our spell is working. We could win or we could fail. But because there are so many more of these than 'the wanteds'—those who want what we have to sell anyway—it stands to reason that their interest level is flimsier. Make it difficult to respond in any way and you will lose these people in droves.

So, do be very sure of your economics and targets before taking out response cards, special offers and other forms of incentives. And be wary of tales from the salesforce that the replies are rotten quality. It's just as likely to be the salesperson who is rotten quality. Look at the figures . . . right across the board.

THE TECHNIQUE OF THE WANTED, THE WASTED AND THE WORKING

Among all the clutter of information that's available—and there's more all the time—do you know who you're writing to? Can you picture them?

Many, many direct response copywriters—often including myself—extol the technique of visualising a single prospective buyer or responder. We fantasise about his or her character; choose his or her clothes; decide on his or her politics and opinions. We invent a person who we think typifies our audience. And a right monster this person can be, too!

Another writer tells me of his own variation on this where he writes to try to achieve a sale with his least-likely-to-buy relative. Whatever works for you!

But this sequence may help you to identify the scope of your task. For it's a fact that on every mailing list—or even database!—whatever your selections, segmentations or profiling, there will still remain only three types of reader. The joy of this rationale is, as you will see, that you need to think about only one of them . . . it makes your job much easier. Sometimes!

The wanted

Let's look at reader type 1. A reader for whom your mailing was WANTED.

He likes you. He likes your company. He knows you. And he approves of you. He likes your product. He probably already has something of yours and he's happy with it.

He likes direct mail. He *reads* direct mail. He likes shopping for lots of things that way. He's comfortable with the whole process.

But more.

He is actually in the market for what you want to sell. Indeed, he had more or less decided to buy one. In fact your mailing arrived that very morning.

I wish there were more of these types around. The fact is, there are never enough of them on *any* mailing list.

So what do we have to say to this person to get the sale?

Answer: next to nothing. As long as we make it easy enough—maybe provide a Telephone Rapid Order Hotline and accept all major credit cards; or be sure to enclose a simple-to-complete order voucher and a first-class reply paid envelope—we should have a sale. Like picking ripe plums!

The wasted

Stand back from reader type 2: the wasted.

He *hates* you. Your company *stinks*. They're cheats, scoundrels and rapscallions. Everyone says so. Your products are the worst, I mean the WORST. He had something from you already. And it broke.

Direct mail? It's not junk. It's worse. He uses better than that for toilet paper. It invades his privacy. He gets at least one full postal van of it every week. And it's all the same—garbage. And as for shopping by post, you must be kidding. They're all crooks—or else they would do what every self-respecting person would do and open a shop.

But more.

Frankly, he wouldn't consider your ignorant suggestion even if he had the quite exorbitant sum you ask for it. And 'let me tell you', the very last thing he needs right now is you wasting his time when he's trying to get to work, the car won't start and the dog's just thrown up on his shoes.

He doesn't approve of credit cards and knows precisely what part of your anatomy the phone was designed for.

Dear reader, we may not pull this one! And when you think about it, we are not dealing just with someone who is going to be difficult to convince, we're looking at someone who is going to be *impossible* to convince. Whatever we say, our approaches are wasted.

Give up! There are, sad to record, always too many of these on any list you may use.

The working

By a process of elimination—the next is the one for whom our message and our offer and our supporting evidence is *working*.

These are the readers you've got to be sure you are writing to. The ones you have to convince. They may be interested. They may buy. They need persuading. They need evidence. They need reasons—good ones. They need to trust and believe in you. But you can do it. It is the number of these readers—the ones on whom we're working—that will make the difference between profit and loss; the difference between success and failure.

So let's spend some time together thinking about how we can achieve the numbers you need.

We'll start with a copywriting formula.

It was, I think, invented just in front of selling itself. But it stands the test of time. And repetition.

It can also be applied effectively to almost any sales situation— mailing, press ads, face-to-face, telephone, whatever. It works equally well to make a sale or to generate an enquiry. It's AIDA. And it stands for:

ATTENTION
INTEREST
DESIRE
ACTION

This formula requires that first you gain the prospect's attention.

Some of the most effective ways to do this are:

- *Powerful use of envelopes*   Copy and art; or just copy. Never art alone. But this must then lead in to the letter headline and opening paragraphs.

- *Benefit-laden promises*   These command attention. Often they can be put across in a dramatic, intriguing way, but they must always be credible. Even if astounding or outstanding, they must not be outlandish!

- *Get an offer into the headline*   But if you can get an offer and a benefit—great. If these are one and the same, even better!

- If your offer is attractive—illustrate it right alongside. Feature a human being for increased readership. But use a caption.

ATTENTION needs more thought so let's take it from the top, literally!

Part One: You still need a headline, of course, but if the deal includes a free offer of something that will illustrate well, then go ahead and illustrate it alongside.

Part Two: Any picture of a human being will attract the eye.

Part Three: Since you've got the eye around, why not use the power of the one thing that gets readership levels second only to a headline—a photo caption.

Next you need to arouse INTEREST. Probably the best way you can do this is to throw another piece of the same meat into the cage. That means, expand upon the self-same benefit—THE MAIN ONE—that you are already running with. Don't be scared to repeat it. And repeat it.

Next we go to DESIRE. What a lovely word! You'll notice it's got two Es. The first is for *Emotion.*

I don't know if you're involved in selling business-to-business or consumer, but whichever it is you'll find a section on how the postures and attitudes vary later. Meanwhile . . .

Let me tell you now that there are two ways to rationalise a sales case—the intellectual and the emotional. Nearly all my money goes on the emotional.

The second E stands for *Enthusiasm.* Here's where you get to work on the canvas of their minds, painting word pictures as you go. Every one a Rembrandt!

Now ACTION. Every salesperson understands the need to ask for the order—AND THEN, GO FOR THE CLOSE. That's why you'll see whole conferences entitled 'CLOSE THAT SALE' and 'THE POWER CLOSE'. What happens when you are in a car showroom? You've expressed interest in the silver whatever with a blue interior. 'Ahhhah', says the salesman. It just so happens that he has one of those in stock. Yes, yes, it has precisely the specification you want (he'll tell you later about the £230 extra for metallic paint) but someone else was interested in the self-same model earlier today. *Fear* sets in.

Well, well, what a surprise. What's he up to? He's after your deposit. That's the kind of action he likes! He knows if he can get your commitment while you're there he's that much nearer the order. It's called striking while the iron is hot!

And so we move from one hot subject to another. Indeed, you could quite easily claim that the next chapter is the hottest of all since we move on to a topic which, many will tell you, is the single most important factor of all.

4

The secrets of lists

DON'T MESS AROUND WITH LISTS WITHOUT A COMPUTER

'Messing around' is all you can do in comparison with achieving the full management and benefit of a list and thereby reaping the full rewards of its potential. You can use non-computer media to hold data, but it can't process it in anything like comparable times.

At present, there is no other practical cost-efficient or sensible media upon which to put a new list—whatever anyone tells you—unless you are trying to avoid the grips of the Data Protection Act which, for some reason, excludes index cards and other, similar, 'manually' held systems. But why would you want to do that?

LISTS? OR DATABASES?

You'll remember that I have already given you my simple descriptions. A list is the whereabouts of people. A database is the whereabouts and the whatabouts. To be successful in direct mail in the future you will have to adopt a database mentality. That means you have to start adding 'the whatabouts' to the name and address information as early as you can in your selling process. But there are some limiting factors to that. They are the individual's basic right to privacy. And the one legal enforcement of that, which adds the individual's right to accuracy. It's called the Data Protection Act.

Although I unswervingly support both, I remain unconvinced that you can legislate for an individual's right to privacy in quite the same way as you can in relation to other data. I believe the interpretation of that right is fundamentally the individual's too. It's up to individuals to decide whether they regard an invasion of privacy as being mailed by anybody at any time, being mailed by certain people or about certain subjects or even at certain times, or whether they really don't give a damn. Having said that, equally I don't believe that an envelope dropping through the letterbox—which you can ignore or not as you choose—constitutes an invasion of privacy. The recipient is, after all, at liberty to dispose of the envelope unopened, or opened and disregarded, as he or she chooses.

There is in most of these matters an acceptable commonsense answer. Most reasonable advertisers know that if they abuse people's rights or offend in any way, they will not achieve their objective. Thus the pressure to succeed will keep reasonable people on the straight and narrow. Public feeling, together with the Data Protection Act, will, in the main, take care of the rats. The great thing is that you and I, as non-rats, do everything we can to uphold standards, and everything we can do to dispose of the rats, otherwise they'll spoil it for the rest of us and turn public opinion against us.

Ironically, whereas I think many extreme consumerists would claim that the age of the database constitutes a real threat of more junk—even a veritable tidal wave—I believe it can be clearly demonstrated that the reverse is more likely; that we move nearer and nearer to getting acceptable propositions to people that are interested by them, with the very minimum of wastage and the very minimum of upset.

How much time and effort should you spend on lists?

There is one extraordinary fact about lists—a situation that has existed as long as I can remember, and which still exists today.

Everybody accepts the list to be the single most important factor in achieving success. However good the offer, the creative, the production and personalisation, if you are mailing to people that can't, don't want to, or just won't buy, you are on a hiding to nothing. Yet, lists have been the most under-developed, under-rated, under-valued part of the industry. It is improving, . . . but slowly. Advertisers blow astronomical sums of money on creative, but balk at the costs of de-duplication. They'll test one simple change of offer, and dash headlong into lists, because they 'feel' right.

A 'good' list is worth its weight in gold

But what does 'good' mean?

Undoubtedly, for most of us, good means responsive. But the factors that affect response go beyond simple 'appropriateness'. Sure, it's a good idea to mail to Eskimos about igloos. But do they want *our* igloos. Not if we spell their name wrong, mail them at an igloo they bought yesterday, or for that matter, mail the igloo they left yesterday!

So there are other things we can do to a list, or make sure that others are doing, to ensure it is 'good'. We shall certainly look at some of those things together, but before we can knock the names into shape we need to find them.

The two principal sources of names

I'll sound rather foolish if I tell you that names come from two sources and two sources only. They are internal and external. That's to say, names that you can access within your company. Or names you have to go outside for. Now the reason I am being so basic and 'obvious' is because so many people overlook the full range of internal sources that are available to them.

So let's assume that you have been given the task of form-ally putting together a mailing list of customers, prospective customers and other contacts for your business. The obvious first place to start is with accounts, the sales ledger. Remember with all these records that the further back you go the greater will be the need to verify the information. Since you will undoubtedly want to build a database in the future, take a good look at all the information you have and make some basic decisions as to what you will wish to store. You will need to consider whether, and if so, for what purpose, you might wish to retrieve it.

Next, the same process with any sales, customer relations or marketing records that are available, going right down to the individuals involved, such as reps or consultants and PR people.

Next look at any agents, outlets or intermediaries and see what you can glean from there. Now it's the turn of administration and service or maintenance teams. Suck out all you can. Examine service and maintenance paperwork and guarantee cards if you have them.

Remember in all this that you must set up a line of communication to ensure that these things will be automatically fed through to you for the future. Think about the ways that outlets or reception areas and maintenance or service teams—anyone exposed to customers or potential customers—can gather names, addresses and as much other useful information as possible.

Regard every contact as a potential for future direct marketing. Just as you will consider all contacts, when they are customers, as an opportunity to repeat sell.

In your search for names make sure that you include telephonists, counter clerks, everyone. Even include the customers themselves. With them you can implement all sorts of fun and games to get them to join in and tell you more about themselves and introduce you to other people they select as being suitable to do business with you. And you'll be surprised just how good (and willing) they are at it. So try member-get-member or customer-get-customer devices.

Leave them space to recommend friends or colleagues on order coupons. Mail them questionnaires to find out their views and feelings. If you can't get a response of between 10 and 40 per cent from a questionnaire or survey mailing, then something is drastically wrong.

And lastly, for the future, don't forget to make the gathering of names, and then the sifting, grading and classifying of them, a way of life.

I can think of only one or two reasons why anyone would want to advertise without a coupon. So why not consider that all your advertising should be couponed? The direct response advertising will naturally be couponed – but then, what about all the *other*

MAILBOX

HOW MANY TIMES CAN YOU MAIL YOUR LIST?

This is a sneaky little question to feed into the Mailbox. And it's one that someone asks in nearly every conference audience. And I can't answer! I can tell you a few 'things' to help you find the answer; the rest, as they say, is up to you!

Thing no. 1 I've not met anyone who has approached the problem intelligently and actually found a ceiling—beyond common sense that is. *Thing no. 2* By common sense, I mean somewhere between 15 to 20 per year. If you want to. And few do.

Thing no. 3 Whether you rent your list can make a difference.

Thing no. 4 Variety of packages, styles and products will help to stretch the tolerance and maintain response rates as you increase. If you are considering sending the same package or the same product all the time, forget 15 to 20. Monitor responses; you'll soon see when they are bored.

Thing no. 5 Remember that as you build up the people who like you and buy from you, so too you will build up those whom you irritate. The response is always a minority. So too, are the nearly offended or nearly irritated. If you let them boil over, some of them will erupt in your direction. Some will reap their revenge in other ways, like moving their bank account from your bank, by not using your credit card, or by avoiding your shops. Or worse, much worse, by anti-wom-ing you. We talked earlier about the power of word of mouth—it works against you too when people are wandering around with such pent-up frustrations. Flush them out and save yourself some money. Use your own mail preference service to get them off the list.

advertising? And if you decide to include a coupon, maybe you can devise something a little stronger than just 'further information' to offer!

Adopt a 'gathering' attitude to all events, activities and functions. For instance, go to exhibitions not just to give out information but to gather as many names of prospects as you can and as much relevant knowledge about them as you can. Your own lists, constructed, cleaned and massaged properly, should always give you the best response. With one possible exception.

From time to time, I have seen even the best customer lists outpulled in what direct marketers call 'affinity' mailings.

This is where the advertiser approaches another list owner and mails out, in the best cases, effectively coupling the power of their own proposition, message and market position together with that of the chosen affinity list owner. Generally speaking, the stronger the endorsement of the third party or affinity organisation the stronger the concept works. Having said that, I must also say that there should be some common ground between the two collaborators. Or, at least, one should be creatable.

OBTAINING LISTS OUTSIDE YOUR OWN BUSINESS

If you don't want to build, there are four principal sources of obtaining lists outside your own business: list owners, list managers, list brokers and list compilers.

In evaluating which of these is the best external source of names for you, I would like you to bear in mind—the very front of your mind—their motivations: who calls their tune; why they are in business; and to whom their first responsibility lies.

LIST OWNERS

There are two kinds. Those who own a list built through their own trading process, and those who own a list that they have compiled for the purpose of renting and selling it. They are distinctly separate types as a rule, bearing in mind—as you have constantly been urged to do throughout this book—the number of exceptions there are to the number of rules!

You have very few problems with the list owners. Other than check out their reputation, you need only ask the right questions and then find which offers nearest to the specification you require and which works best for you. Be prepared for the answer to be both or all. One of the differences, for example, may be that one list offers a high degree of information selectivity and qualification, while another offers little of these but a wider spread of names. Both may work well and the answer may be to vary or alternate your rental of both. On the other hand, it may be better to start with a special purchase deal from both, to merge these with your own lists and then do a deal for the future with them on their new names and their nixies.

Enlightened list owners will not have a problem with this. They may even seek a reciprocal arrangement with you if your market is that close, or your activity level high.

But as far as these owners are concerned, their motivation is to seek maximum sales of their list, to do all they can to keep the list in peak condition, and to keep their customers coming back for more.

I shall now separate those who compile lists for a living and return to them later because I basically regard them as a distinct category.

The motivations of those who have compiled their list through trading will have one fundamentally different aspect; that is, their own future trading potential beyond list rentals. Most owners—particularly publishers and mail order companies—will have built up their list through their own profitable selling to their market. They will have elected, when their list reached a reasonable size, to make it a marketable commodity, and to go into this as an additional profit source. This means two things to you. Firstly, you will never be able to mail anything that competes with their own product range, and, secondly, that their own activities will always take precedence over yours. These two may be so strong as to preclude either of you wanting to do business together. Or, alternatively, it may never be a problem at all.

LIST MANAGERS

List managers are employed by list owners to look after their lists for them. That may simply be to do so for the private use of the list owners or, more commonly when a manager is involved, to keep the list in prime condition for the use of owners as well as to take care of its sale to the marketplace. This will often include the selling and marketing of the list (for which they may go direct or through brokers or both) together with all the administration, handling and processing involved. The involvement of the list owners, where they are employing a list manager, should be limited to demanding their own requirements, monitoring the performance of the manager as their list is trade for them and little else apart from decision making from time to time . . . And banking the proceeds, of course.

List owners should find that a successful manager will not only keep the list in the optimum condition, but effectively return a profit over and above the costs of working the list. Thus, they get the twin benefits of 'free' list maintenance and management for themselves, and an extra bottom line contribution into the bargain.

You might be thinking how this could work for you. We'll look at it shortly.

So, to sum up on list managers, they work for list owners. Their prime concern is the satisfaction of the list owners. You can only ever come, at best, second to that.

LIST BROKERS

If you want to rent lists, as opposed to have anything done to or for your own list, this is where you should turn. And I would urge you to seek out those who belong to the appropriate associations nationally and, perhaps, internationally. In Britain, that will be the British List Brokers Association. The importance of this association is that its members operate within a basic code of conduct, which is, hopefully, a commercial safety net for you.

The 'honest brokers' will be those who understand which side their bread is buttered. Like most direct marketers they will not be after the quick buck. They will want your business. Not once. Not to organise a few tests for you. But for the long term. They will need to understand your business, as well as your direct marketing. Particularly with good, reliable brokers, you should be prepared to disclose your results, your problems and opportunities and your short-, medium- and long-term direct marketing objectives.

As well as giving advice and knowledge, a broker should guide you through the maze of list rentals and take care of the arrangements for you. At worst you should be supplying sample packs for clearance, checking and signing rental agreements, checking deliveries, and paying the bills.

Often imitated but never duplicated

I think that slogan is from the fifties or early sixties. But I can't remember whose it was! I use it to subhead my last but by no means least important thought on external list sources.

Let's talk about duplication for a little.

Everybody shrinks at the thought of duplication, and I can understand that. A list that duplicates with yours is going to cost a fortune in wastage unless, of course, you can remove the duplication. Another reason for the beloved computer! And for high capability software!

Yet, ironically, in 95 per cent of cases the single most likely pointer to a good list is a high degree of duplication with yours. It tells you that there is a greater similarity between the prospective list and your own. And there is generally no reason in my experience to doubt that a list that contains a greater number of actual customers will not equally contain a greater number of potential customers. Having identified that high levels of duplication exist, you then have both to remove it *and* avoid paying for it. Why, after all, should you pay for names you already own? Most list owners, managers and brokers will be open to suggestions. List compilers, in general, haven't got there yet!

The business of business lists

One problem that faces you with business lists is the singular lack of in-depth information available—unless you acquire it yourself. Added to which the lists can be subject to substantial change. The clue to this particular puzzle lies in the fact that although the individuals change, the jobs, functions and tasks remain. Restaurants, snack bars, hotels, etc., may change style or cuisine or ownership. But they tend to continue as they are. Which is why many business mailers will report that names do not outpull simple designations. I have to say that experience here differs enormously, and there is absolutely no substitute for your own experience.

I don't mean so much that one person says one works best and the next person says another. Indeed, my own experience has differed enormously.

If I were to try to pin-point what I think will make the biggest difference, it is probably the use to which you will put the name. In other words, only testing will tell you whether, if using external sources for lists, you should pay extra for named lists. Given a name, it may make no difference whatsoever if you don't really use it. For example, in many business situations, if you only use it on the outer envelope, how many will actually get to see it anyway? On the other hand, if you use it for matching in, personalisation of the letter, a flyer or order device, it may make a lot of difference.

On which point, incidentally, as well as personalising, in business-to-business mail you can 'corporatise' just as well. That is, using the company name on vouchers, letters, flyers, etc., as . . .

'This voucher is for the exclusive use of Hardcastle Engineering Ltd.'

or both personalised and 'corporatised' as . . .

'and so we have extended this invitation not only to you, Mr Smith, but to any other colleagues at Hardcastle Engineering who you feel would benefit by attending.'

WHAT INFORMATION SHOULD YOU STORE ON A DATABASE?

In this, and the following section relating to consumer lists, I am going to provide a checklist of the kind of data that you can consider storing on your business direct mail/marketing database. You may take one look and decide that it's far more than you need, or, indeed, doesn't go far enough. But it is current state of the art. You must additionally consider the items not included that make such a checklist relevant to you. For example, if you are selling retail/supermarket shelving, details of store area by square metre may be useful, or whether they have central buying, or whether any given outlet has its own bakery/fresh produce/butchery, etc., or the number of car parking spaces, or the number of check-outs. Whatever.

In each case, business and consumer, the checklist will be followed by some explanatory notes.

Business database checklist

CORPORATE DATA

- Unique ID number/trans-data link[1]
- Company name
- Street/zone/town or city/state, county or department/ country
- Postal or zip code
- Telephone number(s)/fax number(s)/telex number(s)
- Business or industry classification/SIC codes[2]
- Preferred distribution channelling codes[3]
- Preferred ordering channel codes[4]

- Key contact trans-data codes[5] to personal data/by individual
- Business turnover/number of employees
- Count of duplicate incidence with other files[6]—buyer/enquirer—trans-data link to current employees
- Viewdata/cable subscriber

OPERATIONAL DATA

- Direct/indirect customer
- Acquisition date
- Operational/area code
- Sales/branch/outlet code
- Salesperson/broker/agent codes
- Product or service purchase/enquiry codes
- Fee/commission/credit for sale due/to whom codes
- Business priority level code
- Supply codes . . . equipment/services/maintenance/literature/other
- Media coverage
- Computer system/make/language codes
- Credit control status/limits/excess procedures

CORPORATE RELATIONSHIP DATA BY INDIVIDUAL

- Trans-data link to corporate data[7]
- Acquisition source/method/media codes
- Acquisition offer/promotion code
- Recency of last offer/promotion—success/fail
- Business analysis by product/service
- Recency of last order
- Value of last order
- Last complaint date/reason/resolution codes
- Preferred payment method—bank instruction/credit/cheque/cash
- Business patterns—15 month review by quarters—frequency/value/product (service)

- Recommendations/referrals—MGM/name donor/other
- Count of duplicate incidence with other files—buyer/enquirer[8]

PERSONAL DATA BY INDIVIDUAL

- Trans-data link to corporate data[7]
- Trans-data link to representative database[9]
- Surname
- Title
- Professional qualifications
- Nature of influence—buyer/specifier/finance/other
- Degree of influence on sale(s)—score 1 high/10 low
- Introduction date/employment started/previous job title[10]
- First/second names
- Sex
- Date of birth
- Marital status—married/single/single parent
- Name of spouse
- Occupation of spouse
- Children—number/sexes/ages/first names
- Residential postal/zip code + demographics/acorn/mosaic/pin-point

CUMULATIVE PREVIOUS DATA FROM FORMER EMPLOYEES

- Acquisition sources—method/media/offer/promotion[11]

Notes

1   (Also 7) Trans-data codes are used to link corresponding data between organisations and the individuals involved.
2   SIC (Standard Industrial Classification) codes are a standard method of identifying the business/trade or profession. Some business lists are selectable by SIC code, others are held by SIC order.

3   Distribution channelling codes denote the distribution system(s) or network(s) that is used to supply this customer, e.g. via a particular wholesale/retailer, distributor/dealer or even transport systems, own/Federal Express, etc.

4   Ordering channel codes denote the route(s) through which this organisation likes to order. For instance, via the local representatives, telesales, direct or a particular dealer, distributor, retailer, etc.

5   This is an interim code between the levels at 1 and 7— provides shortform identification of key contacts (often limited to major purchase decision influencers). Although it can provide more, it is often used for name, title, and professional qualifications only.

6   Every time a new file is merged and purged with your own, a count is kept of the incidence of duplication. This is used as an indicator to help in assessing business priority. Also used for targeting.

7   See 1.

8   As an alternative or an addition to 6. Next level of sophistication lowers duplication check success count to individual level where named lists are being merged.

9   Trans-data link code string enables two-way patching for file up-dates, amends and analysis between main file and personal database details held by representative (the computerised little black book!). This supplements main file with on-screen or statistical reporting to include calling information, meeting résumés and agendas.

10   Information to denote service record and whether promoted up or taken on for job.

11   Statistical, historical count, recording success/failure history of additional cumulative information as individuals are deleted from records.

Consumer database checklist

In many ways business list developments have lagged behind even the under-developed, under-invested consumer lists field.

This is an even greater irony, since in business mail the order levels at stake are substantially higher, and therefore the rewards are greater still.

I suggest the invalid, but nonetheless true, reason has to do with the much smaller quantities involved—which in fact make it easier to achieve!

However, for anyone about to make decisions on whether large-scale or up-scale budget allocations for a database are a good idea—and whether the database should be anything as sophisticated as my checklists suggest—let me give you another list. A list of clues to help you make the decision.

- Lists are the single largest criteria that will contribute to the degree of mailing success or failure.
- No other area of direct marketing has been so wickedly, foolishly and unprofessionally under-regarded. Only the US can claim anything like sufficient progress. But then we excuse ourselves by noting, of course, that they've got the numbers.

And so my last clue.

- 1992.

May I suggest one more line to include under 'Personal data by individual'.

- First language/others spoken codes

Let's now consider the all-consuming topic of consumer lists and go straight to the consumer database checklist.

OPERATIONAL DATA

- Unique ID number
- Trans-data link code to other data[1]
- Direct/indirect customer
- Operational/area code

- Sales/branch/outlet code
- Salesperson/broker/agent codes
- Product or service purchase/enquiry codes
- Fee/commission due/to whom codes
- Business priority level code
- Supply codes—equipment/services/literature/other
- TV area/satellite receiver/cable subscriber/viewdata codes
- Media coverage
- Home PC ownership/make/language codes

RELATIONSHIP DATA

- Acquisition source/method/media codes
- Acquisition offer/promotion code
- Recency of last offer/promotion—success/fail
- Business analysis by product/service
- Value of last order
- Date of last order
- Last complaint date/reason/resolution codes
- Preferred payment method—bank instruction/credit card/ cheque/cash
- Business patterns—15 month review by quarters—frequency/value/product (service)
- Credit/payment/debt record
- Recommendations/referrals—MGM/name donor/other

PERSONAL DATA

- Surname
- Title
- Professional qualifications
- Trans-data link to representative or telesales personal database information[2]
- First/second names
- Sex
- Date of birth

- Marital status—married/single/single parent
- Housename or number/street/town or city/state, county or department/country
- Postal/zip code
- Telephone numbers—home/work
- Job status/business or industry/retired codes
- Date of last address change/previous postal code
- Date of last employment change
- Home owned + value/rented/other
- Occupation of spouse
- Children—number/sexes/ages/first names
- Family income band
- Credit/charge/store cards held
- Health record—standard/special (if special, life policy/medical underwriting)
- Residential demographics/acorn/mosaic/pin-point
- Count of duplicate incidence with other files—buyer/enquirer

Notes

1 Trans-data link code to other data—such as individual, partial or complete transaction data or files.
2 Trans-data link code enables two-way patching for file updates, amends and analysis between main file and personal database details held by representative. This supplements main file data with on-screen or statistical reporting to include calling information, appointment résumés and agendas.

Again, as I pointed out with the business-to-business checklist, you will need to look at other data you require to store. It might be residential data, when white goods were purchased, car and motoring information, whether the house is double-glazed, etc. You may wish to have other supplementary lifestyle or psychographic information to assist you in understanding the customer's or prospect's needs.

WHAT ARE GEOGRAPHIC, DEMOGRAPHIC AND PSYCHOGRAPHIC INFORMATION?

. . . And should you bother?

Let's take this question first—should you bother? The answer will depend to some degree on the scale and commitment you are making to consumer direct marketing. But most likely the answer, unless you are dealing exclusively with small local markets, will be 'Yes'.

Let's talk now for the benefit of those involved in European markets. The need to use such targeting systems will increase in 1992. But there are other pressures. For as market potential expands globally—and as manufacturers and service organisations look more seriously at the benefits of international branding—so too, simultaneously, markets are de-massing or fragmenting. For the future, it will be necessary to understand more about smaller groups of consumers within a larger total population.

The targeting opportunities available through geographic, demographic and psychographic data will be enormously valuable for this and will at least see us through the 1990s into the age of interactive viewdata, home terminals and on into the videophone and Home Total Communication Module eras, no doubt. But while we wait for the technocrats to decide our communications fate, let's see what these systems offer for us in the shorter term.

Geographic/demographic systems

In the UK we have ACORN, MOSAIC, PINPOINT, SUPERPROFILES, HOMESCAN, FINPIN, SPECTRA. To start with! In the States ACORN again, PRIZM, VISION, . . . *and more, and more*! If someone could come out with a DIN-type standard, that would be great. Although the thought of DIN-FINPIN does send shivers down the spine!

For many years in the UK, the conventional advertising industry has relied on the most ludicrously out-of-data socio-economic classification. You'll probably have come across them: A, B, C1, C2, D, E. Apart from being barely post-war in their classification of the consumer, they are socially embarrassing!

In order to find something more suitable, more selective, and more effective mainly for direct marketing purposes, a number of suppliers to the industry have invented systems which relate census data to the postal code system. Essentially these differ in that instead of socio-economically defining the individual, they more rigorously analyse the neighbourhood in which a household exists. The British census works in units of about 150-ish households being what is known as an 'enumeration district'. These bear no direct co-relation to the postcode areas but the different systems have, by different methods, achieved workable co-relations.

Having done so they have 'profiled' the areas using the census data, grading postcode areas into a number of neighbourhood types. Some operate 40 or so different types, others up to 150.

I am reluctant to advise you which is best. As such I am not sure there is a best. Certainly, for me, some have performed better than others—but I have enjoyed successes and suffered failures with most of them.

Again, in terms of response uplift, there is no clear winner. I have had one conference delegate assuring me of a 500+ per cent response uplift. I would suggest—knowing the naturally exuberant type—that we divide that by two, and even then I would suggest that this says more about the mistakes he was making before than the strength of the targeting system! I have experienced, typically, anything from nil uplift (even one depression of response) to a 45 per cent uplift.

Psychographic information is essentially behavioural data, generally established through historical or acquired knowledge. It is often confused, but not quite the same I feel, with lifestyle data, which is usually gathered by the circulation of questionnaires or surveys (or trading). The most notable difference in the terminology, as applied by practitioners of such data manipulation, is that the psychographic school base their work on what consumers do, whereas the lifestyle school base it on what consumers *say* they do. You may consider this a fine point.

However, it is certain that there is an expanding use of all of these techniques. And in the face of the de-massification of markets and increasing internationalism among marketers, I have little doubt that all these activities will flourish and become even more widely accepted and adopted.

All the systems tend to work by 'profiling' the whole, or segments, of your existing data bank and ranking the units to which they relate (most often postal code areas) by their similarity of discriminants to your own file or subject segments.

The systems also have something to offer in the list rental field where they can similarly be used to overlay onto a single prospective file, or pre-merged files, to select the most likely respondents. Again these are taken against the profile revealed by your own file or selections of it.

Let's suppose I know where you live or where you are in relation to one of my outlets (geographic data), I know the type of neighbourhood in which you live (demographic data) and the fact that you take two holidays abroad each year, both in Europe, one with your kids and one without (psychographic data). And eminently sensible too, if you don't mind me saying so!

LIST COMPILERS

In this section I am going to run through those lists that are compiled, not generally through trading, but largely from published sources such as directories. The vast majority of these are available for the business and professional markets. Occasionally, you have a choice between, say, magazine subscribers or readers as well, but equally often you will find yourself drawn to the professional list compilers. In the UK we have some noteworthy names.

The Business Database   In other words, the contents of the British Telecom *Yellow Pages* on computer.

- Available with telephone numbers, too!
- Each entry verified by telephone before going on the system for rental.
- Up-dated on a daily basis, although they do not offer names—other than if it's an individual's trading style.

This particular list had its problems in its previous existence but is fast carving a name for itself as value for money and offering wider coverage of some hitherto poorly documented areas (such as retailers). At the time of writing they are operating as BT Connections in Business and offer help with telemarketing in support of their list, and the other way round!

Dun and Bradstreet This is a large database of companies world wide with a comparative wealth of data behind the names. For example, telephone number, turnover, date of foundation, number of staff, SIC code, named executives, etc.

One exciting innovation here for the direct mailer, large, medium or small, is called Duns Direct Access. It offers the ability to access and interrogate on-line Dun and Bradstreet's databases in the UK and other European countries, and to create and download tailor-made marketing lists to your own PC. For regular European users of business lists this is a very useful, flexible and value-for-money way of bringing information for direct mail, telemarketing and sales calling direct on-line into your office at the press of a button (or two!).

Key Postal Advertising This is the name of a leading general supplier of off-the-shelf compiled lists. And a company whose principles (and indeed principals) are respected and admired throughout the industry. They offer high-quality lists covering many hundreds of business classifications and a very usable industrial database with many named executives available.

Market Location Ltd They provide a database loaded with information obtained through field visits. It is linked through to site or location data for sales follow-up and combines a great deal of selectable data as well as executive managerial and SIC coding.

I have chosen to mention just four (and in alphabetical order!), but there are many more. And a host of publishers' files are also available. There are also many specialist areas, such as medical and farming. If you are anxious to track down a shortlist of suitably compiled list suppliers, you would be best advised to contact one of the trade associations.

The snag with many compiled lists is that they are built from directories or other published sources. This is a decreasing problem since the more enlightened directory publishers will make the information available on tape or disk on an on-going basis. One is not therefore so reliant on information that is out-of-date (in direct mail terms) when it is published. Moreover, even when this is not the case, the advent of computer technology in publishing has shortened the time span between the deadline for information gathering and publication itself. Hence they are still relatively out-of-date, but not by so much!

Lastly in this topic, relating as it does predominantly to business mail users of compiled lists, I would urge you to avoid the apparent 'easy way out'. There are some, notably the 'Times Top Thousand' for example, which very rarely give the right answer. This, as a case in point, is so riddled with holding companies, city-type head offices, or registered offices, that it is probably not the best way to market your new shredding machine.

On second thoughts . . .

List rentals

More and more (and for the future probably even more) lists are being rented, and here we present a checklist of questions you should ask *before* you rent a list. There are, of course, others. Specifically you will need to know about costs, timing, availability, and how the list is supplied, to whom they are prepared to release it, what other mailings, especially for competitors, have preceded you (although this had been known to be an advantage rather than otherwise!), and what limitations apply. I suggest that before you place any order, verbal or written, you examine the rental contract in detail.

Mistakes on either side will cause anger, embarrassment and a huge waste of money.

Much of what you need to know about selecting a good list is just old-fashioned common sense, i.e. a list of factory managers supplied by a publisher of a trade magazine with a subscription of £25 per annum will usually be more accurate and more qualified than a similar list from a free controlled circulation journal.

Here are some items to consider when you have found a list that sounds promising for you.

The first question we need to ask is 'Where did the names come from?' Even in these sophisticated days you can still see the odd red face when you ask this simple and basic question.

I'll give you an example. I had a client who was thrilled with a list of people who had obtained tickets for a large business exhibition. Forty thousand of them. For this list he paid a 'trivial' £25 per 1000.

It included his fellow exhibitors, their salesforces, their stand-fitters and their suppliers. It contained each of his large competitors, their salesforces, their stand-fitters and their suppliers. Thirty per cent of the list was outside his existing sales coverage; 7 per cent were overseas visitors. It included every free-loader and everyone who wanted a day out in London. *And* it undoubtedly included some great prospects for him. But what was the real price of this list? As an estimate, probably only 50 per cent were potential buyers. Your first instinct might be to reckon that instead of £25 per 1000, it's really costing £50 per 1000. Not so.

Twenty thousand useless names means more than £3500 of wasted postage, and probably another £4000 to £6000 worth of wasted mail—let's say, for the sake of argument, £7500 in wasted money.

Divide by the 20 000 good addresses, add to the £25 per 1000, now the price is around £400 per 1000! An expensive list by any standards!!

More questions to ask . . .

When was the list compiled or created? Is it an on-going process? How is the file up-dated? Lists are living entities, they start to deteriorate *while* they are being built. They need the addition of new names to keep them fresh and a constant or very regular up-dating process to keep them clean. Does the list owner, for example, mail first class from time to time to flush out nixies? Do they use, and encourage others to use, an 'undelivered' request on the envelope? When they mail do they ask for and facilitate replies that seek new address and other data changes.

How often is the list mailed? What responses are obtained? Remember here that lists most usually become *more* responsive with use, not *less*. But ask what sort of responses others have obtained, in what situation and with what products or services. Don't necessarily be satisfied with the answers you get and, if you're in any doubt or suspicious, ring the advertisers and ask them. Ask, also, whose tests have failed lately—and why.

Ask whether it is a list of purchasers (or subscribers) or responders or enquirers. Purchasers or subscribers who have paid will usually be better than those who haven't, or those who have simply enquired and not converted to sale. All can work, but generally the buyers are best: cash buyers are better than credit. And it is worth asking whether any RFM information is available. If so, whether selections can be made or test segments identified. List owners are usually smart enough to know they can charge a premium for 'hot names'. This is a term used to describe the most recent 'actives' or purchasers. But the top performers in the FM of RFM might also be interesting. That's to say, the most frequent buyers and the higher value transactions.

Is the list geo-demographically or psychographically profiled—or is there any lifestyle information? Even the less sophisticated lists sometimes offer (here comes the *oldest* gag in direct marketing) lists of purchasers broken down by age and sex! What else can they be broken down by(!)?

What quantities or assessments of deliverability are given—and is there any rebate or refund for nixies? Although few list owners will guarantee a percentage of deliverability, they should be prepared to give you some assessment. The most conscientious will offer to refund all or part of the postage to get the gone-aways back. Some will only offer this if nixies exceed the assessed level— and often they will only refund the excess.

After testing, what is the total universe mailable and are there any discounts for multiple or volume use? You will generally be happier to have discovered success with a large volume universe than a small, since the volume lowers roll-out production costs and possibly lowers product or service provision costs too.

Also, check whether they can 'flag' the names you have tested, either for further analysis after the mailing or so that, if you choose, you can leave them out of the roll-out. Again, I must place myself on the fence and say that both have and haven't worked for me in the past. The time between test and roll-out might serve to influence your decision.

Can any other information be supplied that might be useful? An obviously potential Nice One might be telephone numbers.

In what form can the list be supplied? Is it available for merge or purge? Can a 'net' name agreement be negotiated? Obviously, if you are considering any kind of data manipulation or person-alisation you will bc looking at computerised lists. Since we shall be discussing merge/purge below, let's not say anything now other than it means the 'butting up' of one file to others (one is normally yours) to remove the duplication. By negotiating a 'net name' rental agreement, you will effectively only pay for the net off-take from any single list, thus avoiding buying names you already own, and buying the same prospective name twice.

Most list owners and managers will accept 'net name' against a minimum percentage guaranteed off-take. Formulae have been developed to ensure that everyone gets a fair deal in these situations but if you can duck that one, head for a deal that lets you merge in order of the least expensive names first. That way you will, at least in theory, add the maximum of cheap names and the minimum of expensive ones. The sting in the tail is that you sometimes get hit with the guaranteed minimum on the most expensive list!

Lastly, you need to know what their minimum test quantities are and what the costs will be for two activities: the test and a roll-out if successful.

Remember you will evaluate your test against roll-out cost projections, not test costs. But you will still need to know the test costs!

MAILBOX

- When you are advising customers or prospects of your own mail preference service, mention the national service too. It won't involve you in a great deal of cost to provide the name and address, and it will be seen as a caring and thoughtful action. It may also deflect a potential complaint. It offers the consumer the alternative of writing to apply for registration details instead of writing to 'have a go at you'.

- Always make any mail preference service, or similar, a negative option. That's to say, the readers must put pen to paper—or at least take positive action—to implement their wishes.

MERGE/PURGE

And so we emerge at merge/purge, which is woefully complicated now, but is admirably advancing.

Let's start with the basic need. You have a list of customers. You want to increase it by mailing out, achieving orders and adding new names to your file. To do this you are going to mail two lists, which you've already tested, plus three lists you want to test.

You also want those you mail to receive only one mailing. And you want to exclude those on the Mail Preference Service list and a few others who, for any number of reasons—complaints, bad debts, recent nixies, etc.—you have on your 'Stop List'. On the face of it, no problem. There are a number of bureaux who can do it, a number of systems and methods that they will offer, and a number of 'added value' things that can be done at the same time.

But basically (very basically!) the whole lot get 'butted up to each other' on computer and out of the other end spurts your clean list, sorted for postal requirement, free of duplication, everything in apple-pie order—plus, of course, the endless pages of counts and reports.

What has happened is that specialist software has been used to compare the records from all the different sources and eliminate any multiple occurrences. The process is usually achieved through four distinct steps.

Step 1 FORMAT AND EDIT   Records are converted to standard formats, any unwanted or invalid data are stripped out, the postcode is checked (and sometimes corrected) and any oddities are rejected for scrutiny, exclusion, or re-inclusion.

Step 2 DUPLICATE IDENTIFICATION   Exactly as its name suggests, having subjected records to a number of logic-based tests the 'dupes' are found.

Step 3 DIVIDE AND CODE   At this stage the good, the bad (stop list) and the ugly (duplicates) are grouped and the cleaned and approved records are key coded to denote source (and any other required codings).

Step 4   The combined, clean list is ordered to meet the postal requirements for bulk mail price advantages.

The complications I referred to come in two areas: deciding the 'pecking order' of lists being the first. I gave you my thoughts— take the cheapest first. Others will tell you take the biggest list first. Others, still, not to take any of them first, but apportion the duplication throughout so they all share and share the pain alike. Personally, I organise the whole lot through one good broker and take the advice given (which may differ, based on the whims and wishes of the list owners involved).

The next confusion is that of the 'bolt-on goodies'. One temptation is to pre-decline the input lists using one of the consumer selection systems (ACORN, PINPOINT, MOSAIC, etc.) and take, by descending order of appeal, the top decile from each list first, then the second, and so on. Some 'results predictions' claim to be able to identify the best lists for you and to be able to grade them in order of predicted results. It's all done with glue, paper clips, *papier mâché* and some complicated frilly bits that take several different profiles of your list and compare the others for similarities. On the basis of its work it looks into its crystal ball and makes its recommendations. The point of the whole mission is to determine your 'pecking order', making sure you therefore take the maximum from the predicted high response lists.

Yet again, I have to report different successes. On the one hand, the predictions were totally laughable, so much so that I wondered if I was holding the sheet upside down. On the other hand, out of 10 predictions it got 2 transposed, I think the first and the third. The conclusion I came to was that the predictions were more interesting as a computer exercise to determine for large mailings which lists should be shortlisted for testing. But in terms of setting the 'pecking order' priorities, even a misprediction as apparently innocent as transposing third for first and vice versa—however good the score out of 10—could cost more than it could make. It will get better!

Incidentally, the first idea—selecting against your profile—works well. But list owners are not so keen to play!

5

The secrets of testing

The testability of direct mail—when you first realise just how powerful it is, the degree of certainty you can obtain, and its value to your business—is a very enticing and flirtatious quality. You can get quite obsessed by it.

There are plenty of stories of people who have used basic testing techniques to unlock response differentials of 100, 200, 300 per cent and more. Indeed, only recently, I put together a test programme that unlocked a variant offering a 1000 per cent increase to cost-effectiveness.

You can sense the attraction. So let's look at the concept, and the things you need to do to ensure accurate and, as near as possible, repeatable results. And let's look at the kind of things you should test to get the maximum uplift.

WHY SHOULD YOU TEST IN DIRECT MAIL?

Because it's there! In other words, because you can. Let's look at some typical questions that people ask at my conferences and workshops.

- Does envelope printing work—especially to business markets where fewer people see it?
- Does personalisation work—and if so, what style or type should I use?
- How much higher response do you get in a business mailing when you rent a list containing personal names?

- How can I tell which gift will work best—and how many should I get into stock?
- Are you sure this long copy thing works?
- Is it better to put the address on the envelope, on the letter to personalise it, or somewhere else?
- Which of those three lists do you think will 'pull' best?

And of course, this little gem:

- What response do you think I'll get?

Much as I'd love to be able to answer those questions, my advice is always 'Why not test and find out?'

I firmly believe that you should be testing something in every mailing you send out, whether you mail in hundreds or in millions.

Obviously, if you mail in millions, the need, the opportunity and the potential is far, far greater. But if you mail in hundreds, wouldn't you still like to know which type of sales letter, which type of offer, which style of approach works best for you?

I know I couldn't resist!

MAILBOX

DON'T OVERDO YOUR TESTING

Over-enthusiasm and over-ambitious test programmes are bad news! My experience suggests strongly that the thirst for knowledge is great. Until you get the hangover of confusion!

Things to understand before you test

From the outset it needs to be said that testing is a curiously satisfying, illusion-shattering and yet in many ways insubstantial, intangible and frustrating process. And endless; curiously shifting, like the proverbial sands in the desert—but with the odd fixed point.

I think what I'm really trying to warn you about is that testing tends to establish three principal kinds of results.

1 *The constant*   Items which are always worthy of testing and re-testing but which constantly, albeit at varying strengths, give a clear positive or negative result.
2 *The varying*   Other issues, which are often surprising, that tend to give differences because they are specific to a situation, project or time. These confuse wonderfully because just when you think you've discovered something that has been increasing or depressing responses and will yield a significant change, you test again and . . . nothing! Or the opposite! These are the desert sands. Constantly shifting.
3 *The hugely trivial*   These are things that you would think would make a significant difference, but in the event don't.

The first of these, you obviously need to know as much about— and as many of—as possible. That's fine, because, among other things, this book is full of them. And those are precisely the items which I referred to earlier when I said direct marketing speakers deliver them as facts from the rostrum. The very things which enable me to have emphasised statements in this book such as 'LONGER COPY SELLS MORE'. It doesn't alter my view at all that you should go on testing them. Pendulums swing. Attitudes, markets, techniques, change and develop. Results from these tests will tend to appear as small clues, indistinct trends to start with, gaining momentum as time passes. The second type lead me to give advice constantly that test results are for *you*! Not necessarily for anyone else.

These are the things that provoke dangerous ill-informed and unguarded comments on discussion panels. While they are honest comments, they are nonetheless misleading. For example, 'We've tried that, it doesn't work.' Two words more would improve the statement. They are: '. . . for us'— thus removing the implication that if it doesn't work for 'us', it won't work for anybody.

And lastly, the hugely trivial. I am reluctant to list these and the reluctance is born of long and bitter experience leading to the realisation that what is trivial for one advertiser will not be so for another. And, most significantly, what is trivial for one advertiser in one specific situation can become far from trivial for that same advertiser in another.

I repeat, and be warned: what you discover works or does not work for you is just that. *For you.*

Bad testing is better than no testing

This is yet another dangerous statement. You must first understand precisely what I mean, and then decide its relevance to you.

Bad testing, as such, is going to yield bad results. A bad result is going to lead to bad decisions and bad responses in the future.

There are two ways and two ways only to test. Scientifically—to give reliable (statistically valid) results. And unscientifically—to give an experience. In both cases, the test, the analysis of the results, and the interpretation leading to decisions for the future are three inextricable activities.

With unscientific testing, you must proceed very cautiously. You have 'gut-feel' experience, instinct. All those senses to work with; and they are valuable. But you must keep a red light flashing in your head—*all the time.*

With scientific testing, you have quantifiable elements of probability and error, and therefore have much more secure data to work on. You will still need all the instincts and experience I mentioned, to understand what you have discovered, which type of result it is and what use you should make of it.

How to make your testing 'scientific'

As I stated earlier, by scientific I mean statistically valid.

The most important starting point is that you test *enough* to make your test valid. In other words, that the test sample is both a sufficient quantity and also wholly representative and unbiased.

1   ENOUGH IS NOT A LOT—MOST PEOPLE MAIL TOO MANY

I often hear views that 10 or 15 per cent is a good sample size. It may be. It depends. But it has absolutely NO STATISTICAL FOUNDATION. It is a difficult (but imperative to understand) fact that whatever you've heard, whatever you felt right, whatever you've been given to understand—there is NO SIGNIFICANT CO-RELATION for our purposes BETWEEN THE SAMPLE SIZE AND THE TOTAL LIST OR QUANTITY OF NAMES TO BE MAILED.

Confusingly, it is still true that the more names you take, the more reliable your result becomes. But this is simply because it is a *wider* experience not because it is *necessary* experience.

Mathematically, it is accepted that over a given number the wider experience gives proportionately decreasing additional validity. Or, in other words, there is an optimum practical quantity to take.

I shall demonstrate and explain how to calculate this quantity after further notes. But you will find that many people are mailing more than they need at a 10–15 per cent level.

2   YOU MUST MAIL THE RIGHT TYPE OF RECIPIENT

'Right', in this context, is categorically an UNBIASED type. Relax! You don't need to ring round everybody to check out their politics, religion, sexual preferences, colour, mental stability and emotional fabric. Exactly the opposite. It's not the *individuals* who must be representative, it is the *sample*.

Put another way, to ensure the success of our test, we have equally to ensure that the sample chosen from the list is truly representative of the whole list.

Here's what you do. Divide the total quantity to be tested by the number you have calculated as the sample size required. People call this process 'an Nth name selection'. What you will establish by this method is the value of N.

I'll go through that again, with a couple of additional tips.

To ensure the lack of bias, and thereby the true representative significance of your samples, you need only to ensure that it is a random sample. To take a random sample you decide the total quantity of the desired sample size and then take every Nth name from the list.

Example

Total quantity = 100 000
Test required =   5 000

$$\frac{100\,000}{5000} = 20$$

Take every 20th name in sequence ($N = 20$)

The two tips: Firstly, remember the sample size is not an absolute for *carte blanche* testing in itself. You can't test five different—or even two different—factors within the same quantity. You *must* have the full quantity for *each* variation.

Secondly, if you are testing more than one factor, allocate the names in rotation. Thus, if you have decided to test four items in quantities that calculate to 5000, you will wish to take 20 000 from the list. Follow this method:

(a)　Take the 20 000 as prescribed above—in the case of a 100 000 test, every fifth name.

(b)　Then allocate each name sequentially by variant so that, on the file, steps 1 and 2 will look like that shown on Figs 5.1 and 5.2.

Original file

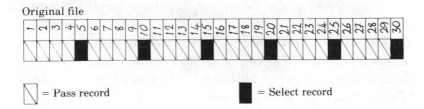

⬜ = Pass record　　　　⬛ = Select record

Figure 5.1　Step one: Take every fifth name

Figure 5.2   Step two: Allocate sequentially

Fairly basic programming will achieve both processes simultaneously and enable off-take sortation into the respective four
samples, as shown in Fig. 5.3.

If you are restless, either you are uncomfortable with figures or
maybe computers—in which case, I do sympathise (I'm not a
whizz with either)—or you fall into the category described by my
third and final point to do with making your test scientific.

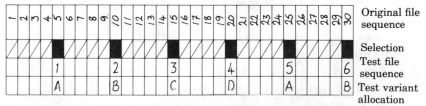

Figure 5.3   Combined process of selection and sequential allocation
together with variant sortation

3   YOU'VE REALISED SCIENTIFIC TESTING IS IMPOSSIBLE FOR YOU

I feel for you but there's nothing I can do, or, for that matter, that
you can do, that will make your testing scientific.

You realised, I expect, with the sort of quantities I was using
that you're going to have a real problem. You've got a list of
maybe 2000. You mail it three or four times a year. Maybe less.
And you thought testing was going to prove to the MD that his
or her subjective judgement—or worse, his wife's or her
husband's—was years out of date, killing response and frustrating beyond belief.

(If you are an MD, no apology. Just make sure the person who does your direct mail doesn't feel like this. I'm about to show them how to pull the wool over your eyes. So do yourself a favour—and let them. It's in your own interest to do so. Take a surreptitious look!)

Here's what you do. Go ahead anyway. You see, only you know that what you're going to embark upon is not scientific. It still sounds very credible. The MD is blissfully unaware that you have calculated (I'll show you how below!) that you need a sample size of 6492 and your list is just one-tenth of that. Or even 6492. And frankly, scientific testing in this situation isn't going to be much help even if your list is 10000.

Likewise, go ahead anyway. The experience is fantastic. And, even if it doesn't point the way as clearly, it will definitely wave an arm in the general direction of what's right, what's wrong, what works, what doesn't, what's good and what's bad.

So if you've got a mailing of 500, go ahead. Test two letters. One short, one long(er!). See what happens if you personalise on the word processor or just print them. Measure the result. Examine it against cost.

But keep reading—for, as you will see, both of these last two factors—measuring results and examining costs—have essential actions attached to them. And what's more, it may help you to use calculations and formulae to establish—by using them in other ways—just how *un*scientific your testing is. You could be surprised and reassured. If not, then at least you'll know the precise mathematical assessment of the risk you take with your testing.

MAILBOX

WHEN YOU BRING A NEW OFFER ON TEST . . .

go back and test an old one too. That means test all three—the new, the control and the one that was the previous control. You'll be surprised just how often 'oldies' can be goodies too.

How ambitious should your testing be?

In direct mail you can test more widely and more precisely than with *any* other advertising medium. It is, as I noted in my opening, a flirtatious quality that the medium holds.

You can read the advice in other books—and of direct marketing, in general, it is sound advice—that you should only test one major factor (or variant) at a time. With direct mail you can do more. But in assessing how much of your mailing should be tests and how much should be the results of previous tests you must carefully consider the need for a control, and the advice of 'The Banker', which I'll explain later.

A single test or a matrix?

For reasons mainly to do with press advertising, which offers very limited testing scope, the single variant process has become known as the 'A/B' split.

It's a simple head-to-head process where you divide your list in two—still on an *N*th name basis (in this case, every other name!) and mail half with each variant.

To test a greater quantity of items is perfectly possible, but is more open to the results being misunderstood or misinterpreted.

To see how it works, look at the matrix in Fig. 5.4. Let's assume that a sample size of 3000 has been calculated and the name allocation process already described is followed. (Remember, each individual variant—in the example of Figure 5.4,

	Offers		
Lists	1	2	3
A	1A	2A	3A
B	1B	2B	3B
C	1C	2C	3C
	9K	9K	9K

Figure 5.4 A simple test matrix

1A/2A/3A/1B/2B, etc.—must mail the full sample size to remain statistically valid.)

The matrix method evokes both focus analysis and tier analysis, which, bearing in mind all that has gone before, can still be quite revealing.

- *Focus analysis* is a direct comparison of each variant. 1A against 1B against each of the remainder.
- *Tier analysis* is the combined effect of the total type of variant: i.e., Combined list A result against combined B against combined C *and* combined offer 1 against combined offer 2 against combined offer 3.

However a matrix test is schematically drawn, analytically examine your results as above.

Production departments may prefer to express the above example in the form shown as Fig. 5.5.

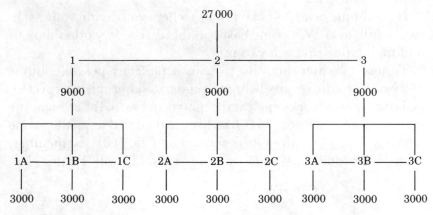

Figure 5.5   Alternative expression of matrix structure

What should you test?

Interesting question! The answer is: 'The things that make the most difference to response.' Sounds fairly natural. But it's a point often overlooked by people. Some favourite red herrings include testing:

- the signatory
- the second (or third or fourth) colour on the letter
- whether to stamp or frank
- the logo position

Take my tip—concentrate on tests to do with the things that will make the most difference. They remain—as they always will—in this order: *the list, the offer, timing and the package.*

Probably the most commonly overlooked of these is timing.

How to test

Basically, there needs to be nothing difficult or complex about testing; that is, unless you choose it to be that way. In other words, it's only as difficult as you make it.

There are five basic ways to assure the most fruitful and least misleading tests. Let's check them out.

1 CODE THE VARIANTS

It stands to reason that if you don't code the test variants to distinguish one from the other you could have problems. In fact there are two reasons to code. The first is to ensure that your mailing test variations go out correctly. The second is to enable you to tell which variations are doing what.

Contents codes

Many people will be testing items that will change several items of print. Thus contents codes are printed on *all* items to ensure that the right letter, with the right leaflet, goes with the right reply card. And they must all be enclosed in the right envelope!

Thus a typical coding system might look like this:

14/8–92/A/4/3

Which is made up as:

14/   = Promotion code
8–92/   = Month and year of mailing
A/   = Offer A, B, C, etc.
4/   = List 1, 2, 3, 4, etc.
3   = Component No.: 1 = Outer envelope
                           2 = Letter
                           3 = Reply slip
                           4 = Gift voucher
                           5 = Reply envelope

Response codes

Whether you decide to have full contents codes or not, the item you really can't escape coding is the reply piece.

And if you're looking for a telephone response you'll have to find some ingenious way of measuring the difference. I guess the most common of all is the Jill Blake, Laura Good method. Phone and ask for Jill Blake. You're a code A! Ask for Laura Good. You're a code B!

2   MINIMISE BIAS

What we're trying to do is ensure the validity of the result, and thereby improve the likelihood of achieving as near as possible the same result from roll-outs as we get from tests. We are also endeavouring *not* to handicap one variant, or possibly give a head-start to another. All this seems very easy at the early planning stage . . . when it's all theory.

With lists, there is not a great deal that can cause bias. You are after all testing the pulling power of that list or segment of the list. The only things likely to creep in to cause a skewed result might be the quality of the addressing itself. Particularly poor or scruffy addressing might depress response; or if one list were to be hand addressed. This is hardly likely these days, but possible! You are trying to get yourself as near as possible into the position of having the only difference between one variant and the other to be the variant itself.

With creative, that shouldn't be a problem—although a few design and copy headaches can be caused getting the balancing act right between merchandising gifts or offers to their best advantage while keeping the overall 'look' and 'feel' to the different packages.

There is no doubt that weaving the gift into the creative approach—or the list characteristics, with visual and verbal links for that matter—can give you a response lift, but usually not great enough to make the difference between a real disaster and a huge success.

3   CALCULATE THE CORRECT SAMPLE SIZE

Here comes some basic maths. Although it's tempting to go into great detail about the laws of probability and bell curves and whatever, I'm working to JFR's law of probability. That is, you probably don't need all the detail. So if you want to work out a sample size I'll tell you how. If you want to *understand* it, then you'll need further reading and you'll find plenty of suitable material in the Bibliography (see page 282)

The basic formula is

$$\text{Sample size} = \frac{\text{CL} \times \text{Response \%} \times \text{Non-response \%}}{(\text{ET})^2}$$

where CL is the confidence level and ET is the error tolerance.

You don't need me to tell you that there's nothing certain in this uncertain world. What is perhaps more surprising is that the oft-berated bunch known as statisticians and mathematicians are among the very first of us to recognise the inescapable truth of this statement.

Yet statistically one can calculate the confidence one can have in a given result or set of results. For us this means simply you can choose what confidence level is acceptable to you for response prediction.

The insertion of the CL figure in the formula is actually the application of a mathematical constant denoting one of the parameters you can set in calculating the sample size you require. Most of the industry work to a 'norm' of 95 per cent confidence. At this level, the value of CL is 3.84, and some other values in common use are:

Confidence level (%)	CL value
75	1.32
90	2.71
93	3.21
95	3.84
99	6.63

Don't worry, if you are still uncertain of what a confidence level is. We'll come back to that after we've looked at . . .

ET stands for ERROR TOLERANCE

Being the wickedly incisive observers of humanity that they are, S&Ms (statisticians and mathematicians) also know that even though you can make predictions with a certain degree of confidence, one cannot always be confident that the predicted result will be absolutely accurate. So, in order to meet the confidence levels (and to be a little more practical about things), we agree that we shall accept some tolerance of error in our prediction. And this error could be either plus or minus the response we want.

– 'Response %' stands for Response %. Not difficult! Drop in the figure or estimated figure.
– 'Non-response %' is simply 100 less the figure above.

Now let's see what kind of statement can be made after we've used the formula. Then I'm sure the meaning and relevance of CL and ET will fall into place.

We'll run through an example and then look at what our S&M friends would have to say about it.

Let's assume that we are happy with the 'norm' confidence level of 95 per cent, and although we're looking for a 2 per cent response, we won't actually commit Hari-Kari if we get 1.5 per cent. So here goes:

$$\text{Sample size} = \frac{3.84 \times 3 \times 97}{(0.5)^2}$$

Therefore, sample size = 4470.

Now what this means to the people in the S&M Dept is that they can issue the following cautious, but optimistic statement . . .

'In this example, all things being equal (which they never are, of course!) if you adopt a sample size of 4470 the response will fall between ±0.5 per cent of 2 per cent (i.e. between 1.5 and 2.5 per cent) 95 times in every 100 if you mail more.'

How do you set the error tolerance?

That's for you to choose. There are a number of popular views on this. So here are two you could consider. For both of these we ignore—as most do—the 'plus' element since over-performance is not generally a problem whereas the minus element is of concern.

Either, set the level based on the differential between break even and the anticipated response or, if you are testing something you expect to give your response a lift, calculate the lift required to cost justify its use as the differential.

Let's just do both of these as examples and you'll see how they work.

Example 1

Parameters: Confidence level 95% (3.84)
    – Error tolerance: Break even for mailing at 2.75%
    – Anticipated response 3%, so say to ±0.25%

Formula: SS $= \dfrac{3.84 \times 3 \times 97}{(0.25)^2}$

$= 17\,880$

Example 2

Parameters: Confidence level 95% (3.84)
– Error tolerance: Testing new flyer designed to lift response in line with or better than cost.
Last result: £20 cost per order at 2.64%
Flyer cost: £40 per 1000
Flyer target: $\dfrac{40 \text{ extra orders}}{20}$ = 2 per 1000 mailed

Response rise required: 0.2% (tolerance parameter)

Formula: SS $= \dfrac{3.84 \times 2.64 \times 97.36}{(0.2)^2}$

$= 25\,675$

What happens if the sample size works out to be too large for practical use?

In this case, the formula is re-jigged to help us assess the degree of risk involved. So it would become (at 95 per cent confidence) . . .

$$ET = \dfrac{3.84 \times \text{Response} \times \text{Non-response}}{\text{Sample size}}$$

Supposing that we had just used the above formula and established our ET of ±0.6 per cent on a 4 per cent response, then our friends over in the S&M Dept would issue something along the lines of the following:

'All things being equal, your result indicates that if you have used the particular sample size at a response rate of 4 per cent, you can be confident that if you mail more of the same, 95 times out of 100 the response will fall somewhere between 3.4 and 4.6 per cent.'

In assessing risk it may help you to gauge the range of ETs when you change the confidence levels in accordance with the options I gave earlier for CLs of 75 per cent up to 99 per cent.

One last thought on sample sizes

Be generous. It is always much better to pay a little extra to test a few more than you need, than it is to have a statistically invalid (in other words *unreliable*) test result.

Perhaps, for you like so many others, the two most difficult things to fix in your head for the future are:

1   There is no valid relationship between the sample and the universe from which it is chosen in relation to its size.
2   The higher the response, the *more* you need to test to maintain validity.

These two attack common sense. You would expect that the bigger the test the bigger the sample that needs to be taken. The mythical 10 per cent seems sensible. Yet it has little bearing whatsoever.

Equally, you would think that the higher the response, the more you had 'got it right', and therefore the need to take large samples would decrease. However, the opposite is true. They once thought the world was flat!

4   MAKE SURE YOU'VE GOT A CONTROL IN YOUR TEST

Where are you going? What are you trying to prove? And where are you coming from?

These hugely philosophical questions, if applied to our lives, could keep us going for hours. They even sound like something from an Open University programme made in the late seventies.

Seriously—what we are leading up to here is something well accepted by botanists, chemists, physicists and all experimentalists the world over.

The fact is that for your test to have any real significance or relevance to the status quo, you must include the status quo in your test.

The reason you need to do this is, as far as possible, to obliterate doubt, or at least quantify it! It follows that you must therefore place the status quo—in effect, a control—in the same environment. Thus it must mail at the same time, in the same conditions as your tests. Then you will be able to determine to some extent where you are, where you came from, and—if you've got your test priorities right—where you're going. And therefore, hopefully, what you should be testing next.

Remember this? *'We seek not that we shall find the answers—simply that we shall understand the questions.'*

An on-going mailing operation should accept this concept. At first, the 'test and learn' opportunities available to the direct marketer seem even more attractive and finite than they are.

Without doubt progress can be made. There are many paths open to us, but it is a *testing* process. That means we shall discover losers as well as winners. It means things will be developed that are a waste of money. It means that prices will be higher because of extra database work, short runs and disproportionate creativity.

As well as a *testing* process, it can also be a *trying* process. For at the end of the day much of the experience, expertise and creative development can, in effect, become 'wasted' by the arrival of, for example, a new production process, or list selection system. So, it should be viewed as an evolutionary process. At times this may seem to be a revolutionary process. A point which leads to . . .

5   THE CONCEPT OF 'THE BANKER'

Testing is an inherently risky business. The over-riding priority must be to protect the bulk of your investment from the unknown, untried and unproven.

It must be accepted that the overall policy should be to change the minimum possible from the known. Indeed, something like 80–90 per cent should be on the same basis as the last, balanced against the results that were obtained.

The discovery of something that works better is an exciting and tempting moment. Imagine. You've been doing things in a particular way for some time when along comes a better product, a new technique, a new creative approach, a list—anything—which seems to offer a significantly better result. 'Why', asks the manager, 'should you go again the old way when we can now offer this new one. It's got to be better.'

The answer is that although new ideas may seem to offer improvement, you can never know until you've tried them. Time after time in my career, I have watched things that everyone thought would prove not just better, but substantially better, go out on test and fail. Classics are . . .

- A new product feature or design that the manufacturer or supplier KNOWS is better than the old. Yet the consumers like the old. They're familiar with it. In fact, they are reluctant and resistant to change.
- A new gift or premium which seems to offer the prospective buyers temptation beyond delight. Whereas what they actually see is too good a deal and it makes them suspicious of the offer and destroys credibility.
- A price-cut or discount which equally destroys credibility. Or worse, shatters the perception of value for money. Or repositions the product so drastically (from, say, luxury to bargain) that they no longer want it.
- A new production process enables massive package cost savings but means that the existing creative and/or personalisation needs to be reshaped. Or worse, introduces more complex or time-consuming response mechanisms for the responder. Typically these might be the switching from a full-blown direct mail package to an all-singing, all-dancing one-piece mailer. It may well slash in-the-mail costs by 20 per cent—but the consumer now needs a week's course in origami to open, digest and respond to it!

So there is a constant need to search out and discover, to push progress and innovation. But each time you fall on a prospective candidate process or item—no matter how spectacular it seems—you are advised to view it with intense suspicion—until it's tested. For those with on-going programmes, there is an answer. For those with continually changing programmes, it is more difficult and requires the very best professional judgement in areas where, probably, the very best professional judges can make the biggest blunders. The consumer is both weird and wonderful. But also fickle.

MAILBOX

KEEPING TESTING COSTS DOWN

When testing, it has been advised that the variants—whatever they are—will give their best results when woven into the package.

However, on a practical level, with testing this isn't always possible. Thus a primary level of testing can be developed to give, what one might describe as, 'soundings'. Perhaps to rule out non-runners rather than precisely identify winners.

For this process, print changes should be kept to the minimum. Or even dropped in as 'over-prints', after a bulk run of common material.

Cheaper still, the test variants can be strapped to a standard package. It is common practice, for example, to merchandise a gift in all items—illustrated and sold throughout the package—on the envelope, letter, leaflet and response device, and perhaps even in a separate gift flyer too.

To obtain 'soundings' one can scale this down. Perhaps the envelope generalising to 'FREE GIFT details inside' or even 'MYSTERY GIFT—revealed inside'. Often you can also refer to a 'gift' in other print items too. In this case my suggestion is in two parts. Firstly, carry a full special gift flyer which thoroughly merchandises the different gifts on test. This will become an easy production task since all other items can be common, and one simply encloses a different gift flyer into each package. A token or stamp to be lifted from the flyer and stuck to the response device will even enable that device to be standard too, and effectively codes it to provide your results data.

However, part two of my advice is: bear with the costs of a changing *response device* anyway. I suggest this for two reasons: primarily because it's a very effective place to merchandise such offers, and also because it acts as a 'code' in itself.

Whatever you decide, if you are considering this very economical primary testing idea, beware that you don't overlook the need to maintain the 'randomness' of the sampling. The most sensible way to achieve this is to pre-sort the addressed items into the samples segments prior to enclosing. Otherwise you'll have the treacherous task of enclosing one varying piece of each of the test alternatives in rotation. Not so easy or controllable!

The additional benefit to this 'economy sounding' method is that one can group varying print items onto a sheet as shown in the example of Fig. 5.6, thus economising on print too.

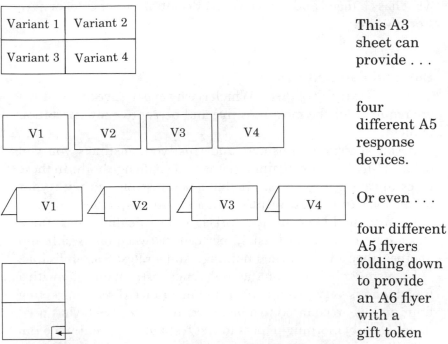

This A3 sheet can provide . . .

four different A5 response devices.

Or even . . .

four different A5 flyers folding down to provide an A6 flyer with a gift token

Figure 5.6   How to economically group varying print items onto one sheet of A3

LOOKING AT RESULTS

Perhaps the first and, indeed, one of the most important things to keep in mind when you look at the results of tests is that you should never look at them in isolation. They will be one or more experiences among a set of other experiences. The learning—which is what you test to achieve—comes from consideration of the results set against two other perspectives: the last—what you have already learned; and the future—what you want to learn next. It is the application of these three tiers of knowledge that creates the most significant growth in you, your experience and thereby your success. You must also be quite sure to be precise about what your test has told you. This falls into two simple areas: what has changed and what has not. Results in either category are worth while.

Lies and damned lies

Test results are full of them. Which is why experience and instinct are required for the most sensitive and perceptive interpretation of them.

If you know your business and trust your instincts you will occasionally come up against results that challenge both. In these cases always try to retest. If that's *not* possible, go with your feelings. Treat the test results with absolute suspicion.

In any case, I have always worked to the rule that unless there was a differential of at least 15 per cent between one result and another, then I had learned nothing. And a retest was advisable.

I remember being up on the conference rostrum one day with a friend who is very prominent in the insurance direct marketing fraternity. He recounted to a bemused audience how he has used national daily morning papers to test testing! Apparently, he ran an A/B split (an opportunity to run an exact split of two alternative approaches offered by some newspapers) but the ad was identical in every respect save for a tiny almost indiscernible single digit code in the bottom of the response coupon.

B outpulled A by nearly 15 per cent!

Just before you retest on exactly the same basis it is worth bearing in mind a piece of advice that is as true for first tests as it is for retests. You should always aim to make test variations as different as possible.

- With or without—not with or with less!
- Long or short—not long or not so long!
- Four colour or single colour—not four colour or three colour!

So just before you proceed with a retest on exactly the same lines, take another look at what you did and see if you can't widen the gap between that and your control.

A wider gap may give you a bigger differential . . . And therefore a more significant result.

Don't forget to project forward

What are you testing for? Normally it will be to determine one of two things:

- Is this worth doing?
- How can I do this better?

To get a sound and reliable answer you must remember that testing costs money. And if you load the future with the costs of the past you may make a wrong decision. And you wouldn't be the first! It is a remarkably common mistake. But a mistake nonetheless.

By this I mean simply that you must examine the economics of your test results against the costs of projecting forward, *not* against the actual costs of the test.

For example, if you carry out a basic viability test—an 'is this worth doing?' test—you could quite easily spend, on a per thousand basis, something like double or treble the costs that repeats in similar or larger quantities would incur.

If you set your results against the higher original costs, you could well mistakenly classify a project as not viable when it is actually perfectly profitable as a forward projection either in larger scale or simply without the start-up or additional costs that testing brings.

These additional costs will include creative work, small quantity or split-run buying and, possibly, extra charges for project management or more complex production.

SOME FAVOURITE TEST SUBJECTS . . .

. . .as well as LISTS and TIMING

Strategic

Mail order v. salesforce (or retailers)
One-stage v. two-stage sale[1]

Product

Deluxe v. regular[2]

Offer

No gift incentive v. discount v. none
High price v. low(er!)
Cash v. credit v. credit cards[3]

Creative

Hard sell v. soft
Closing dates v. early bird[4]
Full colour v. selective colour
Photography v. illustration
Personalisation: with v. without
Copy length: short v. long
Headlines[5]

Format

Reply paid v. not[6]
Multi-piece package v. self-mailer or one piece
Address placing[7]

Notes

1 *One-stage v. two-stage sale*   A lot of products need to be sold in
   two stages. Some just benefit from it. The first stage is the
   generation of the enquiry, the second (following your response
   to stage one) the conversion to sale.

Although this certainly introduces another layer of cost into the proceedings, these can be more than offset by its two benefits:

(a)   There is a substantial cost saving in many cases since complex or expensive sales materials are directed only at those who have expressed a clear interest in what you have to sell and are, therefore, more likely to buy.

(b)   It builds you a list of prospects for repeat approach on this product or fresh approaches on other products, often providing you with useful additional information to make the future approaches on a much more timely, relevant and appropriate basis.

2   *Regular or deluxe—which do you sell first?*   Do you offer the deluxe as the main proposition with an economy option, or the regular as the main proposition with a deluxe option? That's the test!

It's worth noting that a deluxe version will generally give you ±40 per cent of sales.

3   *Cash or credit or . . .*   When testing cash v. credit v. credit cards, if you can't test all three, test both types of credit sale first. Then, whichever wins should be tested against the two cash versions (cash enclosed/bill me later).

Remember, with this test you're not just testing 'what pulls best', you're also testing quantities, economics, fulfilment, money processing and credit costs.

4   *The moral of the early bird*   If you don't know what an early bird is, worm your way through to the creative sections in Chapter 8 where all is revealed! The best way to get there is to keep reading!

5   *Headlines*   Although the current trend (with which I agree, in the main) is to credit creative with a lot less influence than was previously thought, I have seen response improvements of 500 and 600 per cent from simple headline tests.

6   *Reply paid or not?*   This one has more to do with the balance of quantity and quality than whether you should come up with the cost of it. Briefly, I think you should pay!

7   *Address placing*.   On the outer envelope? On the letter to look personalised? On the response device to make it easier to return? This can make a world of difference to response. And, because it is a production decision, it is as much a cost decision as a creative format decision, bearing in mind how the data are held. More advice can be found in both production and creative chapters.

MAILBOX

THE QUICK, CHEAP WAY TO TEST REPEAT MAILINGS

Printing 10000 for your first mailing? Run 11000. Printing 19000? Run 21000. Then mail the balance to a random selection of non-respondents. Code the response items and that'll give you a cheap way of finding out what response a full-scale repeat could get. Run-on print produced at the same time as the original run is very cheap. You'll have to test over a period of one or two months to determine the best gap between your first mailing and your repeat. My experience suggests that this will most likely fall within two to six weeks. Be careful to extract as many as possible of those who have already replied to the first mailing otherwise you could antagonise and place those sales at risk.

One way to get round that is to pop in a short handwritten or typed note (obviously personal and slightly rushed!) which says, 'Since I haven't heard from you yet, I am enclosing a copy of my recent letter, highlighting the benefits of. . .' and then close with a PS that includes: 'Should this letter have crossed in the post with your reply, my sincere apologies.'

The five most important things to remember when testing . . .

1   *Concentrate* on testing the major items: these always centre around the list, the offer, the product, the timing and the (creative) package. The most over-rated of these is creative. The most under-rated is timing.

2   *Test* big differences to get big differences. Two similar creative approaches will yield two similar results. Two similar lists will yield similar results. And so on.

3   *Act* with speed and courage. Test results age quickly. The faster you act the more validity and likelihood there is of you pulling the same again. So don't wait until an entire campaign is complete. Develop a feel for early results and look at the predictive patterns to response. And make early, if brave, decisions.

4   *Don't do what others do.* Test results are invariably very individual. They tell you, at a given time, what your customers or prospects respond to from you. There are inevitably some general tactics and ideas that work well for the majority. But it only takes 51 per cent to be a majority!

5   *Don't look for too much logic* behind test results. There's an awful lot of the emotional in a purchase decision. The head may be logical and therefore more predictable, but the heart is a different matter. You'll gain some clues by watching what other people test. And then watching later what they use again.

TESTING IS NOT A FINITE ACT

Nor, whatever anybody or any book tells you, is it a science. To the advertiser, marketer or seller, testing is an experience-builder, a fine-tuner, a path-finder. And, of course, an extra—something that classical advertisers don't have, at least in any such positive sense, but which, equally, direct marketers accept and revel in as a way of life. On the one hand, it is a vital benefit; on the other, it is a tangled misleading web of confusion.

Grasp its hand. Cautiously. Do not be beguiled by answers it cannot provide. Revel in those it can.

Are you wondering why I talk about testing this way—seemingly shoving you firmly from behind into it, yet standing firmly in front of you like some traffic cop haltingly presenting his 'no entry' palm-up to you? I think what must seem like a dilemma, may actually be clarified with three last thoughts which I will run through.

Nothing stands still for long

People criticise testing. But they can't resist it. The nub of the criticism has to do with the fact that almost as you learn something, so its value starts to fade.

And it's true. All the odds are stacked against you. Speed and courage are the only antidotes. The market is changing. Technology is changing. The competition is changing. Inevitably what works well in one season, one year to one market in one given situation may not have the same significance the next.

Again we come back to the advice that says test the biggest, the most significant things. For these are more solid, and less susceptible to quick change. And make sure you include a control which gives you a yardstick to monitor the combined effect of those changing situations. You will never have enough time, money, or opportunity to test all that you would like to.

Throw away logic!

Testing is an eye-opening process! As you examine the results, you realise that the best thing you can do is throw away logic. If anything, I think one of the greatest lessons I have learned over the years is the difference between a logical reason and a commonsense reason. Mostly, in my experience, it is the commonsense reason that will prevail.

ALL THINGS BEING EQUAL . . .

Remember those words? I last used them to precede the statement from the S&M Dept when we were calculating sample sizes together. 'And they never are' was my rather cynical bracketed remark.

So I will finish out on testing with yet another cautionary set of thoughts. I do so not to put you off, but to make you aware of the realities.

The fact is, you never get the same result twice anyway. And for some reason, as yet unclear to me, response rates out of test always seem to under-pull.

In my experience this under-pull will give you a roll-out result of somewhere between 10 and 20 per cent below the test. I think any number of outside influences, as well as timing, may cause this deviation. What I can't figure out is why it's always an under-pull! In Joan Throckmorton's *Mailing List Strategies* she discusses these same phenomena, and ends with this characteristically frank summation: 'A roll-out which is more than ten times the test quantity can be compared to shooting crap for very high stakes.'

So that's where the mythical 10 per cent sample size comes from! Get me the S&M Dept, right away . . .

6

Secrets about money

I should explain that the following thoughts, and most of the forthcoming calculations, are based on one-off experiences and therefore include no long-term or development factors. Nor do they place any value on pure advertising effect about which we have already pondered.

The first and most important point I wish to make about costings is that you should *always* do them. Right. At the beginning.

HOW TO COST FOR LEAD GENERATION

We'll start with lead generation and tackle mail order second when we've got the grey matter warmed up! For easy reference let's pull back two simple factors mentioned much earlier in the book.

$$\text{Cost per response} = \frac{\text{Cost of mailing}}{\text{Number of replies}}$$

As I said before the above is an interesting yardstick—but not a definitive one.

$$\text{Cost per sale} = \frac{\text{Cost of mailing} + \text{Cost of conversion}}{\text{Number of sales}}$$

When calculating the cost of conversion be sure to include *all* the costs involved. That is, the process as it extends to all those who enquired, not just the smaller number who bought. This ensures that if, for example, you achieve a high response rate but the quality is not up to standard, then the true economics will be reflected—including all the wasted sales costs.

A lot of advertisers wonder whether a small gift or premium as incentive to reply would help. There are four considerations:

1 *Image* In my experience any anti-incentive feeling is usually a problem that lies mostly in the head of the advertiser. Not the recipients of the mailing. They like offers. We *all* like something extra or for nothing! Consider this in relation also to . . .

2 *Your market* Most institutional, government, local authority and civil service personnel are actually forbidden from accepting these offers. A point that can be overcome by explaining, apologising and letting them opt out or by gathering and storing such information until the quantity justifies different 'split-run' approaches.

3 *The effect on conversion rates* The concern of most advertisers thinking about such items is that they will attract insincere enquiries from respondents who will not convert to sale in sufficient numbers. Sometimes this happens. However, by relating the incentive to the subject of the sale, you will find that the mutuality of interest ensures that, even if the recipient is simply 'on the take', at least you have identified an individual with a particular interest.

4 *The effect on the economics of the sale* The economics are not so easily dealt with, since there is no short answer. The best way to find out is to try it. My experiences, in relation to such incentive devices, vary enormously. So test.

Try to get a span of experience in the test, remembering to test 'no incentive' alongside to get a true value measure. Also, be sure that you are testing significant quantities—which are often less than you think you will need.

Thus, you might test equal quantities of:

(a)   No offer
(b)   Product-related offer (product information)
(c)   Product-related offer (low cost gift)
(d)   Product-related offer (higher cost gift)
(e)   Offer not related to product
(f)   The last offer used

The appeal of the offer is very important. As I suggested, it (as well as the rest of your mailing) will affect both quantity and quality. For a motor insurance advertiser, I remember testing no offer, a key ring (quite a natty one!), a pocket road map of Great Britain and a pen-style tyre-pressure gauge. Everybody's money was on the tyre gauge. The indexed results were approximately as follows:

No offer	100
Key ring	80 (yes, *less* than no offer!)
Map	260
Tyre gauge	180

Fascinatingly, the map out-pulled the tyre gauge (some 44 per cent better) and cost about one-third of the price.

I urge you to ignore the *detail* of this particular experience. You must develop your own. All I can assure you of is a set of results often bordering on the perverse! The logic of which I promise can only be understood or rationalised once you've unlocked the answer.

One further point.

How to test sample variants as economically as possible

The more any good incentive is 'bound in' to the sales message the better it will work. I don't use bound-in in the sense that it isn't emphasised and promoted up front. If you want the benefit of a man with a red flag in front of the car, there's no point in allocating him a seat in the back. By 'bound-in' I mean woven in to the sense, the logic, the compulsion of the sales story. It makes *sense* to accept.

Yet, in order to test incentives, this very integration, which so often enhances the effects of an offer, also makes it much more expensive and complex to test.

An offer should be built into the *headline*, the *body copy*, *illustrated* perhaps *on the envelope* and probably in *letter, leaflet, flyers* and on the *order slip*.

So to test several variants cheaply, one must test on the basis of a less integrated offer providing the opportunity to change it cheaply.

Where you have an established winner that is out-pulling or equalling control (which can sustain levels even if it can't improve them), then you know that unless you do something wrong the integration will boost results still further.

Once you have established the value of the effect of the given incentive, then you need to make a judgement based upon conventional value/cost disciplines.

Where should you use incentives?

In a loud voice, I'm tempted to answer *almost anywhere*. The only warning bells are those of credibility (is this really a research questionnaire or are they setting me up for a sale?) and the conversion quality aspect discussed.

Test and find the answers!

However, if you are involved in a two-stage sell (stage one, enquiry generator; stage two, one or more conversion steps) then an incentive that is added to, or completed as a set, by stage two is a good idea. The first must be valuable in its own right.

Example: Stage 1: Free kitchen utensil
            Stage 2: Four more of the same

or   Stage 1: Pocket electronic thermometer
            Stage 2: Home health kit and storage case

or   Stage 1: Booklet *How to Protect Your Belongings*
            Stage 2: Five more companion financial 'How to' books
                and gift box.

Just as you must include in your cost-per-sale calculation the cost of the incentives, so too you must include all the other costs of conversion, whether they be sales visits, phone calls, mailing packs, or whatever. And picking up on my earlier, somewhat basic but necessary point, you must include the costs of all of them to get a true measure of their overall influences on the marketing costs of the completed sale.

How to cost lead generation to obtain budget figures or results targets

The basic formula that I use is not mathematically very bright. But it involves the use of whole percentages, and is easily memorised. It is:

Direct mail cost per sale

$$= \frac{\text{Mailing cost per thousand}}{\text{Response \%}} \times \frac{10}{\text{Conversion rate \%}}$$

Let's suppose we've targeted (or gathered experience that suggests we can achieve) 1.5 per cent response and convert 25 per cent of those to sale. We are trying to establish what the resulting cost per sale will be against a budget mailing cost of £500 per 1000. Therefore:

$$\text{CPS} = \frac{500}{1.5} \times \frac{10}{25}$$

Our direct mail cost per sale will be £133.33.

I am showing you the equation with 'per thousand' and 'per cents' (hence the 'silly' 10) because the business tends to bandy these figures. And, indeed, a lot of costs are organised this way. List rental is '£x per 1000' as often are lettershop and processing costs.

If you prefer to go in units—no problem. Let's take the unit equation with the addition of a premium being used. And this time we'll look at total cost per sale. Again this is a simple case excluding, for example, overhead expenditure in answering sales calls.

Let's therefore start by calculating the cost of the conversion process, which for this example will be a mailed conversion kit with a follow-up going to those who didn't convert after our first attempt.

Suppose from each 1000 mailed we have 15 replies. Each one will involve us in the cost of our first follow-up mailing and, of course, our gifts. Then one in five will buy, the remaining four-fifths will be re-mailed a full conversion kit with some changes. Again one-fifth will buy. Our conversion or follow-up costs will look like this:

Per initial response		*Total*
Conversion mailing	£15.00	
Gift	£4.00	
Subtotal	£19.00	£19.00
Plus second approach		
Conversion mailing No. 2 to 4/5		
4/5 @ £15.00		£12.00
		£31.00

This, plus the mailing cost per response, will give us a total cost per inquiry of (extending our first calculation)

Cost per response (= 500 ÷ 15)	£33.33
Cost per conversion (as above)	£31.00
Total cost per sale	£64.33

Given the concept, you can start to play some 'what if' games. You'll be surprised to see just how little effect is required in ultimate sale terms to justify the extra costs. This remains true, surprisingly, even though in budget terms the cost of gifts and incentives can become significant. Of course, the reverse of the principle is that trimming out the incentive to cut cash can cripple sales. But at the risk of upsetting accountants and penny-pinchers everywhere, by far the most rewarding experience I have had came through *adding* extra pieces. Improving the selling power increases the cost, but ultimately improves the overall *cost-effectiveness*.

Significant cost savings—over and above those of repetition or longer runs, bulk purchasing, and so on—can normally only be made where the job was sloppily organised and managed in the first place. On the other hand, the opportunity to boost cost-effectiveness, given an already efficient and value-for-money vehicle, is a much easier task. In other words, where the job is right in the first place, always think about ways to add value, not to cut costs.

Now we turn to a far more complex and diverse subject. It is my intention here to limit my coverage to the very fundamentals. By far the most succinct—that is, economic but valid—explanation that I have seen written is by Nigel Swabey, and it first appeared as a short(ish!) article in Benn's *Direct Marketing Directory 1987*.

HOW TO COST FOR MAIL ORDER SALES

Rather than endeavour to re-invent Swabey's Wheel for Basic Mail Order Economics, and with grateful acknowledgement to both Nigel Swabey and Benn's *Direct Marketing Directory 1987*, I have selected relevant extracts:

> Ask any direct marketing service company to name the one major complaint they would level against the majority of new clients, and the response you will get (after due mention of the fact that everyone seems to expect 90 days credit these days) is likely to centre on the lack of preparation on the part of the client.
>
> It is not just a question of preparing a comprehensive brief. We all know that an agency's advertising or service can only be as good as the brief it receives. The three-minute brief that ends with that time-honoured phrase 'you know the sort of thing' just will not do in direct marketing. No, it goes deeper than that. What every service company has a right to expect is that the direct marketing client should understand the concept of affordable promotion cost. If your list broker proposes a high quality mailing list at £120 per thousand for a one-time rental,

you need to be able to calculate the impact of that cost on your break-even point. If your advertising agency proposes a free prize draw costing £40,000 for your next mailing programme, you need to be able to calculate the additional response required to cover the cost of the promotion. In short, you need to understand basic mail order maths and the relationship between promotion costs, sales and profits on each new project.

It would be as well for such folk to remember that, for every fortune made in direct marketing, at least two are lost. It is a demanding and exacting business that holds many pitfalls for the unwary.

The real advantage of direct marketing is the sheet measurability of promotional expenditure. As a direct marketer, you enjoy the benefit of instant feedback on your efforts.

The real challenge of this business, however, is in measuring 'results' before the event, as well as after. Provided that you have identified the cost of the product or service being offered, and can predict order processing costs with a reasonable degree of accuracy, you can change any variable in the mix to establish the effect of that variable on your break-even point. You can test the effect of alternative retail prices, alternative types of promotion and the effect of increasing or decreasing the scale of your promotion. When you have determined the optimum mix and are satisfied that the required level of response or sales for break-even is achievable, then—and only then—are you ready to translate your assumptions into a budget and proceed with a test campaign.

It does not matter whether you express your affordable promotion cost as an advertising-to-sales ratio, a sales return on promotional investment, the affordable percentage promotion cost on sales, or as a cost-per-order. The meaning is the same. You have identified the level of orders or sales required to break even on a given promotion expenditure. Without this, you cannot provide an adequate brief to the various agencies you intend to use, and are not equipped to assess the viability of their proposals.

Stage One—Setting the Objectives

The starting point for any break-even analysis on a new project is to establish the overall objective. In the case of a book club, a credit card organisation or a traditional agency mail order catalogue the object may be to limit the cost of recruitment to a maximum cost per member. This cost per member is a reflection of the worth of the member over his life cycle, thus a member spending a total of £100 over an average life cycle might yield a profit of £16 after all operational costs. In order to regenerate the member file, new members need to be recruited at a £6 cost to achieve a net profit of 10% on sales.

The retailers' approach might be rather different. The primary objective of a mail order promotion may be to generate store traffic, and provided that the increase in store traffic can be measured in some way, the retailer may be prepared to tolerate a small loss on his mail order trading operation.

For those companies who are trading at the sharp end of direct response mail order with off-the-page advertising or catalogues, the twin objectives are to recruit new members and to generate a profit on the initial offer. The nature of direct response mail order is such that life-cycle income is by no means assured. In these cases, it may be imprudent to mortgage future profits on your customer file by accepting losses on the initial offer. The object is to achieve a true break-even with no new-member subsidy. Cost-per-order is of course inappropriate as a measure of success in this sector. CPO is a good yardstick where the character and value of the recruitment offer changes little and where average life-cycle income is well established. In direct response mail order trading, the value of the initial order varies with the price of the item on offer, and a more appropriate measurement is one which reflects both response and average order value—such as the advertising-to-sales ratio.

Stage Two—Simple Break-even Analysis

At a very early stage in the development of your promotion, it is worth running a quick check on your assumptions, to make sure that the break-even point is achievable. A great deal of time can be wasted if you proceed to a full costing without a rough break-even analysis.

Figure 6.1 shows a simple break-even calculation on given assumptions. The underlying assumption here is that you are in a position to estimate the gross profit contribution per sale, i.e. the residual profit after deduction of all variable costs of sales including order processing. If, as in the example, the gross

---

Simple breakeven formula

Assumptions:

Promotion costs:	£200 per 1000
Gross profit contribution:	35 per cent of net sales
Average order value:	£40
Returns for refund:	5 per cent

$$\underset{\text{cost}}{\text{Promotion}} \times \underset{\text{contribution percentage}}{\text{Reciprocal of profit}} \times \underset{\text{VAT}}{\text{Uplift for}} \times \underset{\text{returns}}{\text{Uplift for}} = \frac{\text{£ gross sales per '000}}{\text{Averge order value}} = \underset{\text{B/E}}{\text{Orders for}}$$

$$£200 \times \frac{100}{35} \times 1.15 \times \frac{100}{95} = \frac{£691.72}{£40} = 17.29 \text{ per '000 or } 1.73 \text{ per cent B/E response}$$

Formula for 10 per cent profit on net sales (target)

Same assumptions as above.
Promotion costs need to account for 25 per cent of net sales revenue.

$$£200 \times \frac{100}{25} \times 1.15 \times \frac{100}{95} = \frac{£968.42}{£40} = 24.21 \text{ per '000 or } 2.42 \text{ per cent B/E response}$$

Source: *Benn's Direct Marketing Services Directory,* Autumn 1987

Figure 6.1   Simple breakeven calculation

contribution per sale is equivalent to 35% of net sales revenue, break-even is achieved where promotion costs are also equal to 35% of sales. By taking promotion costs and multiplying by the reciprocal (100) divided by 35 you find the level of net sales necessary to sustain promotion costs. The resultant figure is then 'grossed-up' by VAT and refunds to find the gross sales revenue required for break-even. This is then divided by the assumed order value to find the break-even response rate.

Stage Three—Construct a Pro-forma P & L Account

Provided that your trial break-even analysis shows a break-even response rate (or advertising-to-sales ratio) which is realistically achievable, the next step is to draft a pro-forma profit and loss account for the proposed campaign (Figure 6.2). This serves several purposes. Firstly, it provides the financial accountants within your company with a model of the form in which you would like to see the results recorded. Secondly, it acts as a checklist of all overheads and expenses on the campaign. Although the example is shown in simplified form, even this pro-forma draws attention to costs such as the Stock Provision. If you are taking an item into stock, this provision is needed to cover shrinkage, damage in warehouse and write-down on any excess stocks. Thirdly, it provides you with the basis of a formal budget for the campaign, and identifies the six anchor points for your calculations of campaign profitability: Net Sales, Gross Margin, Fulfilment Costs, Gross Contribution, Promotion Costs and Net Profit. All costs and expenses should be indexed to Net Sales to ensure valid comparison of cost ratios on different campaigns.

Stage Four—Record the Assumptions

There are a number of detailed questions that need to be answered before you can proceed with a detailed costing of the project, i.e.:

1. What is the delivered cost? The full cost of the goods or service delivered to your customer, including duties, royalties, service guarantees, packaging, etc.
2. What average order value will be achieved? A compound figure based on the gross selling price plus p&p income, and a units-per-order assumption.
3. What stock provision should be allowed? Based on conditions of purchase from supplier, fragility and value as distress sale.
4. What returns allowance? The amount of provision for the cost of returns, and the handling of returns is a compound figure (see Figure 6.3).
5. What contribution (if any) to fixed overheads? Arbitrary unless the campaign is part of the company's core of business, no contribution if activity is incremental (marginal).

Pro forma profit and loss account cash with order campaign

For financial accounting purposes	£	%	*Simplified for unit profitability analysis*
Gross sales (product)			Selling price
Plus			*Plus*
Postage and packaging income			Postage and packaging charge
Gross sales revenue			Gross sales revenue
Less			*Less*
Refunds			
VAT			VAT
Net sales		100	Net sales
Less			*Less*
Cost of product (including packaging)			Product cost
Postage on despatch of goods			Postage on despatch
Credit card charges			Credit card charges
Provision for cost of returns			Returns allowance
Total cost of sales			Total cost of sales
Gross margin			Gross margin
Less			*Less*
Stock provision			Fulfilment cost
Variable cost of order processing			
Variable cost of warehousing/ despatch			
Gross contribution (to promotion costs, fixed overheads and profit)			Gross contribution
Promotion costs			Promotion costs
Operating profit			
Fixed overheads			
Net profit pre-tax			Net profit pre-tax

Source: *Benn's Direct Marketing Services Directory,* Autumn 1987

Figure 6.2   Pro forma profit and loss account

Returns allowance — refunds and replacements	£ e.g.
Value write-down on goods or refurbishment cost (including any transport cost on returns to supplier)	7.00
Postage in × x per cent	1.10
Postage out	1.80
Order processing charge (in)	0.60
Order processing charge (out)	0.60
Warehouse charge goods inwards	0.30
Warehouse charge goods despatch	0.15
Correspondence charge	1.20
Telephone enquiry on x per cent	0.20
	12.95

Assume 6 per cent incidence of refund or replacement:
£12.95×6 per cent=£0.78 returns allowance per order=2.4 per cent of net sales on £40 average order value.

Source: *Benn's Direct Marketing Services Directory,* Autumn 1987

Figure 6.3   The cost of returns

6   VAT rate? Not forgetting that p&p charges attract VAT at full rate.
7   What allowance for life-cycle income? Any new member subsidy or tolerable loss serves to lower the threshold of response required.
8   What the variable cost of order fulfilment? Including all computer charges, stationery, general correspondence, postage, management time, etc.
9   What is the variable despatch charge? If goods are warehoused, the labour cost on despatch plus storage charges amortised across forecast sales.
10   What credit card charges? A composite figure based on an assumed proportion of all customers settling by credit card.
11   What promotion cost? All creative and production charges, postage, list rental, advertising, print, etc. Postage liability on incoming business reply envelopes is often overlooked in budgeting.

Stage Five—Produce Return on Promotion Investment Summary for Campaign

The ease with which different offers, different lists and different media can be tested in one direct marketing campaign, is such that you need a single schedule

Analysis of distribution, Media, Breakeven Points and Profitability				
Advertising medium/list indentifier	Blogg's Widget Buyers	Quorum Customer List	Insert in *Woman's Realm*	Advert in *Sunday Times*
Method of distribution	Mailing	Mailing	Insert	Advert.
Circulation/ distribution quantity	X,000	Y,000	Z,000	A,000
Forecast % response				
Average £ order value				
Gross sales £ yield per '000				
Net sales £ yield per '000				
Gross £ contribution per '000				
Promotion £ cost per '000				
Total £ cost				
Net profit £ per '000				
Breakeven £ yield per '000 (gross)				
Breakeven % response (gross)				
Total gross £ sales				
Total names recaptured				
Total new names				

Source: Benn's Direct Marketing Services Directory, Autumn 1987

Figure 6.4 Return on promotion investment (ROPI)

which summarises budgeted activity, sales and profitability across the board. This schedule is likely to be the master document for pre-campaign planning and post-campaign analysis of results. The form that we currently use at NS&P is shown in Figure 6.4. The advantage of this schedule is that it enables you to identify at a glance the activities which account for the greatest proportion of total profits. It also identifies the quantity of new customers captured by each activity.

Thank you, Nigel Swabey.

7

Secrets about markets (and people)

For many years I have advised that no major difference exists in creative strategy or tactics between direct mail, whether addressed to consumers, businesses, or indeed, the professions. By far the most common factor is that every mailing will be received (and if we've got it right), opened and acted upon by a human being. Businesses or practices do not make decisions—people do.

It's a far more profitable experience to examine the few real differences that do exist. I will identify these areas as follows: type and level of reader; environment; method of opening and handling; decision process; and buying process.

In order to assess the effects this will have on your approach to mailing, we shall examine the difference between the three types of mail in the light of each of these areas.

To start with, let me introduce you to a little list I've been using in my conferences for some years (see Table 7.1). It was first published in the Post Office Direct Mail Handbook. It's really quite an interesting little résumé that's had a fair amount of exposure already, but in case you haven't seen it before, you might like to check it out.

You'll find Table 7.1 quite interesting, as it focuses mostly on those areas we identified earlier: environment, decision process, etc.

Table 7.1   Consumer reader v. business reader

Characteristics	Consumer reader	Business reader
Type	Human	Human
Failings	Human	Human
Weaknesses	Human	Human
Strengths	Human	Human
Motivations	Human (i.e. greed, lust, self-improvement)	Human (i.e. greed, lust, self-improvement)
Desires	Human	Human
Objectives	Human	Human
Sex	Select one of two	Male predominance decreasing
Language	Normal	Normal with added specialised or technical terms
Purchasing power	Major decisions shared with partner	Major decisions shared or discussed with colleagues or professional advisers
Posture	Generally homely and leisurely	Generally businesslike
Environment	Home	Work
Interests	Self, family, and homely things	Self, business, and company things

HOW DO CONSUMERS DEAL WITH THEIR MAIL?

In all manner of ways. At all manner of times. In all manner of situations!

There's no way we can guess what's happening in their lives—who's in tears, whose father died last night, whose garage caved in, who's getting married today, who's starting a new job, or who's celebrating a fortieth birthday.

But we can find some fixed points among this mass of people— particularly in the way they actually open and set about devouring their mail. It is impossible to predict whether each household is a stacker or a sorter. Stackers tend to sit down with the post and plough through from top to bottom. Sorters divide their post into piles for the various family members. Very few couples choose to 'share' their mail but occasionally, the first one there opens it!

At this point it should be said that millions of households do not get piles of mail. They get, perhaps, one or two items a week. So one division they will make is to distinguish it from The Bad and The Ugly. Because so much direct mail is bright and friendly, colourful and interesting, often with advice or stories or information that make quite a good 'read' anyway, you'd be surprised just how many of these people will actually categorise you as 'The Good'. Into the bargain, these people look forward to mail.

So we have identified one common point of the handling process. The start.

You missed it? Were you paying attention?

It's the name and address block.

Who's it for? Me or one of the others? And, most important— have they spelled my name right? Have they got my address right?

That's why envelope over-printing is so popular in consumer mail. It's a great place to start the sales process. Or arouse curiosity! And, think about it, imagine the space as a poster site and you have a choice: a site on Park Lane where lots of people go, or out in some backwoods spot. Which would you prefer? Obviously, Park Lane. And that's what your envelope front is. Right around the name and address is somewhere we're all going to go. Park Lane!

The next step is fairly predictable too. Again, once they're holding the envelope in their hands, most people behave predictably with it. What do they do? They turn it over. After all, they know the way in is at the back. So there's your next high traffic poster site.

And both of these, strangely, have a quality in common with many posters. People won't dwell there. They're in the process of opening. Time and attention are limited. This is a place for short, simple messages. And, as you will probably have observed, a great many creatives choose to use this space to tease, intrigue or whet the appetite.

Next comes the moment when our potential readers draw out the contents and, if we are successful, start to part with their time. At first, often, without even thinking about it. After all, there are no other ads fighting for attention. Just you. Solus. And, given a clear run, they'll stay with you until that one fatal millisecond when you bore them or simply cease to hold their attention. Then you've got a fight on your hands.

There are some things against which you just can't win: the baby climbing out of the high chair; something burning under the grill; the doorbell. I've never heard of anyone leaning out of their top window in response to the doorbell and shouting 'Come back in ten minutes. I'm just reading this mailing—it's JFR's latest! All about a great new central heating system.'

Once again, we've just walked unsuspectingly past another really important point that's emerging from this short look at how consumers—people!—actually deal with their direct mail.

Here comes a clue—it's one of those luminous bumper stickers you can buy in all the card shops these days . . .

Envelope stuffers do it backwards!

This is true. At least the 'professionals' do it backwards. Most people, I mean those responsible for filling envelopes, don't give it a second thought. Yet since most recipients are going to open your envelope from the back, you'll profit if your message is turned to face them with a handshake and a smile.

There are two more common steps before this opening process becomes such a diverse and individual matter that we can no longer track it. But we can still try to control it, as we'll see later. Indeed, building in a clear reading path is an important creative objective.

People don't dip into envelopes; they try to pull the contents out in one handful. This has most significance with larger envelopes, the point being that there is a distinct danger that small enclosures—such as reply cards—may get left inside and therefore overlooked and discarded. So it is best if small items in big envelopes can be either clipped or 'spot-gummed' to a larger item to avoid this.

However, it is often a temptation in this situation to build a response device into a large item, such as the last fold of a leaflet. This achieves the solution to being left behind or discarded, but it is well known that separate response devices tend to work better than those built in to other components.

While trying to avoid the temptation to produce an all-in-one style of package, you should ensure that what is in the envelope does come out in one easy handful, and that the more we can do to make that handful easy to manage, cope with and understand, the better.

One 'school' tends to profit from the reverse of this advice. It is those—mostly mail order advertisers—who jam pack an envelope virtually to overflowing with a whole gamut of differing verbal and visual stimulations like a lucky dip tub filled to the brim with 'dips' and no wood chips or sawdust to pad it out!

Decisions, decisions! Yes, but whose?

We've seen how with consumer mailings, the physical process of opening your mailing is a fairly predictable process, normally dealt with by the individual addressee you have nominated—The One Person. However, very often, others in the family or household will become involved in the decision process and you must be sure to include them in the scope of your influence. And try to recognise where this might happen. Therefore, for example, if you are mailing parents about a children's Adventure Holiday Camp, remember to include something for the kids too—something that will involve them preferably—as well as giving details of the splendours of the place.

More and more services and products—as the two sexes emancipate—are bought as a result of joint decisions. The days when The Man arranged the insurance and wrote to the bank, while The 'Little Woman' dealt with anything to do with the children's clothes, the vacuum cleaner and food, are mercifully well on their way out. Nowadays many women influence decisions that only a few years ago would have been considered strictly a male responsibility. And the reverse is also true.

There will no doubt remain some bastions of undiscussed decision making, even about joint matters, but one must be conscious of the changes and how matters like this develop. For example, it would be easy to assume that men were still the major influence over some buying. I get about half a dozen or so 'wine' mailings a year (don't ask me why—unless someone has started a new lifestyle database by sifting through dustbins. Now, there's a thought!). I get some from those infamous German wine cellars who have just held—or will shortly be holding—a Mega-Mosel Sweepstake or a Tafel Raffle. My wife, who buys over half (but drinks about a quarter!) of our wine gets no 'wine' mailings at all. Strange since, as a couple, we are fairly typical.

Over 70 per cent of wine decisions in supermarkets these days are made by women. It is, I believe, true that women generally make decisions based more on quality and value than men, but often achieve this by being less brand (or producer) loyal—in other words, more adventurous and less influenced by tradition or habit. They vote, as a recent article on this subject put it so succinctly, 'with their feet and their purses'.

I have decided that brain-death must have occurred deep inside the cellars (or sellers) of Peter Dominic who, for one reason or another over the past decade, must have had my name and address handed to them two or three times or more each year. The result has been not one single contact at national or branch level to make some attempt to influence our household's money away from the increasingly skilfully bought temptations at stores such as Sainsbury's or Waitrose. Perhaps someone will, one day, explain the power of allegiance advertising to them. Or will Sainsbury's, like Marks and Spencer, get there first?

This may be an appropriate time to reveal that at least half the women executives I ask—and I ask a lot!—get infuriated enough to throw out, quite literally, letters that start 'Dear Sir'. Quite right too! One who had taken part in such an 'audience census' was kind enough a few weeks later to send me what she described as a 'red rag to a cow!'. I know what she means. It read . . .

For the attention of the Secretary to the Managing Director

Dear Sir,

Female Sanitary Equipment Supplies

The answer is not, dear reader, to add 'or Madam'!!!

If you're reading this book as someone involved in the marketing functions for, say a large building society or an FMCG marketer, your researchers and analysts will already be way ahead of me—as, no doubt, will you! If perchance you are not so lucky as to have that level of support and influence—or if you're simply a smaller company without the budget for such resources—then you still need to get it right. But you'll do so—as long as people like me remind you!—probably as much out of 'feel' as you will from hard information.

So I would ask you to mark two points from this to influence your thinking.

The first is to give consideration to the person who will be involved in the decision to respond to your proposition. The second, in many ways, a much larger issue (although maybe not so for you particularly) is the consideration—highlighted by my note of brain-death at Peter Dominic's—of the role that direct marketing can, and will, play even in the FMCG fields. This underlines a great deal to do with the changes you will witness and possibly take part in over the next decade plus.

MAILBOX

SOME WRECKERS THAT CAN DAMAGE YOUR EFFORTS

Let's look at how *inconsistent positioning* can make a wrecker:

Successful companies go to a lot of trouble to ensure that they present a consistent corporate front to the world. They prepare a detailed corporate manual for advertising, sales promotion, etc. They spend time, effort and money training salespeople, branch managers, staff and telephone operators. All those who deal with customers. They ensure that every one understands corporate philosophy and policy.

But what happens when you drop the egg of customer perception on the stone floor of inconsistency?

If you present a sophisticated, suave and up-market image to the world at branch level, for example, but send out brash, aggressive mailings to customers at the same time, then the egg of customer perception will fall fairly and squarely with a resounding SPLAT on the stone floor of inconsistency.

Such wreckers can be found in headlines and over-the-top promises. Have you ever been the envy of ALL your friends? Maybe once or twice in a new house or with a new car—nearly. But *all* of them? And because of a thimble collection? SPLAT!

Other wreckers can be found in the way you approach. A charity goes over the top on paper or production quality. SPLAT! Or uses four colour process. SPLAT! Or too much personalisation. SPLAT again!

Next on the list is *thoughtless or even insulting personalisation.*

I was once congratulated on being 'one of the forward thinking executives at . . .'. As MD and chairman at the time, I wasn't too moved by this flattery.

Some months ago, I received a nice wrecker from the building society through which I have my mortgage. They went to the expense of sending me a personalised card to be a member of a club that I've spent 20 years working to leave. It was plainly aimed at the 'first time buyer' level. In my experience, it's better to attach yourself to people's aspirations.

And there was no reason why they couldn't. They would have saved money, and saved face too. They might not be able to select by property value, but I'll bet they can by mortgage level or balance outstanding. Or even monthly repayment. A cut-off half way up the lending scale would have saved probably 25 per cent of their cost and not altered the number of responses one jot.

Mis-spelling a name; or addressing a Mrs as Miss—all these things are gaping cracks in your credibility, . . . as is the next real wrecker.

Duplication   Let's be clear. Duplication is a wonderful thing. The existence of it is a wonderful thing. But letting more than one of the little devils out is a crime.

The only circumstance in which the existence of duplication is not wonderful is, on your own file. It should be avoided at all costs, as doubtless you appreciate.

But the more duplication you find existing between your file and another, the more similarity there is in the type of customers you have. In other words, the more the two market profiles have in common.

Another wrecker often much resented—and I think understandably—by field salespeople is the one that arrives when they are right *in the middle of a negotiation.* Or worse yet, the mailing that arrives extolling your virtues *while a complaint* is being dealt with. Or the *careless and thoughtless* 'your letter is receiving attention' that goes out to a sweet old lady who's writing to tell you that her husband died last week 'just three days after our Diamond Wedding'.

After years and years of devotion to fund raising by mail, let me tell you that there is nothing you can do that will cut out *all* complaints. But you can look at your systems to see, firstly, that these things are dealt with as speedily as possible, and, secondly, that your system—which is nearly always capable of great speed and flexibility in reacting to incoming payments, or especially lack of them—is just as flexible in relation to your customers, or donors, as human beings. So, in the case of our recently widowed lady, it is so easy to de-stream such letters and deal with them more sympathetically, more humanly. Dare I suggest personally?

Doubt is another effective wrecker. Doubt in the customers' or prospects' minds. Perhaps, shame on you, there's something not clear in the mailing. They need some more information, a clarification, or just plain reassurance. Encourage such calls. Let people know that as well as telephone orders you take telephone calls. And if you need them on different phone numbers, no problem. Say so. Of course, you are bound to get the odd ones who confuse the two. So will you ask them to ring the other number? NO! Your enquiry staff should be able to (close sales and) take orders. If you can't give the order staff the basic training required to answer questions, they should at least be able to *transfer* calls.

Some other wreckers

Incredible claims, even if they are true! Obviously *'written' testimonials*, especially if they're true. Rewrite them badly!! And the use of *'Private and Confidential'* or *'Personal'* on the envelope when it's obviously not. Some people claim success with this. I see it as cheating and deceitful. I understand the use of such terms to imply a 'privileged' communication. I cannot condone the abuse of such a privilege. I cannot admire the lack of creative thought that cannot find a better, honest answer.

Of all the things you consider, put consideration of the reader first

This statement is equally true of the consumer and business and professional reader, but needs to be implemented very differently. We are, here, still thinking about the consumer.

I have urged you to think about them, quite literally, *in situ*. To think about their heads and their hearts as well as their wallets!

The last major area in which we need to give them so much consideration is one we have already touched upon. Making it easy to reply, be it by 'phone, visiting an outlet or branch, or by returning an enquiry card or order coupon you enclose. What do they actually have to do?

Your response to this advice will influence your decisions about design and copy certainly, but also about format, contents, and the way in which you use any personalisation techniques. For example, will you use their postal code to insert the address of your nearest branch or outlet as an option to a postal or telephone response? This is quite easily done, and once the programme is prepared you can use it any time for a multitude of reasons. There is nothing to stop you using laser technology to include even a simple digitised map, if you so choose.

You will need to make different decisions depending on whether you are asking for an order or an enquiry. Both purchasers and enquirers will demonstrate over time the amount of 'trouble' or effort they will go to for you. You need to assess this in order to balance what you ask of them. Will you ask them questions that will help you for the future? If you do, you have the opportunity to help them in the future by heeding their answers and therefore ensuring that your communications achieve higher status as 'appropriate advertising'.

My advice is this. Do not cloud this issue—find out how much you can achieve without losing response. Do so all the time in the knowledge that this is a four-cornered fight.

The information you need now, and for the future, are the North and South Poles. The balance of quantity and quality of response discussed previously are the East and West.

The time and effort—or the 'trouble'—that consumers will go to for you is, in general, a specific capacity. The capacity will increase as the relationship you have with them grows or matures. But it is definitive nonetheless. As you make things easier in some ways, so you can ask a little more in others. Develop as much of this capacity as possible.

One useful tip here is to put some friends or colleagues through the task of responding. Time them. Watch them. See what they do. Experience what they go through. In the early days of FREEFONE, for example, it was pretty much a joke that you could spend the same time trying to get through as you could responding twice by post—and this often included a trip to the post-box! Happily it is a different situation today!

When you have observed your 'trial responders', talk to them. Ask them questions. See if they understood what they were supposed to do, and attend to the problems. Then process their responses, and see whether your response handling system works as quickly and as efficiently as it should.

As your mailings go out, the continued observance of response handling will provide very useful information. You will find places where responders 'trip up' because of ambiguous wording, insufficient (or too much) space, or perhaps they 'miss' bits—often important bits, like their credit card expiry date or a much needed signature. After each mailing a discussion with those who handle the response will pay enormous dividends.

But do be wary of some of what they say. Systems or fulfilment teams will often suggest things that make life easier or better for them. One I have come across many, many times is the desire to ensure that all information for an insurance or finance application is available on one side of a sheet. The 'cost' of saving data input personnel the task of turning it over is that the application becomes cramped and difficult to understand, let alone to complete. The result is always a drop in response.

THE DIFFERENCES OF BUSINESS-TO-BUSINESS MAIL

There is one radical difference. Business mail can nearly always be more fun! Not always—nearly always! I think there are two contributory reasons: (1) the orders are bigger, ergo the budgets are bigger, ergo there is more scope to be adventurous; (2) with bigger businesses at least, people are not 'playing' with their own money.

I hope that doesn't sound cynical. I'm sure it's right. And the world of business mail is the richer for it, which probably explains why the instant association with 'junk mail' is a domestic one.

MAILBOX

HOW TO GET PEOPLE TO SHOW YOU THEY'RE INTERESTED—EVEN WHEN THEY DON'T WANT TO BUY OR ENQUIRE

Grabbing the names of people who are interested in you and your products is always a good idea, as we've discussed. This idea might work for you in this hi-tech age.

Someone told me that, of all the scientists ever born on this planet, 90 per cent are still alive today. This highlights the huge mushrooming development of new ideas, new frontiers and new technology.

With it comes the thirst for knowledge, and the need to hear about all the advances and improvements. Preferably in front of the rest of the world.

On your reply cards or coupons place a tick box and a paragraph that says something like this:

FREE TECHNOLOGY UP-DATE SERVICE:
ADVANCE INFORMATION FOR YOU.

As you know, our products and their capabilities are constantly changing and improving to include the very latest technology and design features.

To receive FREE and without obligation a copy of our regular ADVANCE PRODUCT INFORMATION SHEETS please tick this box.

I recommend you check out the provision of the Data Protection Act in relation to this, but you're on to a winner if you get it right.

Business mail may not always be as relevant as we would like, but it is frequently better quality, better produced and more interesting.

HOW DO BUSINESSES AND BUSINESS PEOPLE HANDLE THEIR MAIL?

In most medium-size or small businesses—or even branches of big businesses—the mail is handled in a very similar way to the consumer we have just considered. Probably the single largest difference is that, in the main, the person who opens the envelope is not going to be the one who reads it, . . . or at least, the one we want to read it.

It is therefore understandable that, at my conferences and seminars, the business mail fraternity are less than impressed with my thoughts on the selling power of envelope messages. Yet in most cases, test after test with both types proves this to be cost-effective in both areas. Let us consider why.

Undoubtedly, although I have experienced response lifts of up to 50 per cent through envelope messages alone, this is not every day. They are not generally major response builders. They are, however, usually extremely cost-efficient. The answer to this apparent conundrum lies in the very low additional cost of printing—or even over-printing—envelopes.

The distinction between those two descriptions is that printing refers to the addition of the message during the making (or actually before, albeit sometimes on the same machine) of the envelope. Over-printing is the action of printing onto made-up envelopes. Both are relatively low in cost compared with results obtainable. Printing, as distinct from over-printing, can cost as little as half to one-tenth as much. The printing of envelopes, depending on the complexity of the desired image, when compared with the total cost of a mailing 'in the post' can represent less than a 1 per cent increase in cost, yet its lifting power, when right, is far greater. And that, of course, is what cost-efficiency is about.

Tactically the envelope can be made to be very important, yet, as I have explained, it can be as little as 1 per cent of the total cost. Hence, if an advertiser is expecting, say, a 1.5 per cent response to a mailing, and the envelope knocks that up to anything in excess of 1.515 per cent it has cost justified itself. Or put another way—if you have a mailing of 10000 and you want 150 replies, an envelope message that secures just two more will be a winner. It is not surprising that it nearly always works. It is not surprising that I often describe an envelope message as one of the cheapest forms of advertising you can buy.

Finally, on this point, there are other reasons for wanting to print on to the envelope, and if you desire any of these, then it is entirely possible that all, or a portion, of the printing of the message will effectively be free. And we can prefer nothing better in terms of cost-justification! The reasons I refer to are:

- the need to put your name or identification on the outside
- the need to provide a return address such as 'If undelivered please return to . . .'
- the need to add a postal impression.

You will realise, after this small voyage of discovery into envelope messages, why my views are so clear and unequivocal. Whether you are mailing business or consumers you will, at least nine times out of ten, find that a good or intelligently used envelope message pays for itself. After all, it only has to flex a muscle to achieve your desired response increase.

More than once, even after such an explanation, I have been quizzed again on this by business mail users. 'How', they ask, 'can this be so if no-one but the secretary or the post room get to see it?' My reply is that life is not quite so cut and dried. Nearly every mailing list comprises a mix of businesses, large and small. Some have post rooms. Some do not. Some secretaries include the envelopes in the mail they pass through (especially if it seems to be part of it, or is interesting or amusing); some bosses ask for their mail unopened. The fact is, enough get to see it for it to work—even though 'enough' may not transpire to be very many at all!

The fact, however, that there exists this 'extra step' in the opening process in so many cases is a major difference between the business and consumer direct mail.

MAILBOX

A LEAD GENERATION FORMAT THAT WORKS A TREAT

Although I'm not comfortable with formula-produced creative work, I'm going to pass on one that works most effectively. It achieves the huge benefit of presenting the recipient with a simple package to handle and understand, presents itself in a logical and sensible order, saves money, *and* is easy to respond to! Those are all such good plus points that it has a lot going for it (see Fig. 7.1).

So you see what happens. The recipients see the message alongside the window with their name and address showing through. They turn over (another message if you want) and open. As they take the contents out, the letter folded the way it's shown in Fig. 7.1 presents your big opening—the headline—and already grabs their attention. (I recommend a Z-fold since, if they do flip it to have a quick look without unfolding it, at least the sales message is the right way up. And possibly there's a strong PS working for you there!) You'll notice also, if we consider the roles of the pieces, that: the letter is the salesman; the leaflet tells you more and extends the information; and the reply device is next, all but ready to return. Everything is in the right order. I usually recommend a straightforward business reply design here and that side of the card should face back. Thus, it won't divert anyone who's having a quick flick through, but it simultaneously flags that it is the last piece and that they're supposed to reply. Now all they have to do is decide whether they want to.

Assuming that they do, they'll find you've already done the donkey-work and put their name and address on the reply card making it quick and easy for them to tick a box or two and post it back to you.

Since the card is this way round it's ideally suited for the window envelope I mentioned earlier.

Simple. Neat. Effective!

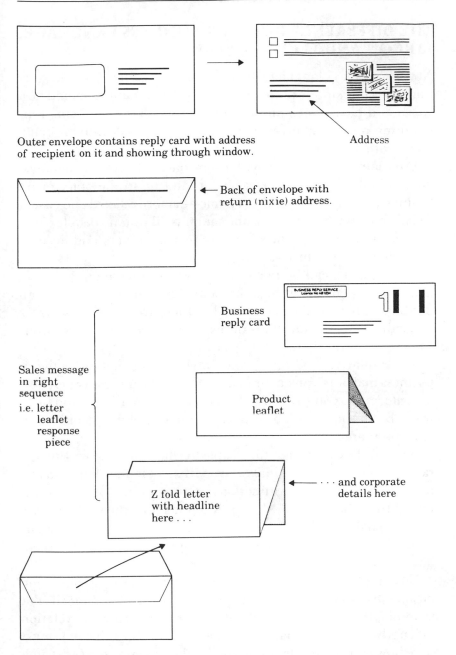

Outer envelope contains reply card with address
of recipient on it and showing through window.

Address

←— Back of envelope with
return (nixie) address.

Business
reply card

Sales message
in right
sequence
i.e. letter
    leaflet
    response
    piece

Product
leaflet

Z fold letter
with headline
here . . .

· · · and corporate
details here

Figure 7.1   A simple lead generation format

THE DIFFERENCE BETWEEN BUSINESS LANGUAGE, JARGON AND TECHNO-SPEAK

Now let's look at language, tone and style. Again we should start from the same simple premise as earlier. Your mailing should be a warm and pleasant communication from one human being representing one company—that's you—to another human being representing another.

I'm a fairly traditional cove for someone with creative leanings. For example, I prefer to wear a suit and tie to the office or on business, yet I go for comfort at home—a more relaxed and casual style, which is why my wardrobe contains, like many people of my age and type, two or three pairs of jeans, trainers and even (a confession!) a tee-shirt or two!

When people call on me at home, we can talk about kids and family and personal things for hours. But at work—although personal or non-business subjects like these are often ice-breakers or parting subjects, one finds the exchanges are normally shorter. Yet they are still there.

So, similarly, I suggest you draw the distinction between business mail and consumer mail. It should be more businesslike; less informal if you so choose. It, too, should wear a suit and tie to work. But it should still be just as personal and human and warm as a communication.

Be clear, however, that the people to whom you are writing are rarely different as individuals at work than at home. They may be more formal, adopt a more serious posture, even puff themselves up a little—but scratch the surface—it's still them! The same things make them laugh; make them angry; make them despair; make them take action; make them aggressive; and make them buy.

Now a lot of people interpret my thoughts here—about being businesslike—in precisely the opposite way to what I mean. For example, they assume—particularly for some reason in relation to length of letters—that to make a letter businesslike you must somehow shorten it. Or traditionalise the typography. Or switch to their 'yours of 5th inst' voice.

Absolutely not.

If you want to be seen as a business stuck in the post-war forties—go ahead. That's what people will think of you when you use that sort of style. It's OK to be sincere and true these days. Faithful dates you a little!

'Oh, I'm long over that. Don't even get withdrawal symptoms any more!' I hear you say. And yet you maybe will find it hard to accept that longer-than-one-page letters are still much the norm these days, too.

'Business people don't have time to read all that stuff,' people

---

MAILBOX

ONE PRODUCT OR MORE?

This is a good question, and is one often asked of me by those planning a mailing. My advice is the same whether you are mailing business-to-business or consumer, lead generation, traffic building, or mail order.

Let's first take out the obvious. I mean, you wouldn't have a single product catalogue. And if you've got 1049 electronic gadgets to sell, you're a catalogue whether you like it or not. Let's also take out essentially or near-essentially linked products—in effect a multi-product purchase such as a PC, screen and printer. Or a stereo and speakers!

I'm thinking more of such people as an insurance broker: 'Shall I sell life, household and motor. Or everything I do? Should I go *one product more?*' Or an office equipment dealer: 'Shall I hit them with the new compact fax machine, *and* the colour copier, *and* the new software packages? Should I go *one product or more?*'

The answer: More. But one at a time!

Generally my experience has been that it's better to put one clear proposition across. Thus, I would define a motor policy and a household policy as two propositions. Each needs to be sold fully; not one confused with the other. Similarly, the fax and copier: supplies, materials, maintenance contracts, etc., I see as 'bolt-ons'. It's the same sale, . . . just as long as things don't get over-complicated.

Lastly on that—don't give up on the bolt-ons! Just because people don't buy at the time doesn't mean they won't in the future. So, taking maintenance or service contracts as our example again, those who didn't buy with the original purchase could well find their minds focused and be prompted into action by a reminder eleven months later when the warranty is about to expire.

tell me. And how right that is. But not because they don't have the time; simply because you haven't earned it. On behalf of house-wives and househusbands everywhere, I reject the implication that people in a domestic situation are more easily convinced that they should give your material the time you want. Indeed, I can quite see many business people parting with the company's time more easily than their own. Broadly speaking though, the yard-stick is the same. If you bore them, if you're not of interest to them, if you can't earn and then hold their attention then you'll get rolled into a ball and tossed into the rubbish bin just the same at work as at home.

Send me a golf trolley offer. I'm not interested. Send me a mailing on bench-mounted centrifugal analysis parameter readers—ditto. Mail me anything to do with new database techniques, or anything to do with communications equipment, or anything to do with making money and, as if by magic, you start with my attention. The rest is up to you. And it's not different at home with hi-fi equipment, anything vaguely gadgety, or to do with food or wine. I'm yours. To start with. The more you appeal to me, the more time I'll give you, wherever I am.

End of story.

DECISIONS, DECISIONS. YES—BUT HOW MUCH FOR?

For the purposes of looking at business mail, I will need to differentiate between mail order and lead generation. Indeed many, far too many, assume that mail order doesn't apply to business mail. They're quite wrong. There are hundreds of companies in computer supplies, factory and office equipment, stationery supplies, etc., who sell very successfully through the traditional mail order vehicle—a catalogue. And there are many people who, for many articles and services, actually prefer to buy that way. As a secretary of mine put it some years ago: 'I like their stuff, hate their salesman. He's got bad breath, BO, a coarse sense of humour, and for some reason he always calls late in the afternoon when I'm hurrying to get the post ready to go.'

Mail order

Consumers have been shopping by mail for some time. It's an accepted method. Those consumers who go to work don't seem to have a problem shopping that way for many work items. But more than that, a lot of things are sold by mail order that are not perceived to be so.

In the consumer field, insurance and financial products are the world's largest mail order product. Yet most insurance and financial sellers refuse to see themselves as partially, or wholly mail order businesses. Charities—who actually have the perfect mail order product—cannot see themselves in that business either. But they are. The direct marketing of an appeal is no different to any other campaign in mail order. The concept of the building of a relationship between the charity and its supporters is very much the same as that between any direct marketer and the customers. The economics are different. There's no product cost involved. The donation, less marketing costs to achieve it and systems costs to process and bank it, is all profit. That is why I describe a charity as having the perfect mail order product. There's no buying or warehousing. No dispatch or shipping. No breakages or warranty claims. No money back refunds or product exchanges or replacements. They are the envy of everyone else in mail order!

In business mail, equally, there are such 'hidden' mail order traders. Their products are books, travel and hotels, lower price consumables, insurance and service or maintenance contracts, conferences, seminars and so on. In fact the business of mail order to businesses has been going on for years!

HOW TO DECIDE BETWEEN MAIL ORDER AND SALESFORCE

Where do you draw the line? How do you decide when to sell by mail order and when to sell through a salesforce? And what mix should be used if you need to do both?

Trial, error and economics will provide the answers. But in both fields, as I mentioned in Chapter 1, there are some surprises—even if they are exceptions to the rule. Christian Brann relates with obvious pride how he was involved in the sale of London Bridge to an American. It was only after the American had bought it, he realised it wasn't Tower Bridge! My own noteworthy, almost mail order, sale was that £1 million hotel site in the Algarve. In most cases the average order value will be a little less than these two I suspect.

The complexity of the sale, the amount of money involved, and the number of decision makers (and decision influencers for that matter) will provide some guidelines. But be prepared for surprises. Mail order, by definition, an order taken by mail (but used with licence to include other non face-to-face media such as the 'phone or fax), does not necessarily have to be supplied by mail. PCs, for example, can be and are sold through mailings and off-the-page. In this case the equipment can be installed by a local agent or dealer, or sent by carrier with set-up instructions for the buyer.

I remember being approached some years ago by a manufacturer of small hand-held scientific electronic instruments. Although this company made and sold a range of equipment up to bench-mounted sophisticated hardware costing many thousands of pounds, they had uncovered a market for their hand-held compact items. These were much lower in price, something around £100. Their salesforce was small and while it offered national coverage the sales teams were all highly skilled engineers (and therefore expensive!) in their own right.

For the high-ticket sophisticated equipment this was a necessity to serve the market adequately. For the smaller, low-ticket sales, it was an economic impossibility. In other words, they couldn't afford to send a sales engineer to sell one of the smaller products. Their profit was gone before the engineer was more than a few miles down the road. Their problem was two-fold. Would scientists and lab technicians buy by mail order? And if so, would they buy this kind of product?

A programme of testing was developed and happily provided positive and profitable directions. It was fascinating to watch this client develop into the mail order business. Particularly to watch how, through testing, they discovered that the more they used classic consumer mail order techniques the better it worked. But we learned quite clearly that although '14 days free trial' and 'send no money' coupled with 'no quibble guarantees' and other devices worked well, they had to wear their 'suits and ties' to work too. Very soon these mailings were strategically and tactically indistinguishable from consumer mail order packages. But they definitely looked, well . . . more businesslike!

One more thought while I recall this experience, since it might be something you could try yourself—to businesses or consumers. The manufacturer arranged for a telesales call towards the end of the trial period. This was smart thinking since it enabled the telesales operator to:

- answer any technical points or queries in using the equipment. This improved the 'stick' rate and cut returns by over 30 per cent.
- go for a second sale. It was surprising how many other people in the same company wanted details or indeed wanted to order based on their colleague's purchase.
- remind the buyer that there was shortly an invoice to be paid. And check that, if necessary to smooth payment, a purchase order was initiated by the buyer's company.

Anyone for Ten-X? Another interesting by-product emerged from the telesales follow-up. It transpired that many of the purchasers of the small equipment were also prospects for the more sophisticated bench-mounted expensive models. By talking to the purchasers of the compact models, sales appointments could be made for the sales engineers to go in. This resulted in extremely high success rates—yet again proving the Ten-X factor. It was much easier to sell to an existing customer. This manufacturer had unearthed a lead generation programme for higher range models that was effectively better even than self-liquidating; it made a profit!

From your existing sales experience, you will know how many decision makers and influencers are involved, how much money must be found for the purchase, and how necessary the face-to-face meeting is to the sale. In my experience, if you have not tried to sell direct, you will most likely have an exaggerated view of the need for a sales meeting. So, if you've even the first idea that your product or service could be sold through direct methods, go ahead and explore them. The 'strike' rate may be lower, but so are the costs. But be sure to turn back to the section on economics first of all and do your sums. You may well be very pleasantly surprised. See what break evens are necessary. Determine how much you will need to spend to test. And don't penny pinch. This kind of test could change your way of trading for years ahead, and become a huge source of profit.

Even if not, it is far, far better to spend out and obtain an answer you can trust, than to face retesting because you don't think you got it right, or find that a large investment in roll-outs, dispatch packing and handling systems and staff, etc., is all to no avail. But my worst fear of all is that, through not having used a large enough shovel, you will not dig deeply enough to find the gold!

One of the decision factors—that of the number of people who will be involved in a purchase—is something you must also consider in business mail lead generation.

I made the point earlier that it is extraordinary just how much people expect of a mailing. It is equally extraordinary how often it delivers. No one would dream of putting their ad on TV or radio once. Few people display just one poster. Most people appreciate that ads should appear in consumer or trade journals more than once for maximum effect. Yet they send out one mailing! Equally, to sell a major piece of capital equipment that might have productivity, financial, quality control, and environmental advantages for the buyer, they send out one mailing to get the salesperson in. Very often it will pay to adopt a multi-channel approach. Mail to the financial executive with the financial advantages first, and include a brief run through of the others. Mail to the production chief, selling the quality and productivity and environmental benefits—and a brief run through of the others. Mail to the sales director, running through the speed, quality and product cost benefits, and mention all the others. And so on. Taking each individual potential influencer, reshuffle the benefits for the best priority for their individual interest.

This multi-channel approach accepts that different people in the different companies in your marketplace will buy for different reasons. Let them tell you what they are. So, if you get replies from two people in the same company, do just one thing: put them at the top of the pile! . . . And get round there *fast*.

This system works most effectively. Yet often I see people assuming that one single mailing addressed to 'The Managing

---

MAILBOX

ON COMPLAINTS . . .

I have already started to communicate to you the quite exceptional power of direct mail. There is a downside to this.

It is unavoidable, particularly in view of the very personal nature of our central communication device—the letter—that the more effective you are, the more people will read what you have to say and respond to it.

That includes the negative responses as well as the positive. As you build response, so often you will build complaints. You can't cut them out; you *can* be prepared and deal pleasantly with them. This experience remains constant without any question of your mailing being provocative or contentious or offensive. It's obviously even worse if you are any one of those three.

It is also worth remembering that most charities reckon to 'turn' complaints, and receive (often very) large donations from such people. Now there's a gauntlet thrown down to your salesforce! But gently does it, eh?

Director' will do the trick. It is true that in general things will travel 'down' a company quite easily, yet they find it very difficult to go up. In other words, an item passed down from above—the MD, chairman or secretaries—rarely gets ignored. The same is not always true in reverse.

I remember hearing of the US company who mailed junior management about a week in advance of board directors. With utter candour an accompanying letter explained 'since we will be mailing the enclosed details in a few days to your Chief Executive and his fellow Directors, we felt you might like to return the enclosed enquiry card for advance details. That way you'll have all the data at your fingertips when that memo arrives, or more likely, you get that phone call from on high.' Good old fashioned blackmail!

LADIES AND GENTLEMEN

Direct marketing men enjoy the company, skills and effectiveness of many, many women. I am on record (well, video actually!) as telling the world that, in my view, women are better at direct marketing than men. It has something to do with their mentality— a great deal of it to do with abundant common sense, sensitivity and intuitiveness. In these qualities alone (and speaking for all *man*kind as you will notice I like to from time to time!) men can only stand in admiration and respect. No more so than in this world of direct marketing.

I remember, in the early days of *The Secrets of Effective Direct Mail*, conference audiences would be 90 per cent men and 10 per cent women.

Nowadays, it's normally 60/40. At least in the UK. Occasionally it's 40/60. But it's not far from half and half. Are women more thirsty for knowledge—or are there more of them in this business? I suspect both! Certainly we have more female business leaders than most industries. I would guess at better than double the average. No wonder, as an industry, we frown on 'Dear Sir' letters!, which is actually my point to you. It's not just direct marketing, and strangely, it's not just men who forget how many businesswomen there are out there. Women secretaries do it too! And a female telesales caller once asked a female executive I know to put her through to her print buyer. Or, if *he* was busy, *his boss* would do. The lady on the line, a head print buyer responsible for some millions of pounds worth of print a year, hung up. And who could blame her!

It was therefore a relatively rare experience when I was able, at a Federation of Wholesalers annual conference a year or so ago, to greet my morning's audience of 150 delegates with complete accuracy and say 'Lady and gentlemen, good morning'.

BACK TO TROUBLE AND STRIFE

There is no link to Cockney rhyming slang! By trouble and strife, I'm back to the trouble your readers have to go to in order to respond to your mailing.

If you're selling mail order, one difference may be that your customer will need to draw up a purchase order. It is for this reason that the fax machine is already proving enormously successful. In one test I worked on for an industrial mail order catalogue, a display panel about one and a half inches deep and two inches across was used to provide details of his new 'Fax Orderline'. Over 40 per cent of the resulting orders came in by Fax.

Whether for lead generation or mail order, the advice I gave in relation to ease of reply is just as valid in a business-to-business context. Credit cards can prove a useful inclusion, making payment of smaller sums easy—especially internationally.

Where does the professional fit in all this?

Something of a hybrid. With one or two oddities. Doctors, for example, are pretty odd! One of my most successful headlines selling insurance to doctors was 'Are Doctors the sickest people in the land?'!

Professionals as a group are much more difficult to gauge. Thus, the more you can do to encourage any field sales staff you have to feed back information, the better off you are. Here, on one mailing list, you can range from names of one-man-bands to huge practices with lots of staff. Accountants and architects are also good examples. Some published data are available to help you make assessments. The number of partners is one popular, if crude, yardstick.

And what of those who work from home? It's a decreasing quantity, but doctors must be a prime example of this. Some, particularly urban practices, have clustered together in bright new health centres. Others still use the downstairs front room as the waiting room, and the one behind as their surgery. So do dentists, but the proportions are different.

Do we treat them as businesses or consumers?

I find that professional people enjoy being thought of as 'professional'. Most of them have studied hard and long to achieve their qualifications. And many, particularly the successful—and I believe this point to be most significant—are successful in their own name. If most others do well they do it with the spotlight on the company. If you're happy with a purchase, you think well of Boots, or Sainsbury's, or Marks and Spencer's, but not the pleasant young man who served you. His name may have been on his badge, but a week later you've forgotten it.

Hordes of professional people trade in their own names, and are proud of it. So get their names right—but also get their qualifications right. Be aware of the professionals' quirks and ways. Even though consultants and surgeons are doctors to most of us, we insult them by addressing them that way. And be aware, too—or maybe I should have said 'be wary too'—of the systems and procedures they have. With the medical field that might be the 'supplies' chain—the buying procedures of the various health authorities and the bureaucracy. It is considered 'bad form', for example, to mail to hospital officers without having first sent details to the supplies officers.

Over at the RIBA, to help architects handle and 'store and retrieve' all that product information, some bright spark invented a filing system which most of them use or refer to. SFB codes, as they're called, are applied to leaflets and product details, which is why so many publications churned out by people who want architects to specify their goods, print what I would describe as a two-tier rectangular box, top right front of their material. Inside is the SFB code for their product to ensure that it gets filed properly. That's fine if you want your information filed, of course. In direct marketing we tend—as a rule—not to like that very much. Too many of us have found ourselves tucked behind the clock, lost on top of the fridge/freezer and shoved into a drawer in the hall. We prefer action. Will putting an SFB code on get you filed *instead* of acted upon? Possibly even filtered out by some diligent soul before the real prospect gets to see it?

You must think about what you want. You must get to know the ins and outs of the professional life of a dentist, vet, solicitor and their colleagues before you can sell to them most effectively.

Through the last few pages we've been examining the differences between consumer and business mail. With the exception of the few, mainly practical points I've made to you, it has—I hope—become clear that there is indeed very little difference between them.

8

JFR's creative secrets

Firstly, as we arrive at my creative secrets, I'd like to discuss one of the most overlooked aspects of the creative task. Perhaps, since it has as much to do with the kind of things that classical advertising people deal with, it is not often appreciated as part of the direct marketing brief. However, I assure you it is. I am referring to positioning.

The importance of positioning is in direct proportion to the importance of your products to the prospective buyer: offers,

---

MAILBOX

YOUR SINS WILL FIND YOU OUT

Occasionally the market will position you first! When British Airways came out with 'We'll take more care of you' the frequent travellers WoM'ed them to death (WoM = word of mouth). Up the Loyalty Ladder, advocates do it for your benefit. Off the ladder, reverse advocates can kill. Remember: make customers happy and they'll each tell two or three people, make them unhappy, and they'll each tell fourteen!

BA were hoist with their own petard. They set about solving the problem the right way. They started to live up to the slogan. Turned opinion round. Advocacy (and terrific PR) took over. And zap. Now they're the world's favourite airline. Not difficult when you're the world's largest airline! Verisimilitude appears to rule OK.

In all things tell the truth.
Be who and what you are.

---

products, guarantees, price, timing, the message—those things that are the bricks of a successful sale. Positioning is the cement that binds, and adds strength.

I remember seeing a Public Service TV commercial from the States of the late 1950s or thereabouts. Tough but lardy star of the series, 'Highway Patrol', Broderick Crawford, reminded us 'It takes 4374 nuts to hold a car together. But only one to spread it across the road.'

It's the same with positioning. There are probably 4374 things you can do to position everything correctly in a mailing—and then one careless decision or forgotten action will 'spread it across the road'. All the way to the rubbish bin.

WHAT IS POSITIONING?

There was a two-word headline in the nationals recently. Potentially it was a contradiction. Yet because the advertisers had very well positioned themselves, for me at least, they could get away with it.

The two-word headline was simply this:

Harrods Sale

Did I read the ads, check the prices and reductions, make any decisions expecting anything other than I found? Was I looking for prices cheaper than Curry's or Comet or Argos? Or the postal bargains page? No. I was looking not to pick up a bargain from Harrods, but a Harrods bargain. A perfect piece of positioning.

I would suggest that this is a subject so fundamental to success in any advertising or selling function that you would do well to read the well-known book on the subject: *Positioning—the Battle for your Mind*. Again (happily for them) it's published by McGraw-Hill and written by Al Reis and Jack Trout. It is an excellent and convincing book, if a little padded out, on a paramount and fundamentally essential advertising constituent.

WHY IS POSITIONING IMPORTANT?

Let me tell you the parable of the PC salesman. It all started with a mailing. Not a brilliant one; but with two huge advantages. I wanted what they had to sell, and they got their timing right.

The product was a personal computer and a few bits of software.

I sent off the reply paid card. The rep 'phoned to make an appointment. He explained the process: he would personally demonstrate the equipment. He would then leave it with me for a few days. He'd then ring to check, if he hadn't heard from me before, whether I wanted to keep it. The paperwork could all be done by post.

It *hung* right.

It was a proposition made simply, quickly and with confidence. It was easy and convenient. The price was fair. It meant I could play with and feel the product hands on. He sounded a nice guy (very important to the emotional side). So I accepted.

You wouldn't believe the mess that turned up! From the stains on his tie; to the off-white shirt (it was only just off-white on its first day of wear) to the frayed cuffs. His suit was much shinier than his car.

So while he's de-boxing, I'm de-bunking. While he's setting up, I'm climbing down. His appearance had destroyed the magic words. It hung right. Now it was no longer hanging—it lay shattered on the floor. So here's why positioning is important. And long term. Positioning is for life.

YOU CANNOT DESTROY YOUR POSITION IN SOMEONE'S MIND—YOU
CAN ONLY MOVE IT

And once in the negative hemisphere, it's a truly difficult task to get it back. Sinners *can* become saints, but it's a long hard slog.

Think about it. I wanted to buy what this man had to sell. Yet evidence had undone it all. Stupid, silly little things. The stained tie; the frayed cuffs; the tired, shiny suit; and the rest.

I suppose you could argue that he could have got round it by playing the absent-minded professor type: 'I may not look great, but I know my stuff.' You know the routine. But he thought he was a salesman.

So I saw frayed cuffs. I thought other things. What kind of company lets a man like this out on the road? And I knew, I mean, I KNEW the answer. A sloppy company. A company with low standards. A company with lousy back-up, extended response times, etc. And a lost sale.

Well, not quite true. He sold the PC. But for another company. I bought the same elsewhere.

MAILBOX

DON'T BUCK THE TREND. SOME THINGS JUST ARE

For a charity, we asked people, 'What colour is cancer?' Nine out of ten said 'Yellow'.

For a holiday company: 'What colour is a holiday?' Eleven out of ten (I agreed) said 'Orange'. Every time I tell this story half say they think blue. But only after they know about the orange!

HOW DO YOU ACHIEVE CORRECT POSITIONING?

Firstly, you must decide what position you want to occupy inside the head of your prospects or customers—and even that distinction will make a difference. Secondly, you must live and breathe it.

Some people—even recent books on this self-same subject—will lie to you. I quote from one fellow guru: 'Positioning should be expressed through a short simple statement. . . .'

What utter, utter rubbish. As good a copywriter as the issuer of that nonsense is, I defy anyone to write the 'short simple statement' that could have recovered the sale for our PC salesman. Other, perhaps, than 'I know I've lost the sale—so please accept this PC as a gift.' Positioning is not everything. But it is as important to truly competent advertising, direct or otherwise, as oxygen is to life.

In direct mail you achieve positioning by careful attention to everything: the typefaces; the tone of the voice; the nature of the offer; the weight, colour and feel of the paper; the quality of the design and print. Everything.

Your market will ask, does it *hang* right? They'll piece together evidence like a jurist at a murder trial. Do they trust you? Do they believe you? Do they want you in their home or office? Do they want to make a *relationship* (remember that one) with you? And what type of relationship—long and happy? Or a one-off? Can they have faith in you? All these questions must be satisfied by your mailing.

The relevance of this is that when recipients hold your mailing, they hold YOU, your company. When you think they hold your mailing in their hands, they don't. All their senses and instincts are at work. You are in their minds. They'll poke and prod and scavenge to find you out. To catch you false-footed. To disbelieve your claim. To establish the sneaky trick in your offer. Everything they see before them will enable them to make snap judgements and form mental pictures of you and your business. Positioning and much more of the creative process will provide them with their answers. Make sure they are the answers you want them to have!

MAILBOX

Years ago, Leyland teamed up with the AA to give 'Supercover' with a Leyland car purchase. The Supercover symbol was formed of a pair of cupped hands—the gentle giant protection. When Fiat did the same thing (or near enough) they pictured an AA man in the glove compartment, suggesting that a Fiat without an AA man was the same as a Fiat without wheels. Maybe they know something we don't.

THE CONCEPT OF THREE-PHASE CREATIVITY

I believe that most written advertising—direct response or other—is tackled by its readers in three distinct phases. They are the GLANCE, the SCAN and the READ.

There are two important points about this theory. Firstly, readers have gearboxes in their heads and there are only three positions—a bit like those old Daf cars—forward, neutral and reverse. Or even, YES, MAYBE and NO. Secondly, the theory clarifies the true role of creative in the wider process and says why you must put your proposition up front. It makes sense that if you're going to ask people to give their time to you, they should at least know what it's about. Most often, this has two ways of happening and it is an interesting analysis of an advertiser's confidence. Those with a strong offer come out with it fast. Those with a weak offer build up to it slowly! Thus, we arrive at the conclusion that the function of creative is to *present* your proposition (in non-direct, your message) and to *persuade* as many readers as possible to accept it.

There are, of course, many techniques to achieve these two functions. But the most important part is to recognise that we must achieve success not once, not twice, but three times as our readers go through the stages of reading. We must succeed as they *glance* at it, to get them to move on. We must succeed when they *scan* it, to get them to move on. And we must succeed when they *read* it, to get them to absorb, accept and act.

The numbers will decrease at each stage. But you have to make sure that, as the numbers dwindle, your effort increases in its influence on those that remain.

Over the course of this chapter, we shall take a look at some of the ways you can set about this task. In one section, for example, we shall see how our understanding of human nature can be used. How our reactions to certain stimuli can be used. And also what emotions and desires will drive us to act.

Now, however, I would like to present you with three personal methods that have helped me over the years. These three, plus the age-old but still perfect AIDA formula (see page 86), plus Bob Stone's Seven Key Points, are the only five methods I carry with me. These five methods should enable you to crack any direct mail problem and can be adopted for most other direct response situations too.

NOW BUY!   *N*oticed
            *O*pened
            *W*anted

            *B*elieved
            *U*nderstood
            *Y*es'd

Noticed   Will you get noticed when you arrive on the mat? Or, if you think your envelope might not get seen, how can you get yourself to stand out or be placed on the top of the pile? Why not try to win in both situations?

Opened   What have you done to *ensure* that you will be? And then what single thing will attract or impress above all else at the Opening Moment?

   This latter question is a vital one that is often overlooked or ignored. But more often still is totally misunderstood by both copywriters and designers alike, as you will see later in the section dealing with human nature.

Wanted   You need to approach 'wanted' in two ways. (1) What can you do to make your mailing wanted? If they want to read, there's much more chance they'll want to respond. (2) Have you done everything in your power to make the product or service wanted?

Believed   Avoid the incredible. Back up your sales story with undeniable fact. In place of opinion and rhetoric, give evidence: testimonials and case histories, for example.

Understood   You must be; your proposition must be. What to do must be. Use clear, simple, jargon-free conversational language, and clean, easy-to-follow layouts that make your message easy to absorb.

Yes'd   What have you given people to say 'Yes' to? Have you phrased your proposition so that 'Yes' is the obvious, attractive and desirable thing to say?

   If you have, you've 'yes'd 'em'.

THE GOLDEN STRATEGY

*G*rab attention
*O*pen strongly
*L*ead logically
*D*emand action
*E*ncourage response
*N*eed it now

Grab attention   What can you do to grab attention—*and* hold it?

Open strongly   Maybe you can solve that problem by doing this. But, do this one anyway. The biggest possible benefit to the reader is probably the strongest opener at your disposal.

Lead logically   A sound sales case generally has a logical sequence to it. Find it and follow it. But more; make sure the composition of your mailing package follows it. This is one of the main pitfalls of taking a general product leaflet and simply strapping on a letter and reply card and accepting it as a mailing. I'll bet that if you look at 95 per cent of these sort of packs the letter and the leaflet present different product rationales in different sequences. One has to be right. Or at least better! They may be in harmony. But what you need is unison.

Demand action   Just no getting away from it, the need to demand action from the reader, to spell out what you want, to make it attractive, desirable and urgent, crops up in nearly every worthwhile formula, checklist and, for that matter, textbook!

   You *know* why.

Encourage response   There are so many ways to nudge, push, prompt, cajole, tease or urge a reply. Offer a gift or an incentive.

Make a special offer, discount or saving. And, on top of that, you will encourage more to reply by making the physical act of replying simple in every way. Do they have to respond by mail? Maybe the 'phone? Or local branch or outlet? Will you take a credit card payment? Can a business respond by fax? All of these can only happen if you provide the information. And forget which one is best for you. Organise your response handling around the one that is best for *them*.

Need it now   That's the level of excitement, enthusiasm and desire you've got to aim for. You've got to make them say 'I need it now'. Can you use a time-close? Will you make some extra or bonus available if they act within the time limit?

And lastly on this aspect, if you've managed to get someone to say 'I need it now', at least pay them the courtesy of a prompt, efficient delivery or response. Otherwise all the hard work you've done will drive them elsewhere to satisfy the need. To your competitors, for example. Or other sources.

Let's take a creative . . .

APPROACH   *A*rrive

*P*ropose

*P*ersuade

*R*eassure

*O*rganise an opportunity

*A*sk for the order (or enquiry)

*C*larify

*H*elp

Arrive   Have you done all you can to ensure that you've arrived in the right hands at the right time? And what steps have you taken to make the right impression—not just of your mailing, but of your company, and what you have to say? Do you look important enough to merit their investment of time and energy and attention?

Propose   Let them know *fast* what's in it for them. There is no single bigger turn on for the readers than for them to ask 'What's

in it for me?', which they will *all* do immediately, and for you to
come out with a strong, credible and wantable answer.

Persuade   Now set about a confirming process for those in YES
gear and a convincing process for those in MAYBE or neutral gear.
As we saw earlier in the book, your success with this group will
make or break your mailing. Each one counts. So assess your
benefits in the right order and set them out one by one. Cover
them *all*, and have the courage of your convictions. It's cost you a
lot of money to get in front of the reader, so put your mouth (or
pen!) where your money is. Remember, benefits *never* bore.
Benefits never put people off. Just as long as they are real,
believable, desirable . . . and at the end of the day, you can
deliver.

Reassure   If you were in the reader's situation what would worry
you? Small print? The thought of a medical? Whether you could
afford it? Whether a salesperson will call? If the product's new—
does it really work, will I get maintenance problems, or teething
troubles? If it's old, how soon will it be replaced with the new
model? If it's far away—like a distant holiday—who'll look after
us, handle languages, etc.? If it's complicated—that it's worth the
trouble and paperwork? Whatever the potential worries, address
them, reassure your readers that you understand, that you have
the answers and that they won't be intimidated, embarrassed,
regretful or let down.

   Guarantees are very reassuring. So are Free Trials (with other
benefits too!).

Organise an opportunity   To get people to act, they need reasons.
One reason should be your proposition. But we want people to act
now. Therefore we have to make it opportune (well-timed) for
them to do so. Now will be the moment to orchestrate an
opportunity for them—in other words, to add an extra level to
your proposition which makes the whole concept a good one, but
even better if taken now. An opportunity is by definition 'especially favourable'. Probably the direct marketing stalwarts here

are the bonus offer, the time-close, and the limited edition. They are very powerful but all too easily dismissed as 'mail order techniques'—which they certainly are, but there are so many ways of devising all three of these for situations at all levels of society, and whether consumer, professional or business-to-business. For one thing is certain, we all hate to lose. And we all like to win. Here your task is to lubricate these desires.

Ask for the order (or response)   Talk about response as if you expect it, not as if it will surprise you! It's a small point, but the number of times I see this . . .

   'If you return the reply paid card enclosed . . .'

The very use of the word 'if' unravels almost everything you've done so far. It suggests that there is a course other than the response. It suggests that *you* believe they might not want to accept your proposition. It suggests that really it might not be all that it's cracked up to be. Have you been lying? What does this say . . .

'*When* you return the enclosed replay paid card . . .'

It's an entirely different set of implications. More confident. More positive.

   Closing dates are normally good for response. There is nearly always a genuine need for one. Sometimes, because it has a special offer or terms; sometimes because you are using incentives where supplies are limited. However, it is often wise to 'cover' yourself with any non-standard offer by specifying the duration of availability. I would counsel you though, if you're dealing with a financial service, to beware of the Financial Service Act which prohibits 'artificial' closing dates. But you may lose quite a profitable 'tail' of business if you don't get your timings right. Too short loses business. Not everybody wants to reply to suit your schedule and you must respect that. Too long and it won't have the desired 'hurry up' effect. Indeed, people may actually delay responding because you've told them you'll give them 12 weeks to do so. And once they've put you on one side, whatever their intentions at the time, you will have your likelihood of response reduced to about one-tenth.

What has become known as 'the early bird' is one answer to this problem and usefully leaves the door ajar for those who want to reply in their own good time. An 'early bird' is an extra offer for acting within the time frame. But you make it abundantly clear that it's the extra offer that closes on the chosen date, the proposition is acceptable at any time.

Another, rather obvious (but still overlooked by many) way of asking for order or response is to provide the means for it to happen. And indeed to explain how they achieve it. Hence:

Clarify   There are two things to clarify. You need to be absolutely certain that you have made your proposition, offer and terms clear to them. The best way to do this is to run through them *totally* again. Don't worry about repeating yourself. But it will need to be kept interesting. So use different words to do it. You also need to be certain that the response methods and procedures are clear to them. The blatant way to do this is most successful. That's why you see this headline so often: *'How to apply'*. Again, this is easy to convert to other situations.

> 'Please complete and return the enclosed application promptly. You'll find a reply envelope enclosed and no stamp or addressing is needed. Please also be sure to sign and date the . . .'

Or the executive version!

> 'Please ask your secretary to fax your acceptance within the next 48 hours. Simply complete the five questions relating to your current financial policy, and naturally we guarantee absolute confidentiality. However, I must point out that places will be given on a strictly "first come" basis. Since I feel your presence is particularly important, and to assure your registration, please ask your secretary to provide your American Express, Diners Club, Access or Visa number and expiry date.'

As you draw to the close of your message it's quite possible to find ways of weaving the last three together—that is, organise an opportunity, ask for the order and clarify why and how they should respond.

Help   The more you can do to help, the better. This extends from helping them to afford your product or service, to helping them get answers to questions (a telephone Hotline?) or just helping them to respond by providing the wherewithal, advice and convenience.

Last, by courtesy of Bob Stone, the seven key points.

I joined an audience of 500 or so direct marketing evangelists some years ago to hear Bob set out these seven key points. It just didn't occur to him that he was teaching Grandma to suck eggs because Bob KNOWS the strength of this formula. *His* formula.

This is the one that has never failed me yet. Whenever I get stuck, or whenever I can't find a way out, this is the routine I turn to. And it *always* works for me. What's more, it works equally well as the sales strategy for a single letter or a complete package. Often both—especially when they are working together.

Bob Stone's Seven Key Points
1   Put the *main* benefit first.
2   Enlarge upon the *main* benefit, and bring in the *secondary* benefits.
3   Tell the reader *precisely* what he or she will get.
4   Back up your story with case histories and endorsements.
5   Tell your reader what he or she might lose if he or she *doesn't* act.
6   Sum-up *restating* the benefits—but in a *different* way.
7   Incite *immediate* action.

Five great problem solvers
I believe any one of these formulae can help you. Take your pick

from my three—BUY NOW, GOLDEN or APPROACH, or use AIDA or Bob Stone's SEVEN KEY POINTS. You'll probably find that you 'bed down' with one. But here's the important part. When you've completed your work (or you've had it presented to you by your supplier) use two of the others and score the proposed mailing on all three.

Sure, the formulae are all headed in the same direction. That's OK, so are you! But their perspective and emphasis is different. So you're judging from different angles!

Now let's start to take a look at ten things with CREATIVITY in mind. We'll start with the most significant aspect of creativity: the one that is so important it must influence and lead your problem-solving, solution-finding steps in all the other nine creative issues of which you must be mindful. I suggest that every decision you make, every action you take, and every thought you have should be made . . .

1 WITH THE *READER* IN MIND

The best advice I have ever given anybody, and that includes myself, was first crystallised while writing some years ago for the first printing of the *Post Office Direct Mail Handbook*. It is this:

WRITE WHAT THE READER WANTS TO READ

NOT

WHAT THE WRITER WANTS TO WRITE

Depending on your level of personal modesty, you will find the next statement anywhere between easy or hard to take!

People are ALWAYS more interested in themselves than they are in you. That applies to even the most deserving charitable cause.

So we're back to what's in it for them. The biggest mistake when analysing or appraising this statement is to assume that you should take it as advice that can only be answered on a material level. And, that it is black and white. Neither is true. However, it can be followed in many, many ways. But at the end of it all, it should tell the recipients what they want to hear (or read). It should explain how their lives will benefit, be enriched or improved through accepting what you have to offer.

Take this tip seriously and use it to question every decision. Seeing things from the readers' points of view, putting them first, will never do you any harm. It will always serve you in the end. So extend this simple philosophy away beyond the copy—to the graphics; to the development of the proposition; to the format. Throughout!

2   WITH *COPY* IN MIND

The largest single difference between ordinary advertising copy and direct response advertising copy is that ours *sells*. What it sells is the proposition, irrespective of whether that proposition entices the reader to buy, enquire, or visit a store or exhibition. You name it, we'll sell it!

In direct mail creativity, copy is far, far more important than art. Pictures don't sell. Design doesn't sell. Pictures might explain, demonstrate, or illustrate. Those things help a sale. They don't make one. Pictures certainly grab attention, as we'll discuss later. It is the use, with copy, that you make of the *attention* that is more important.

Design doesn't sell. Not in direct mail. It positions. It supports copy. It displays your wares. It humanises, creates mood, eases the task of reading. But it doesn't sell. It certainly contributes; you might say it smooths the way to the sale. But it doesn't sell.

Copy sells for you
Direct mail is a words medium. You will be amazed at the word power that is available to you, and just how many words you can get people to read. Very few good mailings (or for that matter press ads and other kindred manifestations of the direct marketing way) feature anything that comes near to good writing. We chuck away the grammar textbooks. We ignore convention. We use punctuation in ways that would make our old English masters

cringe. It is possible to achieve both, but it cannot be coincidence that talented writers and talented direct marketing writers are two different things. My feeling is that most of the truly talented writers in direct marketing only ever get half way up the ladder. That's probably because there are two more important attributes in our copy-writing league. You must have a headful of ideas. And you must be able to sell.

All you have to do that is any different to any other sales situation, is to use these ideas to sell ON PAPER.

Since I cannot write your copy for you, I propose now to give you a short checklist of advice I have been given, thoughts I have developed, and experiences I have gained. Whether you arc facing what might seem the daunting prospect of writing a mailing, deciding which presentation to accept, or trying to assess some work you've been given, this list will help you.

Seventeen Dos. Plus ten Don'ts. That's 27 ways to make copy irresistible. Just for you!!

To start with, let's check out some 'Dos' . . .

1 *Plan what you want to say*
Develop a rationale that would convince *you* to accept the offer. Then work on it. But be flexible. Often you will stumble on a better, stronger or more appealing idea half way through what you have already started. Write both. And then choose.

2 *Develop a flowing style*
Not smooth or bland, but pleasant and charming. In letters, be conversational and personal without being impertinent or cheeky.

3 *Write long and edit back if you need to*
NEVER the other way round. If your copy runs short but you feel you did the job, the designer will be delighted! And the reader won't mind either.

4   *Make yourself easy to read and understand*
The easiest sentences to understand are just eight words long. At 32 words they've lost you.

5   *Concentrate on communicating well*
Forget about grammar. Worry more about flow, being understood, and communicating well. One acid test is to read copy aloud or, better still, get someone else to. Where this reader trips up, so will others.

6   *Be warm and sunny-natured*
Then let yourself shine through. It's infectious. Just as telesales people are advised to 'smile' on the phone!

7   *Avoid the crescendo*
Crescendo letters arrive on my desk every other day. They look a bit like this . . .

Dear Managing Director

We were founded over 20 years ago and have now become the world's leading supplier of gringing machinery.

We have 75 staff at our Warrington headquarters which, when it was built, was the most modern gringing machinery plant in Europe. It is conveniently situated near the M62.

In order to extend our reputation into allied areas of gringing, we recently opened a new gringing pipework cleansing facility a few miles further south on the motorway.

Here we have achieved notable success and received much acclaim for our pioneering pipe-flocking processes.

I am pleased to enclose our latest brochure which tells you more about our gringing success story. If you would like further information please return the enclosed card and we will tell you the full gringing story.

FOR AND ON BEHALF OF
Premier Gringing Ltd

(Signature)

Managing Director

PS   A display of our gringing equipment and pipework will be at Olympia for International GRINGEX 2000. We have taken a stand this year for the first time to tell more people about our gringing. Will you visit us?

OK—it's a slight exaggeration! But you can see what I mean. First, it's written from the wrong side. Second, the crescendo gradually builds up to what has to be the main event. An invitation to an exhibition.

In 99 cases out of 100, this kind of letter should be stood on its head. People do not start out interested. They start out indifferent. We have to earn their attention. They start out looking for excuses to bin us. So the strongest way to come out fighting is to hit them with the biggest benefit. That provides—or should provide—your trump card. In one go it answers what's in it for them AND earns you time to explain, justify, give more *reasons to read*.

The best reasons to read are benefits. There are others. Curiosity. News value. Scandal even! But one reason to read is never enough. Jo Sugarmann described this process as the 'greased chute'. I have also heard it described as the 'string of pearls'. Each sentence has two objectives: to make its point; and buy readership of the next sentence.

8 *Use link-words and phrases*
They help to 'grease the chute'. Start paragraphs with these—and; but; also; what's more; for example. You may have had problems with this style at school—but school's out! And use punctuation and text marks too. There are all manner of devices . . .

. . . which just tell the reader to keep going!

9 *Use simple language*
And simple construction. This kind of thing. It's so easy to handle.

Especially in comparison with the much longer and, from a constructional aspect, markedly more complex style of sentences that barely give the unfortunate individual trying to cope with them a chance to breathe and which become, therefore, asphyxiating in more ways than one!

10 *Humanise wherever possible*
Bring in personalities and names. Do away with 'our Sales

Department can . . .'—use—'Jenny Pearce, your personal Customer Service Manager, can . . .'.

11 *Snuggle up with the reader!*
Do away with '. . . it's got many features . . .'—use—'. . . let's run through the features together . . .'

12 *Use active words*
Tick. Send. Act. Claim. Take. Grab. Select. Slash.

13 *Sprinkle the evergreen 'turn-ons' plentifully around*
YOU. NEW. NOW. FREE. INTRODUCING. ANNOUNCING. SAVE.
    Use 'unique' very carefully. It is an evergreen. With severe leaf mould!

14 *Picture your reader*
Hold imaginary sales chats with them. Fantasise the sale in your head. And then write about it.

15 *Paint word pictures*
Try to find words that are evocative and inspiring. Which do you want your policy to be, the one that pays 'a regular monthly benefit', or 'a fountain of money, placing hard cash in your hands each and every month'?

16 *Be ruthless*
Strip out waffle or padding. But don't take out chute grease. And be careful not to de-humanise, cool or get in the way of the flowing style. The yardstick: is it of benefit, is it interesting, does it convince, does it hold them, is it there to lubricate? If it doesn't do one of these, it doesn't deserve to get printed.
    You can often strike out whole paragraphs measuring against this yardstick. Interestingly, with amateur or classic ad writers' work, they are mostly to be found at the beginning. Funny that!

17 *Ensure that the copy works on all three levels*
This you should do with the layout artist/designer (see 'Human nature' on page 220).

If you're not sure whether it succeeds, use the 'snatch test'. Give it to someone. Count five seconds. Snatch it back. If they can't tell you what it's about, you've failed!

MAILBOX

LONG OR CURIOSITY HEADLINES

It's quite a fascinating business writing a book. Like detective work, I suppose you can gradually start to piece together the past, and see where others have been before you. You can see where they've sought guidance to plug gaps in their experience or have just taken the lazy way out by adapting someone else's thinking, together with the odd story or two.

With some things, there's no escaping repetition or even rip-etition. AIDA. The Loyalty Ladder. And so on. Thus when my own experience differs from other authors', I feel beholden to tell you about it, with the proviso that it does differ.

Long headlines are an example. I've had enormous success with headlines as long as two or three sentences. You do have to make absolutely certain that they're clear and understandable and digestible, but in my experience they work brilliantly. Although when you are tempted to run a long headline, do make sure the typography is of the most excellent quality. With no fancy bits! Fancy bits may please designers, but not readers. Nor do word-plays and puns.

The other difference I wish to report that flies in the face of another often repeated doctrine is that of the 'curiosity' headline. Again, as long as the curiosity wraps around a clear benefit proposition these headlines have worked for me.

The keyword is benefit. As a wet-behind-the-ears copywriter myself in the very early seventies, I remember being so pleased with a headline for Hertz Truck rental promoting their refrigerated vehicles.

It proclaimed . . .

'From Hertz. The Coolest Deal Yet!'

Firstly, as I learned from one complainant, it should have had a question mark after it to be legal, decent, honest and truthful! But I also know now that it would have worked much better as:

SAVE 25% WHEN YOU
RENT A REFRIGERATED TRUCK
FROM HERTZ TODAY

And here come the Don'ts . . .

18   *Don't use incredible, or uncaring words or phrases*
Avoid the time-weary as opposed to the time-honoured. Do
you honestly want to do business with people who offer

- THIS WORLD-BEATING COTTON WOOL BALL (The USA's
  latest secret weapon?)
- THE MOST DYNAMIC GARDEN PIECE YOU'LL EVER OWN
  (What's a garden piece?)
- ONE TASTE WHISKS YOU TO PALM FRINGED, SUN-SOAKED
  LAGOONS (I can only handle one lagoon at a time)
- THE BANK ACCOUNT THAT'S LIKE A PERMANENT FRIEND (A
  high-interest friend, yet?)
- IT'S THE DOG FOOD BREEDERS PREFER (Yeah! But how do
  the mutts feel about it?)

19   *Don't use word-play, puns or be clever*
It doesn't work. Nuff said!

20   *Don't use too many 'me-words'*
I; MY; WE; OUR. It's supposed to be all about *them*. The
readers! So by all means use enough of these to be personal,
but don't go overboard. YOU and YOURS is fine! They can
be used as much as you like—especially at the beginning of
paragraphs, a place where 'me-words' should only rarely be
found.

21   *Don't use negative words*
Change the aspect from which you are writing around to the
positive.

22   *Don't use abstract or needlessly complex words and descriptions*
Do you really mean 'seating arrangements', or chairs?

23   *Don't use 'Etc.'*
It's fine in books! But in a mailing it means you've left
something unsaid, partially explained . . . or worse, you've
left the readers something to work out for themselves.

24   *Don't forget. You'll lose more readers in the first 50 words than you will in the rest*
So turn up the heat. Put plenty of thought and effort into headlines.

Either Mr Ogilvy himself, or someone else of Ogilverian disposition, once explained that: 'When you've written the headline you've spent 70 per cent of the client's budget.' This does not indicate the prices of the agency. It's to demonstrate how important the headline is.

25   *Don't worry about length of copy*
Worry more about whether it's interesting, paced and easy to read.

26   *Don't leave questions unanswered*
To the direct mail copywriter a 'Questions and Answer' routine is like a favourite old pair of shoes. We'll slip into 'em at first excuse. But also, you should ensure throughout that you are provoking questions in the readers' minds. One of the best ways to return their attention and interest is to pose or manipulate a question to which they need an answer. The secret is not to withhold all the answers to the end! The secret is to make sure that in every answer, you carefully plant the next question.

There are some questions that will occur to the readers anyway. They are suggested by the very structure of your mailing, perhaps the components, its shape, format, design, or function.

Courtesy of Siegfried Voegele, here's a useful checklist, presented component by component, of the questions that will quite naturally occur to the readers.
Envelope
1   Is this for me?
2   Who is it from? (You may choose to answer this later!)

And your *existing* customers:
3(a) What's it all about today?
4(a) Am I interested in this?

And *cold* prospects:

3(b) What's in this envelope?

4(b) More important—what's in it for me?

Letter

1   Why are they writing to me?

2   What's so interesting about this? (i.e. put your main benefit first)

3   Who signed this letter?

4   Shall I go on reading?

5   Do I need this?

6   Again—what's in it for me?

7   Can they prove it? Where's the evidence?

8   What am I supposed to do?

Leaflet

1   How did I get along without this up to now?

2   Why will this make things better tomorrow?

3   What's in it for me?

4   And who says so?

5   And who can prove it?

6   Is it exactly what I need?

7   Should I react?

8   Is this urgent?

9   How do I respond?

Response device

1   What must I do with this? (All the way through your package you should talk about response as if it is expected)

2   How much . . . what's the price?

3   Must I sign?

4   What is the risk once I sign? (You'll say none, of course!)

5   What happens next?

6   Do I have to make any decisions? (Preferably not)

7   Must I fill in, or just check my address?

8   Must I pay postage?

9   Is it urgent? (Yes, yes, yes!!!)

27   *Don't make a monkey out of yourself*

(Or: why so many copywriters have long arms!)

People are very nice sometimes. Even the people you're
going to write to. They'll do just as you say. Follow you
lemming-like. So when, in paragraph three of your letter you
casually invite them to 'take a look at the stunning new villas
in this year's exciting brochure enclosed . . .', they will.

More often than not, most of them, right there, right then.

It's usually the very last thing you want them to do.
Having spent a great deal of time and effort getting them into
the letter, you would much rather they carried on with that.
Because the trouble is, they won't come back to it. And you,
knowing that the brochure was going to 300 000 new prospects as well as the 50 491 customers from the previous two
years, only mentioned the special offer for past customers in
the letter. And now they'll never get to know.

Think about it. A simple rearrangement of your copy will
make sure you give them the right advice. Be sure to build
into copy and design the visual and verbal signposts that will
help the majority of readers to get the whole story. Build in as
many as possible, in the most logical, convincing sequence.
Otherwise, they'll miss loads of good reasons to respond!

Lastly, if you write a fair amount of copy, you might like to get
hold of a little paperback gem called *Words that Sell*. It's the
brainchild of an American copywriter called Richard Bayan.
You'll find details in the Bibliography. And probably your fastest
way to get a copy would be from the British Direct Marketing
Association in London on (071) 630 7322. Failing that, I know it is
also available via Hoke Communications Inc. in the US who take
all major credit cards. And telephone orders! From the UK the
number is 010 1 516 746 6700 and the time difference is around
five hours. I'm not on commission! It's just a jolly useful
'thesaurus-style' moneymaker of a book. For you and him!

MAILBOX

USE LAYOUT FOR EMPHASIS

Have you ever noticed how many direct mail letters use indented paragraphs?

They work well to add emphasis to the importance of particular passages. I've always worked to three paragraph widths, which have the added benefit of adding shape and interest to the layout of a letter. As do indented paragraph openings. Generally the more tidied up copy looks the more boring and solid and heavy it looks—so justify left but 'ragged right'!

Here is my paragraph grid (not to scale):

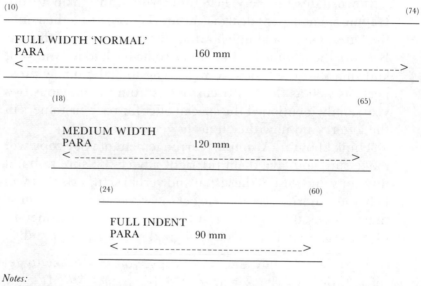

Notes:
1   Minimum type size, 10 point.
2   Use a serif typeface.
3   Minimum left and right hand margins, 25 mm (i.e. 10 spaces in on 10 point).
4   Figures in bracket show spaces in from left edge.
5   Layout on 'centred' format.

Figure 8.1   JFR's paragraph grid

3 WITH *DESIGN* IN MIND

Copywriters—that is, direct marketing copywriters anyway—are quite brutal with designers. This, for many years, has kept most of the really talented designers out of direct mail in particular. They felt it was dull, style-ised and boring.

They were right. However, three things have happened that are decidedly good news and show all the signs of proving that design has a valuable, indeed vital, part to play in the world of direct mail—even if it is a supporting role. These changes haven't altered the fact that it's a double act. The copy is Holmes; the graphics, Watson. The copy is Gin; and the design is Tonic.

The changes that are slowly improving the level and quality of design in direct mail, and in fact direct marketing as a whole, are these:

- More young people, often very talented, are coming into direct marketing.
- Some of the better classical advertising art directors and their teams have been bitten by the 'direct' bug.
- As the 'establishment' advertising names—clients and agencies—move into 'direct' they will not tolerate what they perceive as the inferior graphic standards of direct advertising.

For years, especially when the influence of creative was so vastly over-rated, the dominant copy-ists (make that domineering copyists) insisted that the pretty and the neat, tidy, smarter, more aesthetic didn't sell so well. It actually got in the way of copy.

There remains truth in this. And therefore I place the credit for this surge in graphic standards at the feet of all those designers who manage to find ways to work within the often artistically constraining walls of direct mail, but still demonstrate their freshness, flair and ingenuity.

Long may it continue. But never in the cause of good design. Always in the cause of a good response!

Let's look at the function of the design element of a direct mail package—as a part of the total sales effort. Then we'll look at a design checklist, to go with the copy checklist you've just seen.

For a number of years now I have identified the functions of design in direct mail thus:

- to get the words read
- to enhance, illustrate, dramatise and emphasise the proposition
- to illustrate, clarify and endorse the text
- to show the reader the way to go, and how to deal with the various pieces
- to indicate and encourage the desired response.

There are others, of course. But we are essentially dealing with a very practical approach to design, followed by a highly informed and aware typographic mentality, then followed by 'how it looks', which is to many 'lay' people what they think is meant by design. A good-looking piece is well designed. An ugly piece is badly designed.

I can't agree with this. The classical advertising business is the living example. Most of the design is pretty, or nice looking. But at least 50 per cent is so appalling as, in my view, to constitute professional negligence. I mean purely as examples of design in its wider sense. That's why it's so rewarding to watch the more skilled and talented designers now working down a path that says it does not have to be a conflict.

It is possible to meet the demanding requirements of the direct marketing world. And satisfy the noble and refined aesthetic desires of the artier factions of design.

Direct marketing design—at least at the more tasteful, quality end—tends to settle rather more easily with the classical approach. That doesn't mean it should be stuffy. It does mean it should generally make looking at it a pleasant experience. It should look inviting and attractive. It should work with the materials to aid the product/service/corporate positioning.

To achieve our objectives, all a designer, typographer, or artist

---

MAILBOX

AVOID STANDARD COMPANY LETTERHEADINGS

So often their design gets in the way of Eye Track Management. Often your logo and name will do just as much for you as the whole lot. Relegate boring address information, telephone numbers, and your registered address and incorporation number to the bottom. Who needs your address and phone number unless you've given them a reason to contact you anyway? Clear them away! Now you've got a great big hole. Fill it up with a great big benefit laden headline!!

---

has to do is think. . . . not about their own desires, or purposes, but about *the reader's*.

And probably the most compromising factor of all of these is that the design should not be so striking as to distract the reader, or get in the way of the copy. We don't want to hear 'what a lovely brochure', we want to hear 'what a lovely hotel', or holiday, or nest of tables, or headscarf. That's all!

At last it seems that it is not too much to ask. There are designers who can do it. Most of them are ridiculously young. But then they haven't hardened to a school yet. If you've been a rebel, or convention fighter, or devil-may-care genius for 20 years, I suppose it gets to be a habit.

In direct marketing we were going through that era of over-obsession with rolled-up-sleeve creative, absolute infatuation with the position of the full stop and apostrophe. The design element had been forced into near submission. So it was bound to make less difference when you tinkered with design, than copy. They were operating in a subterranean tunnel of blandness and mediocrity. We direct copywriters, who are after all the barrow-boys of the advertising business, were more than happy to chase the maximum response. And it always worked. The louder, brasher, and more blatant we got, the more response went up. It was a vicious spiral downwards from quality. Never mind the quality, feel this great stack of reply cards.

Despite all this progress in the design and art side, I cannot say that I feel copy skills moving so distinctly in any direction—other, perhaps, than to be grappling with the technological break-throughs.

Yet I cannot get away from one fundamental. Nor can those who know anything about direct mail, from Claude Hopkins in 1923, to Ogilvy in his time, and to my contemporaries now. In direct mail it is inescapable. *The copy has to sell.* Design has to join in and help. But then I'm the kind of believer in sexual equality that likes to open doors for ladies!

MAILBOX

DON'T FORGET MATERIALS

Your paper merchant can become a friend. One great way to make impact is the vast array of different textures and weights and colours available to you. But remember my earlier advice. When they hold your mailing in their hands they hold your company representative. If they don't know you, the materials (not just paper, but typography too) will be a major piece of evidence.

Number one on the checklist is much along the same path . . .

Designer Dos and Don'ts

1 *Use the 'reward' psychology*
Conventional advertising and marketing design operate largely on the psychology of approval. The nicer we look, and the prettier we are, the more they will like us. If they like us they will admire us greatly and do as we ask.
Result: 'What a lovely brochure.'
Direct marketing operates more on the reward psychology. 'Hey look! If you do that, you'll get this.' It's a very much more basic. In design terms it translates principally as action-based formats and those rather less than subtle headline styles and forceful, powerful layouts.

Let's look at an example. A classical designer wants to make sure that something looks as nice as possible when it arrives. He or she will design into the brochure (often as the last fold or an A4 concertina leaflet, for example) a reply card. To make it come together as a piece of design they have created a layout that runs across the entire spread. Perhaps it is a tint or illustration softened into the background, or maybe the copy is carefully ranged around a colour pic of your building, or the massed bands of the product range. You know the sort of thing. The design encompasses the whole spread.

This psychology is wrong because the action you want — the card ripped off and returned—is at complete loggerheads with the designer's achievement. So the reader has to spoil or mutilate the work to do what is necessary. And to compound the felony, the better the job the designer does, the worse the conflict; the less likely it is that people will want to mutilate it or spoil it.

That is one of the contributory factors to my advice to keep reply cards separate. No one has to spoil anything to take the action. . . . plus some other reasons we'll come to.

But designers can move one step further. You must have seen all those leaflets and inserts where the reply cards hang off, flapping about like that cartoon of the last leaves on the autumn tree. They beg to be torn off. In fact, if the design is right, people will tear them off anyway, even if they're not responding. Why? Because they don't look right. They look awkward and out of place. In fact, if you were just to tear that last bit off it would actually look better.

Bullseye!

Right into the deepest mire of what we were looking at a few moments ago. At the very heart of this piece of advice is the need for the designer to create a piece that looks awkward, clumsy and unwieldy, so that when the reader looks at it, the blossoming conscious desire to respond is egged-on by the subliminal desire to improve the shape and design of the piece. The two are in concert. Take the action. *Reward*. You move nearer to the offer. *Reward.* Suddenly you've made that thing look better. Now what will you do with that enquiry card you're holding in your left hand?

Did I hear a cry from the back? A still small voice suggesting that no hard-headed right-minded person—consumer or business—is going to spend money just to make a leaflet look better and because they couldn't think of what to do with a reply card in their left hand. Correct. My point is, what are you giving them? Is it a magical mystery tour, or an assault course?

2   *Make your packages readable*
I won't even mention fine typefaces, reversed white out of 'thin' four-colour process. I promise!

No. This 'do' is all about using simple, clear typefaces, preferably serif which people (everybody, according to Graeme McCorkell, apart from the Swiss) find easier to read. Nothing less than eight point if typeset, ten point if typewritten. And work to reasonable column widths. That's why newspapers and magazines use such narrow columns. So should you! Use distinct colours for type. No fancy stuff. Don't ever make copy blend into the design.

3   *Use shape and folds and construction to 'present' the rationale for you*
In copy 'dos' we learned to develop a rationale. In other words, to orchestrate our sales story; to lead readers down a natural path of persuasion. Designers can do a fantastic job here, developing formats and paper folds so that, as the paper unfolds, so too does the sales story.

4   *Establish the role of each component*
Think about the tasks and objectives of each individual component. Is it to inform, to entertain, to involve, to announce, to celebrate, to invite, to impress? Use design and choice of materials to make this role clear. Make the fun elements look like fun and the technical pieces look technical.

Above all else, appreciate that mailings have a character. The various components should all work together even though each may perform a different individual task.

Remember, too, that when people hold the mailing in their hands, they should *feel* your company. That's about positioning, image, style, tone-of-voice and personality. Whether the letter comes from the chairman or the area sales manager should make a difference.

5   *Use illustration and photography to score points, not just for imagery*
The sales story will benefit from illustration—photographic or otherwise—to add understanding. Remember that the picture will get looked at well in advance of most of the copy. Photographs generally work better than illustration as such. To waste either in 'theme-ing' or 'mood-ing' will be bad for you. Use them carefully when and where they will add maximum emphasis to the story.

Remember the dual role. Photos and illustrations tend to get looked at twice at least: once very early on, then again, but by smaller quantities of people who are, nonetheless, of greater significance when the copy is being read seriously.

They must work to the objectives of both situations. Theme-ing and mood-ing can be dealt with quite well by backgrounds, choice of models, props, and all the details that are so important.

6   *Don't leave out the human race*
People warm up print. They attract the eye. They convince.

Who wants to eat in a restaurant with nobody in it? Who wants to sail on a boat that nobody else sails on? Who wants to drive a car that nobody else seems to want? Who wants to fly on a plane that nobody else seems to want to fly on? Get some people power!

There are six design pointers. Much more for the design-conscious momentarily!

4   WITH *HUMAN NATURE* IN MIND

Confession. One of my conference routines was stolen from California's Ray Jutkins. To make a point, Ray asks the audience to think, instantaneously, of four things.

He gives them subject-headers, and they have to write the first thing that comes into their heads.

'Gimme a colour!' asks Ray.

'OK. Now give me a flower.'

'Next, a piece of furniture.'

And so on.

Most people—never all, but the majority choose the same: RED, ROSE, CHAIR.

Some things just are so. We react naturally to certain stimuli, just as we always have. It's just human nature.

Now let me tell you a little more about someone I mentioned earlier, Professor Siegfried Voegele.

Siegfried is a technician in creative strategies—particularly in direct mail. And he's quite brilliant. He's also very aware of his second skill: he's a great communicator. Siegfried and I spend more time nodding and smiling at each other than anything else. He wishes me a good session as I go into the one I'm leading. I reciprocate. Whenever I get the chance to spend even ten minutes in any of his sessions it would take more than wild horses to keep me away. If you ever get the chance yourself, don't miss him.

So for the next few minutes I'd like to run through a blend of our ideas. But a great deal of the hard evidence of what I'm going to show you is courtesy of Siegfried Voegele, or rather, in particular, his scientific approach to studying how people handle and read their direct mail and other forms of direct marketing.

I'd like to address human nature from two aspects. First . . .

The concept of eye track management

There are some things I just can't resist: stealing the top strawberry in a bowl; a good glimpse of female cleavage; making light of a difficult situation; and any opportunity to swim. I like to do a couple of kilometres most days, so it needs to be warm, because something else I can't resist are creature comforts!

How about you? I expect you can think of some things you can't resist.

There are probably going to be some things that neither of us can resist. Because one of the things we've got in common is that we're all human beings. We respond to those things in a particular (in fact a predictable) way because it's just human nature to do so.

And these reflexes stretch across all boundaries—geographic, ethnic, and social.

The point is that the most natural and involuntary human reflexes can be manipulated in our favour. So we want to manipulate these to get the reader moving in the right direction. We want to make sure that the reader goes where we want them to go or where we are waiting for them.

To discover where and what these places are, Siegfried has carried out some ingenious experiments with an eye-movement recorder.

A memorable experience for me was a live demonstration organised at the Montreux Symposium one year. In front of an audience of about 200, Siegfried subjected a Swiss lady to the test.

Blissfully unaware of what she was supposed to do—and with four close circuit TV cameras, one showing the eye movements related to the pages she looked at—she went through piles of magazines and mailings demonstrating with innocent Swiss precision what Siegfried wished to demonstrate.

I'll take you through some of it now, then you'll realise, perhaps, just how ignorant most advertising layouts are, and how you can in future improve the work you do or use.

Our objective will be to make sure that the readers' attention—where their eyes go—is, or is made to be, in harmony with our sales rationale, enabling us to achieve, as was suggested earlier, our aim to lead the readers logically along our path to persuasion.

GLANCE, SCAN, READ

In the early glancing process, Siegfried has identified 'fixing points'. That is his name for those places where the reader's eye will alight momentarily to absorb information—be it words or visual. This is a horrendously fast event. It should frighten copywriters to the very core.

The eye rests on each fixing point for just two-tenths of a second. The tolerance level per A4 spread is about ten fixing points. Your work lives or dies in just two seconds! With an A3 spread the tolerance level goes up to about 15. So you've got three seconds. Good luck!

Then, with the speed of light, the Glancer's brain makes a decision.

Go again or quit? With Germanic logic, Siegfried attributes the decision making to a count. More than five out of ten, and your A4 sheet gets up-graded to a scan. Less, and you die. I suspect that it is not quite that clear cut. I believe it more likely that one very strong success out of ten can buy you a reprieve.

The second trip round—the scan—gives you more time, but not that much! The scan is all about gathering hard evidence to justify a read. It will include much more copy. The glance was picking up odd words, maybe a full phrase but not much else other than feeding the visual sense. Here whole headlines, photo-captions, subheads and so on will be read.

How you fare from here on is down to you. With some you'll get the in-depth read. Some will still not decide without a pre-read. Then they'll go for the body copy and diagrams and more complicated pictures and illustrations.

YOU NEED TO USE 'EYECATCHERS' TO GET THE HIGHEST SCORE!

This isn't all news. But it's a valuable confirmation nonetheless. Let's look at this list of ten eyecatchers, and discuss some of them.

1   *Big pictures beat small pictures*
    We all know *that*. Sure we do. All except the agency that gives

us an ad with a small black and white picture and places it in a magazine notorious for lavish big colour spreads—and we paid extra for a right-hand page!

2 *Colour pictures beat black and white*

3 *Warm colours beat cool colours*

4 *Pictures of humans beat pictures of products*
Memo: if, in the same shot, the product doesn't *really* stand out, readers may only see the human *not* the product!

5 *Pictures of lots of people beat pictures of a few*
Suggestion: get a football team to endorse the product. *And* remember what I said about empty planes and restaurants!

6 *Portraits beat whole body pictures*
This is mainly because we can see faces, particularly eyes.

7 *Solids beat copy*
What to do: use headlines reversed out of solids.

8 *Vertical shapes beat horizontal*
Apparently this goes back to the fact that once upon a time we reckoned anything standing was a threat.
Anything lying down was not.

9 *Circles beat rectangles*
This one, I am told, is a sexual preference. Don't worry, it was your forefathers' fault!

10 *Short headlines beat long headlines*
Now here's an interesting one, because most direct marketing know-alls (like me) will tell you that *longer* headlines work best.
    Let's play with this one a little.
    We're discussing eye-pulling power here, not response-pulling power. Thus, you can still stack up a high success rate on the fixing point test while, at the same time, ignoring one or more of them.

Try to imagine this. You have a full page A4 in front of you. Across the top left to a width of two-thirds you have a longish headline, say three lines deep. Ranged with it in depth, to the right, you have a picture, in colour, of a group of people. The headline is printed black against white, but with the last two words of the middle line emphasised in bright red. They are 'YOURS FREE'. The photo has a short caption: '£1 million! You could join these 17 lucky winners.'

What's going to happen? Answer: your long headline isn't going to get fully read until second time round. But the number of successful fixing points will get more people to go round the second time!

These 'eyecatchers' are not arranged in any order. And the list is not exhaustive.

MAILBOX

BEWARE THE *DANGER* FIXING POINTS!

These are the unintentional ones. The most common are those paragraphs that end with a new line only one word long. No problem if the word's a good one but, unless you are careful, even the apparently positive will work against you. For example . . .

be pleased you did and we can help you to avoid
danger

and that means one more benefit. You won't pay out
high charges.

then it's guaranteed that we take out all the
risk.

Your fixing points here say DANGER, HIGH CHARGES, RISK. Not good for building readership or response!

We'll discuss eye track management further when we consider letters, but for the moment let's look at some more human nature.

Some of your best friends are human . . .

Always remember not to get over-involved with your actual product or service. Remember, the people you're writing to are *individuals* and, as such, are susceptible to all the traditional weaknesses and needs. Think beyond the immediate benefits that you have to offer and consider how these will relate to their character and personality.

Here is a brief checklist of what most human beings like in life:

- Money
- Status
- Comfort
- Sex
- Toys and games
- Possessions

They like visible evidence of their ability to acquire things and maintain a culture.

- People like knowledge, new information, practical and DIY skills, intellectual enjoyment and satisfaction.
- People like security, protection, being prepared, having reserves or safety devices, feeling safe, avoiding discomfort, embarrassment, risk and worry.
- People like to feel fulfilled, creative, individual, happy and self-confident. They like to get away, to escape, to avoid pressures or sometimes even decisions. They like to be free.
- People like to be accepted, popular, to receive praise, to be stylish, fashionable, or up-to-date; they like to achieve status and authority and respectability—sometimes even unrespectability or notoriety! They like to be seen to be helping others. They like to help themselves.
- People like to be one-up, to be sensible, organised, well equipped, faster—to have got a better deal, to be better prepared, to be warned in advance or to know about something before others. They like to feel cosy, smug and satisfied.

They like to please their peers, to be seen as efficient and smart.

And despite all this, they like to be liked!

5   WITH *IDEAS* IN MIND

Getting an idea is a problem for some people. Getting too many is a problem for others. One of the great assets of direct marketing is the ability to test lots of ideas to establish those that really are worthwhile.

I may as well be blunt. I find ideas happen in particular places. I commuted daily across one particular level crossing on the Brighton/Portsmouth line. It was almost always closed—nine times out of ten. At first it irritated. Then I became resigned to it. Later I loved it. It became one of my great idea places. There are others. Two are the bath and the loo!

There are also idea times. One of my favourites is last thing at night (well, nearly last thing!). I nearly always end the day with a scotch. We Capricorns love routine. As my mind empties the day, it starts to generate ideas like crazy. Another time is in the early hours of the morning. Sometimes they are so strong they literally wake me up—or seem to. I always forget these ideas because I drift back to sleep, so a scrap pad and pencil by the bed is a 'good idea'!

I also have ideas just as I wake. These stay with me. I guess they are the result of a night's mental data processing.

Sometimes however, the loo, the level crossing and my late night 'quiet moment' fail me, . . . or the timing doesn't suit, . . . or perhaps it's other people's ideas that are required—particularly if the idea I'm seeking is to do with something I'm very much involved in.

Personally, I've always found my best ideas work better for other people than they do for me. One of my most expensive ideas—I lost a lot of money!—was in the mid-sixties trying to sell fashion wigs by mail order. One friend told me it was a hair-brained scheme. On both counts I was forced to agree.

Other people's ideas can be great problem solvers. So here's an idea to generate ideas when you're too close to . . .

See the wood from the trees

Use it particularly when you are closely involved with whatever it is you are selling or promoting. It will pay you to examine carefully the many different aspects that your products or services have from the point of view of the buyer. It is always very different to the seller.

One of the best ways to examine new opportunities, new angles and new strategies for promotion is the brainstorming technique. Gather together your creative team, your production team, your client service people—even a few customers if you're feeling adventurous—and take another look at what you're trying to promote. Turn it upside down. Inside out.

Here are a few triggers for brainstorming sessions.

- *Increase it!*
  Make it bigger; give it more value; add to it; multiply it; make it more frequent; give it more strength; make it higher; make it wider, longer or fatter!

- *Decrease it!*
  Omit something; halve it; make it smaller; divide it into pieces or parts; make it more compact; condense it; understate it!

- *All-in-one?*
  Put your ideas together; put all the elements together; put all the separate bits and pieces together; sell as a complete piece!

- *Modify it?*
  Add a new twist or flavour; give it new form, design or shape; change its appeal to the eye, the ear, taste, smell or feel!

- *Change it around?*
  Can you put something else first; can you change the sequence or order; can you change the frequency or timing?

- *Try a substitute!*
  What else can you use instead; or who else?; or where else?
  What other element can be included or left out?

- *How about a different angle?*
  Don't accept the obvious; try the absolute opposite; turn it
  upside down; turn it inside out; how about backwards? Turn
  it around; try the unexpected or even sometimes the unac-
  ceptable?

- *Make sure you've asked these!*
  Why; when; where; who; what; how; what about; what if;
  what else.

In order to make a brainstorming session work well, you
should select your participants carefully. You must describe
your problems to them clearly. You must create a casual
atmosphere and get your participants relaxed before this
session gets underway.

It is not necessarily a bad idea to provide drinks and start with
a joke session or a few anecdotes.

Make sure everyone is encouraged to speak. Compliment
them. React positively. Never make negative comments.

Encourage innovation and effort. Encourage building on other
people's ideas and suggestions. Make notes unobtrusively rather
than record or video the session. Never come to any conclusions
during the session. Lock out senior management!

6   WITH *A PROPOSITION* IN MIND

I'm not going to spend a great deal more time on propositions. I
am going to give you a little lecture—in the emphatic tone of voice
that mothers use when they are explaining to children how to
cross the road.

Not a bad analogy really since the life of your mailing is at stake. So look left (list and/or database!), look right (proposition/offer!) and go if its clear (package and timing!). Here's about all that matters:

1 Think a great deal about constructing a proposition that people will want to accept. The more you can do to relate that proposition to your audience (or segments of audience) the better it will work.

2 Consider what you can do to enhance it with an offer that will attract action and have a clearly established link with either the product/service that you are selling, or the people you are selling to. Why not both?

3 Develop a clear and explicit rationale for both proposition and offer.

4 Sell it. Sell the proposition harder than the product or service. Sell it in front. Sell it first. Sell it fast. And sell it thoroughly.

7 WITH *LETTERS* IN MIND

Letters are undoubtedly, undisputedly and consistently the single strongest weapon in the creative armoury. A good letter is a joy to read or, at very least, a pleasure. It is so formidable for a number of reasons:

1 People's natural instinct is to head for the letter first, often shunning more than casual glances of your other items in favour of it.

    This is simply the conditioning of time. We expect letters in the post. We know they'll explain what it's about. So if there's any news, or anything significant, or anything important, it'll be in there.

2 Letters often look the easiest to cope with, the least threatening or blatantly trying to 'sell'. This is not always true. But there is a 'comfort' factor to a letter which, once we've established that it's good news not bad, we enjoy and attracts us.

3   This is enhanced and forwarded by the fact that letters come from people. Leaflets are issued by companies. Letters are sent by individuals—even if they are obviously mass produced. They have signatures. They talk in a light (sometimes chatty) style. So there's obviously a person there. A person behind it. A person involved.

Logically, of course, this is true of all the other items too! They just don't show it so engagingly!

Let's look at some more of Siegfried Voegele's evidence. Because there's no doubt that eye track management on this item is of huge importance. For so many readers it will be where positive or negative decisions for the glance–scan–read process will be made.

One of the big differences with letters as opposed to other printed or published items is the number of historically conditioned (I call them *Involuntary*) fixing points. For example:

- The recipient's name and address block
- Your name and address
- The signature
- The name and title of the signatory
- A PS.

You can create other fixing points (I call these *Voluntary* fixing points). For example:

- Indented paragraphs
- Underlining
- Capital letters
- Handwritten margin notes
- A Johnson box

```
* * * * * * * * * * * * * * * * * *
*                                 *
*    That's one of these . . . often used   *
*       for highlighting, particularly at   *
*          the beginning of a letter        *
*                                 *
* * * * * * * * * * * * * * * * * *
```

- All those **<!!>?@*-ing things around the keyboard

We also know the eye start positions—where the eye will come in—and where it will go out if it's left to its own devices (see Fig. 8.2). So you see, taking A4, as an example, it is possible to manage

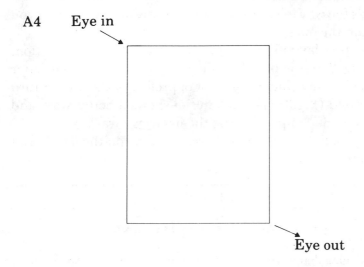

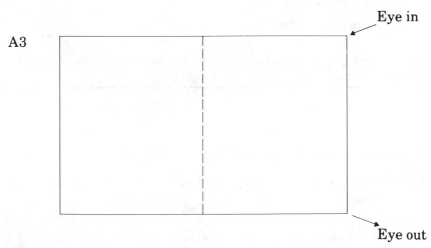

Figure 8.2 The natural eye path

an eye track in order to boost our score with the readers, and move them along the glance–scan–read path.

The numbers will dive—no, plummet—during these first seconds whatever you do. So saving just the odd extra reader or two is important. Don't be disheartened by the number of cop-outs. That's the way it is. As long as you have done everything you can to retain the ones you want.

Here are three layouts showing a simple use of this information. The first (Fig. 8.3)—a 'before'—shows a typical single page letter format which many (including a lot of professionals) would turn out; the second (Fig. 8.4)—an 'after'—shows a better way; and the third (Fig. 8.5) superimposes the likely eye tracks.

Spend lots and lots and lots of creative time on the letter. It'll *pay* you back handsomely.

MAILBOX

KEEP THE MOMENTUM GOING

Don't do anything that might encourage the reader to quit. In fact try to do the opposite. Use run-on hooks, for example. That's breaking at a page end, mid-sentence, mid-paragraph. If possible try to build some intrigue or curiosity into the 'hook' too. Such as . . .

'. . . benefits too. And, of course, you could win . . .
/over please

Don't number pages, unless you are using separate sheets where it will help to clarify or avoid confusion.

---

8   WITH *PERSONALISATION* IN MIND

I remember inventing a term to describe my attitude towards personalisation—or rather, what it should achieve. The term is 'techno-creativity'.

Personalisation, in my book [*sic*], is not about sticking some-one's name and address on the top of a letter, together with a

Figure 8.3 An innocently designed letter-style page ignoring eye-path principles

Figure 8.4   A layout which follows the eye management concept

EYE IN

OWN THIS PERSONALISED
DIRECT MARKETING LIBRARY
FOR JUST £99.95.
SAVE OVER £25.00. CLAIM TODAY.

Dear Marketer

BONUS
FREE!

EVERY ASPECT OF
DIRECT
MARKETING
EXPERTLY AND
COMPREHENSIVELY
REVEALED..

★DIRECT MAIL

★DATABASE

★TELEMARKETING

★OFF-THE-PAGE

★ELECTRONIC
MEDIA

RETURN YOUR
BONUS OFFER
CLAIM NOW

SAVE
£25.00
PLUS!

EYE OUT

Figure 8.5   So a typical 'glance' might follow this easy path for the eye.
(But note just how disruptive the salutation might prove to the
first glance eye path.)

personal salutation. That's 'matching in'—a process which modern computer printing has made easy and cheap and fast. But it's *not* personalisation.

In an earlier chapter, I referred to days gone by when one of the services on offer from direct mail producers was a litho-printed letter with the name, address and personal salutation 'matched in' on the top. We were trying to give the readers the impression that someone had sat down and typed a letter to each of them. I wonder how many are fooled today. I wonder how many will be fooled in five years' time, or even ten.

However, as laser and ink-jet caught on, their uses became more inventive and so their users more skilled. So, as well as for selectivity, simple file information can be regurgitated in text matter: age, sex, job title, business activity, make of car, and so on.

The game of the name is 'personalisation'

The change-over to appropriate advertising has, in a very modest way, started. Some few years ago now, readers observed that letters from direct mailers were no longer just written at them. In some pioneering way they were beginning to be written *about* them. So what had started out as a desire to make letters that *looked* original, evolved to the present where they *are* original. Again.

Not only is my letter appropriate to me, it is appropriate to me only. If someone else received it, he or she could only be interested out of sheer nosiness!

During that evolution the objective of personalisation changed. Originally it was used so that a mailing wouldn't look like a mailing. It still is.

Then, as it all started to look like that, personalisation was used to grab attention. It still is.

Then, as it all started to look like that, personalisation was used to make replying and buying easier. It still is.

However, nowadays, as well as all those with the parallel development of database marketing, we are on the brink of *individualisation*. As markets fragment, so the front ends of those who wish to communicate with them must fragment too. The size and reach of the fragments will be determined by two criteria: the intensity of the relationship and the desired effectiveness of the communications within the relationship. Hence the very careful need to understand, manage, control and develop the technology of the communications, for it is this that will enable us to understand the needs of each market fragment, and to respond to those needs.

Now let's see what relevance that has to the production of personalised mailings. Firstly, it will determine marketing and sales objectives. This guides what you have to do. Next you have to decide how you will achieve your objectives, and how you will use the resources available to you. From this will develop a communications strategy, and from that strategy, it will become clear to what use you will put the resource of information. Will it be to segment the market? What are the common aspects of the segments—and are they completely or partially common? What is the most effective way to relate the exclusively tailored proposition to the segments?

You will be endeavouring, using the media at your disposal, to cluster groups of individuals together. This makes the communication process more economical. You will be trying to develop an acceptable proposition (and here I use the word acceptable in its most literal sense). Next comes the task of putting that proposition across in the most acceptable way. And after that we also have to make the act of accepting as acceptable as possible!

From all of this will come the conclusions that are necessary to decide whether you will use some form of personalisation and what you want to achieve. Remember, the effects it can create are:

1   To make the letter personal in varying degrees
2   To grab attention and stimulate interest
3   To transmit information (often administrative data)

4   To tailor, communicate, enhance and relate the proposition
5   To facilitate acceptance of the proposition.

I once came out with this immortal line:

'I had forgotten how bad my memory is!'

What I'm building up to here is yet another acronym. I find they help me to carry thoughts in my head.

Since I have yet another circulating the whispering gallery that is my cerebellum right now, and it's for personalisation, we may as well verbalise it.

The MIGHT of personalisation.

*M*atch-in
*I*ndividualise
*G*rab attention
*H*elp response
*T*ransmit information

Those are the same five uses as above, in a different order! So that is the basic 'menu'. What creative have to do is to decide with you which of these, often more than one, are required.

Certain choices—'individualise', for example—can achieve a bucketful of 'grab attention' at the same time.

But creative will obviously make a more proficient job of presenting the personalisation if they have a clear idea of why it is being used. For instance, if you've picked T—Transmit Information—and you're going to announce the price increase of a subscription, it will need to be handled differently in comparison to someone who is going to declare a record dividend on a savings plan or unit trust.

Personalisation needs to complement all manner of things: such as style, tone of voice, positioning, and image. It needs to be influenced by the list or database, the character of the audience and the relationship you have with them, the nature of the proposition and the personality of the package.

It is one of the major development areas for creativity in direct marketing and endorses the need for a new breed of practical, ingenious, technically detail-conscious creative mind that wants to enjoy the benefits of new technology. That is precisely why I invented the phrase 'techno-creativity'.

It describes the future of creativity in direct marketing, and no more so than in direct mail.

MAILBOX

SOME TIPS FOR PERSONALISATION

- Do all you can to make sure that whoever is creating your mailing understands the production and computer disciplines. This will ensure that their ideas are practical and should, if they are truly creative people, still mean that their ideas are stimulating and challenging in every way.
- Think carefully about pioneering. Remember the risks increase at the same time as the potential rewards. But the latter—the rewards—don't always follow.
- You may ultimately feel forced to use personalisation for the wrong reason. An awful lot of advertisers produce full colour leaflets simply because the noise level is so high. In other words, their competitors all use four colour, so they feel obliged to follow suit.

I know that a number of advertisers feel this way about personalisation. I do sympathise with the feeling. If you decide to do it for the same (wrong) reason, that doesn't mean you should be slap-dash. It's important to get it right. At least it then stands a chance of paying you back with a profit.

- The more heavily that you use personalisation, the harder you will fall (measured on a scale of indignant complaint letters!) if you get even the slightest detail wrong, inaccurate or mis-spelt.

Personalised or not, it is a fact that the higher the response, usually the higher the complaints. This, while regrettable, usually indicates the higher levels of readership and is therefore a sorry side-effect of success. Whatever you do, however legal, decent, honest and truthful, somebody will dislike it enough to complain!

9   WITH *THE PACKAGE* IN MIND

With some occasional exceptions a 'package' should be a cohesive sales machine or enquiry generator, with each component performing a task.

- *Envelopes* intrigue, lead the reader in, or introduce.
- *Letters* announce. Explain. Invite. Encourage action.
- *Leaflets* tell. Describe. Expand. Give detail. Illustrate and stimulate.
- *Flyers and other devices* emphasise. Highlight. Carry urgent Stop Press. Provide extra final detail. Or a last push for response.
- *Reply devices* re-sell. Take orders. Encourage a dialogue. Re-illustrate offers. Reassure responders.
- *Reply envelopes* bring replies, money and sensitive data.

But they all have to pull together. If you have been able to identify one clear offer/proposition they should all work together, gradually moving the reader's mind nearer to a decision—the decision to respond to that proposition.

When establishing the functions of the various pieces one must be clear that, for example, a flyer being used to emphasise a point does not overpower the leaflet or letter so that, in effect, the point becomes greater than the reason for making it.

Endeavour to make each item in your package a stand-alone

MAILBOX

LIFT LETTERS

Now and again you can steal the dynamic readership levels of the letter and spread it around a little with a second letter. And you'll grab the same if not more. This is a technique pioneered by the publishing fraternity with the now famous 'Only read this if you've decided not to buy . . .'.

The rules are:

1 Don't confuse the reader about which is the main letter.
2 Reassure the reader (guarantee?).
3 Remind the reader (main benefit—ONE MORE TIME!!).

---

item. Meaning simply that whichever one is picked up, looked at first, returned to after a telephone call, or catches the eye when emptying the waste paper basket (NEVER give up!), the reader can still grasp the proposition and find out where and how to get it.

If you build in a whole heap of eyecatchers, they will go on catching eyes until they reach the rubbish dump or incinerator.

10 WITH *RESPONSE* IN MIND

The response device needs to ask for the order. It needs to close the sale. It needs to stand alone. It needs to perform its task with the minimum of fuss or effort by the responder. And lastly (meaning literally *last*ly—give it final priority), it needs to be economically and conveniently processed by you when it is returned.

Here's a checklist of ideas to help you achieve those objectives.

Response device checklist

1 *Keep it nice. And clean*
   Design is all important here. Yet a lot of designers rush out the response piece, either because they get bored with it, because it's no fun designing forms, or because they think it's a fairly trivial piece of detail.

   Wrong. It needs to look just as attractive, logical, open and inviting as the other items. Bearing in mind all it has to do, that's often a real designer's challenge.

2 *Keep it simple*
   It needs to look happy, colourful and friendly but not confusing. So use colour in the twin roles of making it cheerful and also making it easier to understand and follow.

3 *Give sufficient space*
   The responders should not be forced to cramp or abbreviate their name and address details or their order or response requests.

Don't lose orders for items because you didn't allow enough lines. Ask them to write in BLOCK CAPITALS.

4   *Identify it*
Make sure the response item stands out and is clearly headed. Avoid the word form if you can. Slip, coupon, request, claim, application are all more positive, inviting and less formal.

5   *Make sure they don't miss bits*
You can use emphatic arrows to highlight important bits like signatures or postal codes. Or place tinted crosses like your accountant or solicitor does in pencil to show you where to sign.

You can achieve a great deal with background tints—for example, leaving all the sections they have to fill in as white sections out of a light background. This has the added advantage of making a large piece look less than it does as a whole. One only notices the white spaces!

6   *Give clear instructions or advice*
If you have something that requires difficult, time-consuming or hard-to-find information, be helpful.

Nothing beats a step-by-step guide, the 1–2–3 of How to Apply. If necessary give additional tips and hints alongside tricky bits. Such as '. . . your bank sort code is the six-digit code, top right of your cheques'.

If you are in Britain, then make sure the space you leave them to fill in looks like this:

☐☐–☐☐–☐☐

not like

☐☐☐☐☐☐

or even this

☐──────────☐

7 *Fill in their name and address together with a fast-find computer code for response handling*
You'll boost response by filling in the basic details for them. If you can design the document so that the name and address block shows through an envelope window, you'll do yourself another favour.

But find some discrete place to print a code that will also speed up your access of their record when you need to.

8 *Remember the keycodes you need*
This is definitely the place for codes. But don't make people feel like you used to work at The Inland Revenue, or, for that matter, that they are just a set of numbers to you.

9 *Code mailing responses for a fast handling stream*
If you use reply envelopes for other things, or you want to apply different priorities to response handling, code the outer envelopes or return address sides for your mail handling staff. This can be achieved by a simple change of colour. A side stripe or corner flash and so on. Or a different department name in the address!

10 *Encourage the personal contact*
Be sure to give them a named individual to ring. And a number!

You will have spent some time humanising the package, don't stop at the reply device. Print a name for them to return it to. One person sent them the letter. Let them reply to one person, too. If they can be the same, that's great.

11 *Tell them how to pay*
Make payment easy. Accept credit cards (and telephone orders!). Additionally, test 'Send no money now' if it's feasible or appropriate. Bad debt certainly goes up. But so does response. See if one outweighs the other.

12 *Go for extra or bigger sales*
Offer deluxe versions, or even—just like they do by the

check-outs at your local store—tempt with an impulse purchase. . . . even if it's only 'Gift Wrapped' or 'Express Delivery'—both at a good profit for you, of course.

Much better to go for 'real' extras. You'll be surprised how this can bump up order values. An Order Slip is a very 'hot' sales area.

13 *Remember their worries*
Keep on reassuring. This document, at one level or another, is often a commitment from them to you. Repeat any guarantee here, for sure.

14 *Remember the common courtesies*
Say 'Thank You'. Tell them how quickly you will deliver or respond. Ask for their day/early evening phone numbers, if appropriate. And don't abuse this information.

15 *Ask for further information—but not intrusively, or if you've already got a lot*
The name of a friend. A forthcoming or recent address change.

. . . And one final hurdle

That concludes the creative secrets and almost concludes all the essential secrets that I can pack between these covers. However, there remains one last set of secrets that I'd like to reveal. Because, having gone to all this trouble to plan and create your mailing, we now have to produce and get in the post, on time and without errors. It's actually quite a complicated business in one way or another—but we'll do our best to make it as painless as possible. Read on. You are almost there!!

9

Secrets to get your mailing out

You have now arrived at a chapter where my knowledge and the assistance I can give you is to be used in a particular way: that is, to supplement everything you can discover for yourself and to guide and help with the relationships you develop with your collaborators and suppliers. This should assure a greater under-standing of your objectives—not only your practical production objectives, but also your business and campaign objectives.

You should view each of your suppliers' skills, resources and capabilities as a craftsman's tool box. You are the Architect—the visionary; they are the builders. So the first and most important piece of advice I can give you is: show them the 'models, sketches and building plans'.

The successful production of mailings is only partly about the 'bricks and mortar'. It is also about money. And, setting aside the materials, it is about co-operation, communication and team-work.

Direct Mail is complicated. It involves a whole gamut of skills and many technologies: research; copywriting; graphics; photo-graphy and photographic reproduction; typesetting; printing; envelope manufacture; paper manufacture; computer work and data processing; database or list management and broking; ad-dressing; labelling—manual or mechanical; enclosing; postal sorting, and so on.

It's also still a developing industry. Worse than that, it is a very rapidly developing industry. When you are sourcing and buying direct mail services of any sort, you should recognise this as a risk and proceed accordingly.

You must explain your needs in minute detail and allow plenty of time in your schedules to cope with all the awkward formats and processing involved.

MAKING YOUR PLANS

Despite all this talk of technology and pioneering, one part of the production process has remained a stalwart for producers for years. I am referring to an old and tested friend: The Reverse Timetable. I don't know whose idea it was. I do know only that almost everybody uses it. So now we'll run through it together and comment on a few things as we go.

Time—and the management of it—is a perennial problem for anyone organising a mailing. There's never enough of it. And even if you lay your plans well, building in plenty of 'spare' for slippage and proofing and all the other things that cause delay and discussion and rethinking and reorganisation—and often invite unnecessary comment, change and procrastination—it somehow nearly always seems to end up with a breakneck deadline or two for someone or something along the way. It's normally the poor old lettershop at the end of the chain that is left with the daunting task of achieving the impossible. They have a very stressful way of working and living!

There are methods and wrinkles to cope with late mailing panics, yet still maintain a 'landing' or 'drop' date. That's the day(s) you want the mail to be received by the addressees. For example, you could up-grade from second- to first-class mail. Or, in Britain, from Mailsort 3 to one of the discounted standard class services equivalent to first- or second-class mail (Mailsort 1 or 2). There is no problem if the envelopes are going to be stamped or franked. You can even stamp over a previously printed postage mark. It doesn't look so good, but it gets there on time! Failing that, you've a fast label printing job to organise and then arrange to affix them, placing the postal impression label for the newly selected faster service over the impression that was originally printed on the envelope.

THE TRUSTY REVERSE TIMETABLE

It would be very nice to be able to sit down, look at today's date, ring everybody up or have a meeting and then add all the times up and work out when you can get the mail out. Life is all too rarely like that. Nobody wants a potential, or tested and proven, sales boosting idea in three to four months' time. They want it now; or tomorrow; or, failing that, ASAP—which is Adspeak for yesterday! The job of the production team—inside or out—is to do it for you. To achieve the impossible each and every day of their working lives!

Thus we turn conventional time-keeping on its head. And start from the other end.

1 The arrival ('drop' or 'landing') dates

When all is well with the postal service, these dates are fairly predictable.

I'll remind you that business mail is generally best received on a Wednesday, second best Tuesday and Thursday, and worst Monday and Friday. Anyone who mails first class on a Friday is wasting money—unless they want to get to a business that is open on a Saturday or arrive on the worst day of the week.

Consumer best days are Friday and Saturday. The rest of the week is much the same. In terms of months—again with some exceptions—the industry seems agreed that the two best periods of the year are mid-January through to mid-May. And the second week of September through to the first week of December. You will need to overlay onto that your own seasonal aspects.

If you're in mail order, as I commented earlier, short daylight periods or rain, indeed any kind of moderately inclement weather, will help. But just take it as a bonus! There is no need for a hotline to the Met Office. Bank Holiday weekends are something of a problem. Some report excellent results; others catastrophes.

If you are a charity, you will probably already know that Christmas and, in Britain anyway, Easter lift responses. But you need to link, creatively or in theme of appeal, to get the best out of it. This seems to remain the same despite the fact that everyone's doing it. Possibly the sheer weight of fund-raising mail at these peak times has a bludgeoning effect on the marketplace, sufficient to provide the response lift it does, regardless of the fact that the 'kitty' is being shared between so many more.

2   The mailing date

No need to explain this! But what should you have taken care of by the time this all important day arrives?

First you need to have taken care of the postage bill. Let-tershops, unless you have an account with the Post Office, will normally have asked you to pay for the postage in advance. If you haven't, they are perfectly within their rights not to release the mail.

By now your response procedures must be ready to happen, whatever they are. Telesales must be briefed, rehearsed, and standing by. Fulfilment packages must be printed, prepared and ready to go. The analysis procedures must be set up. Samples must have been taken out and placed on file. Advance copies must have been sent to any parties requiring them.

3   Finish enclosing date

My own preference is always to aim to make this at least 24 hours in front of the release date—which effectively should mean, in working-day terms, that it's two days prior to the date of mailing (i.e. mail 25th—finish enclosing by close of play 23rd). If you are using a new supplier or if there's anything tricky or unusual about your requirements, you can avoid potential disaster by visiting the lettershop on the intervening day and taking some random samples from the finished job, just to be doubly safe. I warn you now, nothing creates a faster, deeper sinking feeling or is more stomach-churning for client or supplier than to find a problem at this stage!

4   Enclosing start date

Some time during the 48 hours before this date, you must have gone through the coding details, quantity and counts expected and required. And also by this time have notified the lettershop of any special requirements, such as Stop Lists (those you want taken out at the last minute). This is not always possible to deal with at this stage, and such things are much better dealt with at the time of list preparation.

Often, specials, perhaps for your salesforce or dealers and distributors, are to be included in the mailing. Again, for preference these are better dealt with and inserted into the main listings as a part of the list preparation. But if you want a different letter, or extra or different enclosures inserted, they will need to be kept separate until after enclosing and then merged with the main mailing.

Naturally all your materials will also need to be printed, finished and delivered by this date. If you can arrange for these to be a good 24 hours in advance it will enable the lettershop to check properly that all deliveries are full and complete, perform check counts against delivery notes and assemble and group any variants or segments together. If you have a complicated test structure, allow 48 hours. It is always true that the less time there is, the more errors occur.

The batching and grouping of materials prior to manual or mechanical enclosing is always considerably less risky if codes run throughout the components, enabling the lettershop to check quickly, simply and accurately that given pieces are actually supposed to be with each other and are going into the right envelopes.

Labelling is often carried out in advance of enclosing and if this is the case your label carrier—usually the response coupon, or outer envelope or letter—will be required earlier.

I am a great advocate of pre-production meetings involving as many suppliers as possible, but this cannot always happen. In any case, always make sure that enclosing samples are received from the lettershop for you to check. If you have time, my best advice is to visit them the day before the enclosing starts to 'sign off' an enclosing sample or samples for each and every variant of the mailing. These should be prepared by the lettershop in accordance with their initial written job instructions which, in turn, should be prepared from dummies that you will have sent to them earlier.

It is too late at this stage to be showing them what you want. The method I have suggested actually 'proves' their own internal translation of your dummy and instructions. When sending dummies to them, whether printed, made up from proofs, or 'dummied up' from photocopies of the artwork, always send *two* sets of each variation. Use a highlighter pen to indicate variations and notable codes. The first set should be made up as required but left unsealed. The second set arranged to protrude about half-way out of the envelope and should be stapled through each corner, effectively holding everything in place.

This gives them one sample to play with and examine, and another which demonstrates the precise enclosing order and pattern you want. The stapled sample is free from the hazard of some well-intentioned person trying to 'improve' your wishes or just failing to note every detail exactly as they take apart the sample to see what's what and how it's formed.

At an earlier stage you will have agreed with the lettershop the 'overs' they need. To remove any misunderstandings later, it will pay you to ensure that you have given them clear instructions as to your requirements for any surplus materials prior to the enclosing getting underway.

5   Print completion date(s)

Often printers, realising that the print is moving from one 'trade' shop to another, skimp on the packaging, and because the client will never get to see it, they are rarely found out. To avoid this happening be sure you have given them clear instructions for the packing just as you will have done for the printing. Otherwise to meet the quantities, your mailing house will have to resort to enclosing dog-eared, damaged, torn and crumpled pieces. Badly packed and damaged enclosures may also slow down or make mechanical enclosing impossible, which will result in extra cost and delay.

Your printers should be instructed to supply you with finished samples as soon as they come off the machine so that you can prepare 'live' samples for the lettershop.

And one last thing. Make sure your printers understand what you mean by a completion date. Is it the date you want the printing complete, or the delivery complete? You know what you mean. And, probably, they know what you mean. But the comparison can nearly always buy them a couple of days and nobody quite knows who's to blame—except the lettershop, who receive your 'phone call to ask if they can trim a couple of days. That's the problem with being last in line!!

6   Machine proofing start/finish

Machine proofing is unnecessary for straightforward items or reprints. However, if you have four-colour process items, anything vaguely tricky, different or unusual, be sure to build in both the time and the costs. Duo-tones, for example, can lead to bitter disappointment or outright success. And not much in the middle.

But do understand what this proof stage is about. It is to proof the technical side of the printing and whether the 'process work', the designer's bright ideas, etc., have worked. It is *not* for checking copy or whether the label position fits the envelope window. All these things should have been done long, long ago. Moreover, others such as sponsors, third parties or any colleagues in your own company who see these proofs, should have been made very aware that they cannot make detail changes at this stage.

This means that you must have told them at the artwork approval stage that it was their last chance. Many, on the other hand, seem happy to delegate colour proofing to their agencies or sometimes for expediency to the printers themselves. This I cannot recommend for any reason.

7   Artwork handover date

It really does all have to be 100 per cent by now, which is why I recommend scheduling at least one amendment stage. And although it may have to be used for other things eventually, I propose you should originally schedule two.

8   Second amendment stage

This is essentially a double-checking stage. Nonetheless I propose that you go through an exact repeat of the stage I'm going to describe next. You'll remember that as this is a reverse timetable, it will actually precede!

9   First amendment stage

Allow enough time. Although, naturally, other parties can check the artwork, photocopies are often sufficient. But if it's necessary that they see illustrations you could get colour photocopies rather than risk coffee stains or worse on the originals. I have more than once seen people actually marking comment or opinions on the original drawings!

Don't pass transparencies around; have colour prints made from them, otherwise they'll get scratched, damaged or lost. It is essential for your budget and your sanity that you co-ordinate and merge all the different changes and comments before going back to the studio with them. And if necessary pass these around for confirmation, too. Otherwise, in order to keep to scheduled commitments, you will be tempted or obliged to pass corrections through in waves. It is frustrating and infuriating for the studio to have to reset or layout something that they have just reset and relaid out earlier that day. For you it is expensive. And unnecessary.

Occasionally, you will also find that one person's or department's amendments or changes impact on another's. This is deadly to timing; thus, if you can merge all amendments, gather all those whose approvals are required, and then run through everything with the studio or agency in attendance. This can save a lot of heartache and budget problems.

I would like to add a word of explanation here for those who are surprised to see, at amendment stages, that their agency or copy and art teams want to change things too. 'I paid you to get it right, I didn't expect to get to look at the proofs with *your* amendments marked on it' was a comment once fired at me. Personally, I like to work with people who think while they work. So if when they look over the job they spot mistakes, or want to make some suggestions for making improvements, I think they should be welcomed. More than that, few writers—however good they are— don't pick up work a few days or weeks after they've written it and decide something would be just that bit better if . . . And, I know designers and artists feel the same way.

Things look different typeset as opposed to typewritten. Things look different as artwork than they do as roughs or visuals. Although part of the advertising writer's and designer's task is to be able to envisage the item in print *when it is created*, that is not something one can always do well, even with years of experience.

10   Finished artwork completion date

Make sure in advance whether artwork will be camera-ready or not. If not, your printer or process house will require extra time to make plates. This can also add substantially to the costs. So if the studio have quoted 'camera ready', hold them to it. Which means either they take the job back to finish out or they must meet the charges for doing it.

In order to provide the best finished result, a lot of processes and requirements might be better or more accurately carried out 'on camera'.

11   Finished artwork start date

In the same way that a lettershop will need all the finished print before they can start enclosing into envelopes, so you should work to provide *all* the materials for the studio.

This includes giving them the visual or finished colour rough to work from. They cannot do their job properly without it. If the MD wants it to show the next door neighbour, the sales director wants to show it to the sales managers and one of your third party intermediaries or co-sponsors for another reason, give colour copies, or have slides made for the sales conference. Give the originals back to the studio, and make sure anybody wanting to indicate changes does so on the photocopies, not on the original. Otherwise confusion will abound.

In relation to copy, you should always maintain a master, dated and with an issue number, as you and other parties make changes. Days before handing it over to the studio, circulate the final consolidated clean typescript punctuated and emphasised exactly as you want the set type to be.

Make sure everybody understands that this is their last chance. Be rigid about this and eventually everyone will realise it's for a good reason. Life will instantly become a lot less hassle further on down the production line when time is running out.

12   Copy and visuals completion and production

Don't ever accept original creative work any way other than face-to-face at a meeting or presentation. Don't judge your suppliers' work by committee; endeavour to make their first run through fairly intimate, preferably just you and possibly one other key influence, but no more. In my experience, if you get more, the weaker, less senior or personally insecure individuals will feel the need to criticise to justify their presence at the meeting. The more noise they make and the more problems they can create the more they see themselves demonstrating their need to be involved for the future. And people of this type always prefer their own ideas to everyone else's!!

I once had a client who, when my agency handed over any artwork, attached a sticker to it with no less than 13 spaces for approval signatures. It effectively invited 13 opinions. This happened whether or not the individuals concerned had any need to see, influence over, or responsibility for the creative item. It was crazy; and it cost the company a fortune in time and money. What made it worse was that the boss's position was number 13. So 12 executives used this to demonstrate to their boss their eagle-eye, marketing ability, legal prowess, sales flair and heaven knows what else. You won't need a schedule if you let this happen. You'll need another time round on planet Earth. So keep it down to a minimum. And make sure the most senior people see it first!

13 Creative briefing

In an earlier chapter I have given my own preference for a creative brief. It is wide-ranging in scope, and gives lots of detail.

However in the same way as a meeting is required to *receive* the creative work, I recommend that you organise one to *get it started*. Creatives need to be motivated, enthused and excited. You'll never do that over the phone or in the post. Don't hurry these meetings. Encourage banter, humour and informality. Encourage your agency or studio to involve directly the team who will do the job rather than let an account executive or account manager translate the brief on. It never passes on well.

14   Written brief ready

I said earlier that the brief should be written. It must also be agreed. It will help you to ensure that your brief does not contain any surprises for anyone. My advice is to get a 'sign off' of the brief itself from anyone and everyone who will later sign off copy and visuals or even artwork.

There are lots more production tips and points to come. Many of them to do with scheduling and planning. All of them will help you to stick to a schedule. But none of them, not even all together, will actually enable you to keep to the schedule written on Day 1.

You'll see why this is such an unlikely achievement under the next heading. If you've already faced this task, you'll know how true this is.

Scheduling is a repetitive exercise. You need to keep re-scheduling and re-issuing copies to ALL parties. However, two dates should be treated as sacrosanct from the beginning: the landing date; and the mailing date. In all others, be flexible for your own benefit. Flexible, but strict.

And above all else, encourage teamwork and team spirit. Don't tolerate suppliers jostling with each other to score points. They'll work best for you when they're concentrating on the job, not on poking each other in the eye. And whether you succeed or fail, share the ups and downs with the team. Make them sweat when you sweat. Treat them when you've won.

BE PREPARED

To be prepared, you need to understand what's going to happen. Let me show you, step by step. This is a workflow plan which will give you some idea of all the different stages, steps and pitfalls.

1.0   *Mailing production*
1.1   Preliminary discussion
1.2   Method of approach developed—strategy prepared
1.3   Strategy discussed, amended and approved

1.4   Brief prepared, circulated, discussed, amended and approved

1.5   Briefing meeting—creatives and as many others involved as possible. Discussion to cover all aspects but *must* include budgets and lists/database capabilities and timing

1.6   Mailing concepts developed, formats agreed, outline production specification prepared

1.7   Production specification passed to suppliers for estimating with outline timing requirements

1.8   Estimates received

1.9   Creative concepts reviewed against prices and any discrepancies or specification or cost problems considered and resolved

1.10 First timing schedule issued

1.11 Creative given go ahead

1.12 Copy and visuals presented

1.13 Photocopies and full specification passed to suppliers for submission of first written estimates

1.14 Copy and visuals processed to full approval, materials gathered, studio briefed to proceed to finished artwork

1.15 Schedule reviewed and reissued if appropriate

1.16 List or database specification finalised
       <Go to 2.0 list routine>

1.17 Finished artwork received. Photocopies to all appropriate parties

1.18 Amendments gathered, merged and consolidated

1.19 Final changes and amends recirculated

1.20 Studio briefed for amends. Schedule reviewed and reissued if appropriate

1.21 As 1.17 to 1.20 until approval received from all parties

1.22 *Signed* proofs obtained as appropriate

1.23 Meeting to pass finished artwork for printing. Prices and timing checked and problems resolved

1.24 Revised photocopies, coding instructions and any other 'special treatments' or requirements reinstructed to suppliers

1.25 Process work carried out and completed

1.26 Machine and/or colour proofs prepared, circulated and signed off

1.27 If any amends—review and reissue schedule if appropriate. Postage payment checked

1.28 Final samples prepared for lettershop from machine proofs and or photocopies

1.29 Print complete, finished samples checked and circulated. Lettershop instructions rechecked. Deliveries confirmed. Quantities and coding details reverified. Made-up samples signed off

1.30 Lettershop commenced, mailing dates and response handling details rechecked

1.31 Lettershop complete. Counts completed and checked. Spot check on finished items. Release sanctioned

1.32 Release confirmed. Postal dockets received. Response handling alerted

1.33 Invoices received, verified and passed

1.34 Cost discrepancies analysed and noted

1.35 Guardbook entries, with job history and log entered

1.36 Responses processed. Surplus material arrangements checked and confirmed

1.37 Response pattern logged and reports prepared

1.38 One month from mailing: interim figures reviewed and reports passed

1.39 First debriefing: all suppliers attend—report on response to date and feedback. Financials circulated

1.40 Two months after: final figures reviewed, responses and financials circulated

1.41 Final debriefing with computer analysis and review and reports circulated and discussed

1.42 Nixies dealt with

1.43 Guard book entry finalised

2.0 *Lists/database* <from 1.16>
2.1 List and data specification agreed

2.2   All segmentation, availability, coding and costs drawn up

2.3   List owners circulated with copy and visuals for approval

2.4   List details, segmentation, codings, prices and dates final-
      ised. Addressing or tapes ordered

2.5   If appropriate, mag tape dump and record formats checked.
      Details passed to computer print bureau

2.6   Go ahead to bureau with instructions issued *per tape* includ-
      ing coding details

3.0   *Personalisation/addressing* <from 1.5>

3.1   Requirement feasibility checked and costs estimated

3.2   Bureau confirmed all details of selections, formats, codes,
      mail preference and samples (copies of copy and visuals at
      the least) agreed

3.3   Bureau estimate, timing, provisos received and verified

3.4   List security requirements reviewed and instigated

3.5   Bureau receive copies of finished artwork for addressed/
      personalised items. Production details checked thoroughly

3.6   Format proofs received, reviewed and approved

3.7   Live proofs on actual printed stocks prepared, reviewed and
      approved. Timing checked if amends required

3.8   OK to run

3.9   Run computer, counts and samples provided, checked and
      verified

3.10 Finished production delivered in to lettershop

3.11 Deliveries checked for quality and against quantity counts

Sixty steps to follow. So you see, there's a lot to do. A lot to get
right. Don't let the apparent complexity of the task worry you. It's
a system you need. Once you develop one and you discipline
yourself not to skip the safety steps, you'll find it's all easy and
most of it's fun too!

CHOOSING THE METHODS OF PRINTING

Let's divide this into printing proper—you know, what printers
do!—and computer printing. Conventional printing first.

I don't feel it falls within the remit of this book to turn you into a grade one print expert. And there's no need to. What I would like to do is give you four things to think about.

1   Get to understand your printers' machinery, capabilities and sheet sizes

There's no substitute for stimulating ingenuity, solving problems, and getting value for money—all of which are important factors in the successful realisation of a good mailing. Moreover, an enormous number of the problems that you will face at that tricky Step 1.9 will be solved by knowing precisely what capabilities your printers have.

More important still, you should ensure that whoever is responsible for the concepts and formats of your mailings, *and* whoever is responsible for producing the finished artwork, also get to know your printers just as intimately as I am suggesting you do.

You will quickly get to 'milk' the best combination of value-for-money print and practical creativity (something with which the world is not always overflowing!).

You will know what they can do easily, cheaply and quickly. You will also know what processes need to be 'put out', what folds they can handle quickly, what goes out, and so on.

You will learn all the different suitable permutations available from their machinery. Although I encourage standardisation of sizes (it avoids wastage) as a rule, there are some alternative ways to use flat paper, effectively 'grouping' components out of the same flat sheet rather than printing them separately (see Fig. 9.1). And if you can't avoid wastage, then rather than just cut it off and lose it, see what else can be done. Do you need any compliment slips or memos, or remittance advices?

If not, gum and pad them; or give suitably sized offcuts to local schools or charities—they are always welcome.

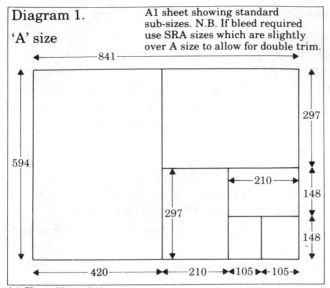

A1 Sheet 594 × 841
All measurements in millimetres.

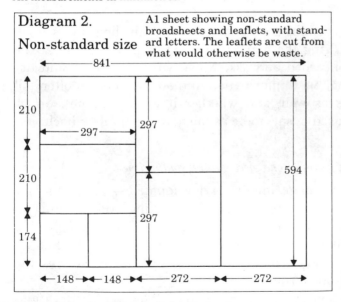

Figure 9.1   Standard and alternative formats

2   Get to know your printers' range of finishing equipment and its capabilities

Again, this also applies to your creative team. If your printers have good contacts with trade finishing houses, visit them and get to know what their capabilities are. Encourage both to keep you up-to-date with the new and different things they're doing. If possible get them to send you samples regularly.

3   Become a sample 'squirrel' and hoard samples

Keep masses of samples—yours and other people's. Examine the mail you get at home and at work. Don't think twice about using other people's good ideas, or at least testing them to see how they work for you.

Go through them from time to time and remind yourself of what can be done. And, most important, encourage others to raid your hoard. Don't let them take the samples away. Only the ideas.

If you see something good and you can't think how it was done, or who did it, ring the marketing team or print buyers at the advertisers concerned and ask. Most will be flattered and delighted to oblige with information and advice. They'll often tell you the snags as well, and whether it worked or not. So be prepared (pleased even!) to be as open and helpful yourself.

4   Discover the world of one-piece mailers and in-line origami

There has been a huge amount of development—principally for longer runs—in the area of reel-fed printing and finishing to produce a mass of different devices that can be folded and glued in a wealth of different formats that will, from one length of paper normally up to about a metre, offer a fascinating and very usable range of all-in-one formats.

There are devices that can be torn down one perforation, releasing separate items—such as a letter, booklet, order coupon and reply envelope. Many of these make excellent inserts and house-to-house pieces since the components do not get separated and lost. Equally, many can be addressed and personalised to provide very low-cost and quite effective direct mail packages.

You'll be amazed at the huge array of capabilities available from scratch 'n' reveal, numbered or adhesive items (stamps, stickers, game pieces, etc.), and little gimmicks and gadgets that modern adhesive technologies and modern paper-processing equipment can provide.

AND THEN THERE'S COMPUTER PRINTING

With some subjects these days, one is hesitant almost to put pen to paper with any positive statement, or place anything on record as fact. The whole database and computer field provokes such feelings. But, there are some basics which it will be helpful for you to know. Let's start with laser printers.

LASER PRINTERS

They are high-resolution (therefore high-quality) printers, relatively cheap in production, and certainly the bigger machines are fast. Importantly, along with ink and bubble jet, they provide the most variable of variable text facilities.

There are principally two kinds of process: 'hot' and 'cold'. They come either as sheet fed or as continuous stationery. The hot process is aptly described since the fusion of the image to the paper takes place under the influence of over 200 degrees Celsius. This has led to some problems, technically speaking, with conventional printing inks and papers but, if in doubt, one can run-on extra proofs prior to printing for a test. With the 'cold' process the fusion is caused chemically.

The laser process uses an electrostatically charged drum which, as it revolves, collects a toner powder as directed by the laser beam. The toner is then transferred to the paper and the image is fixed or 'fused' to the paper. If you think of it as a damned clever photocopier which copies the computer generated 'image' you won't be far off!

Probably the biggest drawback is the limitation in paper stock that can be fed through. Paper and inks need to be tested, but folds, creases or perforations can cause problems.

Sheet fed machines will cope with standard letterheads and also can handle 'duplex' printing where the items are personalised on both sides of the sheet.

DOT-MATRIX PRINTERS

At the time of writing, I generally don't regard dot-matrix printer quality as suitable. This may change with developments. Certainly they are cheap, but the finished print looks it!

DAISYWHEEL PRINTERS

They are slow, and therefore expensive; yet they provide the very highest quality. However, modern laser printing is not far off the quality, with the benefits of speed and price.

IMPACT PRINTERS

In Direct Mail production the day of the impact printer is drawing to a close. Just about the only saving grace is that they are cheap. And quality wise, there are only two things worse. Dot Matrix. And my handwriting.

INK-JET PRINTERS

Ink-jet and laser have for some time been battling for supremacy as the mainline. In the seventies, in-car entertainment was making up its mind between 8-track and cassette. In the eighties, video had VHS and BETA. In direct marketing it's ink-jet versus laser.

Ink-jet gives a lower quality, but the highest speed. And yet ink-jet will probably be the first to bring us colour as an option. The process has already been used to produce full colour out of three, not four colours). And it's impressive.

The process is actually the most definitive and controlled piece of spraying I've ever seen. The ink is literally 'fired' at the paper by an 'ink gun' which is, mercifully, controlled by the computer. So-called 'bubble jet' printers are also available and you may care to examine these for features of compactness and cost.

DIRECT MAIL HAS TO BE CAREFULLY PRODUCED

My experience has been that the production team can, if involved sufficiently, become a vast bank of creative solutions. And this goes for the industry's suppliers too. They are always looking for the next horizon.

My suggestion is to make good friends with the production team. Encourage and support and listen to them. In most cases you or I will be the cause of their headaches and heart attacks. Not the work we give them. But the task we give them.

Here are a few tips to help your jobs go through a little more smoothly . . .

Avoid unnecessary four-colour process demands
Designers are notorious for pushing the aesthetic through, not just in front of the practical or functional, often at the cost of it. Resist this.

Watch particularly for choices of tints and background colours that are difficult and slow for printers to get right. Four-colour processors and printers need to concentrate on getting the people and the products looking good. The flesh tones should not be too pale or blushed. If they're trying to get a delicate and difficult shade of off-pink grey to hold to the match specified as well, you'll end up with a compromise. Encourage your designers, when a complex job comes along, to go to the process house or department and see it through.

Don't let designers force through white-out text in four-colour process areas where the background is busy, varying in contrast, or just not strong enough to 'hold out' the copy. On top of this, they often seem to choose fine, 'thin' typefaces which, with the slightest movement of register, start to fill in and blur.

All of these things—and many more, which are nothing more than designers' whims—simply make reading the copy more difficult. You will have enough trouble getting enough people to read enough of your copy without anyone making it more diffi-cult. I promise! The art team's job is to make it an easier, more desirable thing to do. Making it pretty is going to do some of that; making it pretty difficult is not.

NEVER CHECK ANYTHING

Get out of the habit of checking things. Make your standard double-checking. Involve those who aren't involved. Get their opinions as well as their corrections. I'm sure you have experi-enced the feeling of complete disbelief when somebody points at a wrong word or spelling in something you know you read and checked not once, not twice, but half a dozen times.

You can't do anything about that, your brain is picking up what it knows should be there. But others don't know. They read with a critical innocence you can never have.

These matters are important, not just to get the job right, but also to save lives! The responsibility for artwork being correct always lies with the client—*not* with the studio; *not* with the typesetters; *not* even with the agency. It's down to the client. So if there's a reprint, that's down to the client too. It's a responsibility not to be shirked, made light of or even delegated. And a responsibility that makes double-checking instead of checking well worth while.

Does the response device work?
Does it fit the return envelope and is it as easy as you can possibly

make it to complete? Can recipients clearly see what they have to do to buy or enquire from you? And is it easy for them to do? Always give them plenty of room for their name, address and other details.

When using boxed spaces for the recipient to complete, allow a minimum of 5 mm in box depth—and ideally, 6 or 7 mm. A millimetre is only a small thing, but it can make a big difference to the number of replies.

And does it fit the reply envelope? You might think these little things are too silly to mention in a book. I've seen them all and disagree!

I remember a beautiful example of an A5 (that's half A4) response card, printed on heavy weight board. Together with a D/L (or one third A4) reply paid envelope! And if you think that's bad, how about the really bright insurance company that recently asked me to reply on a standard business reply card . . . and *enclose* a cheque!! Nice one.

Just as bad are the vast numbers—even pros, who should know better—who produce response pieces on high gloss-finish card so that my pentel or biro smudges. And if you think I'm being hypercritical, let me tell you that no one likes to look stupid! So if we smudge or spoil a reply, more often than not we don't bother sending it in. After all, we know you'll mail us again. Mailings are like London buses, aren't they?

A buyer or responder needs to feel safe, relaxed, and in control. That's most of what the need for simplicity and clarity is about. So the next time a studio or agency submits a reply device that gives an applicant an inch and a half to fill in his or her full names, the same for the company name, four inches for the telephone number and another four inches for the postal code, you know what to say!

Make sure everyone is aware of the codes and their meanings

Use scratch coding, it's cheaper than plate changes. Make sure the code only alters in one colour. Make sure that every single piece of the package carries the code. This cuts down the risk of incorrect pieces being included in incorrect packages.

Here is an example of a cheap scratch coding system for the litho printing process. To get ten different codes the printer merely has to stop the machine at the required quantities, and delete one numeral from the plate:

0123456789   Code 9
012345678   Code 8
01234567   Code 7
and so on

The list of typical mistakes is also the list of common mistakes

Perversely, the very qualities that make the best mailings—the human qualities—when turned to the business of production are also the same failings—the human failings—that can cause havoc and cost a fortune! So, if I list a few typical mistakes, you'll probably recognise them as common mistakes.

- spelling errors or literals spotted *after* the job is printed.

- Poor quality print through wrong or badly chosen paper and materials.
- Devices that don't pop-up, appear, release or unfold correctly, because no one made working dummies.
- Mini-cab, bike and courier bills to cover late delivery of proofs, separations or plates (often due to one of the first three above).

Those are the types of mistake I mean. I've no doubt that they will be with us until Lotus come up with a software suite that writes the brief, creates the job, proofs it and produces the mailing for us—on which day they will probably also bring out one that writes books, making the likes of me redundant. And knocking me off my hobby-horse!

But there is still one last piece of advice.

Check through the bills

This procedure is not to check that you've been charged correctly. Hopefully you'll be doing that anyway. It's to draw up a list of expenses incurred over budget—extras, corrections or errors—or to improve quality or pull back lost time.

Don't use this list as the agenda for a mud-slinging meeting with suppliers. Use it as the agenda for 'How can we do it better next time?'

Such meetings tend to start with all the enthusiasm of a new client/agency or supplier relationship, and dwindle to nothing as time passes. Make it a regular procedure and you'll feel the benefit, either because it will start to eradicate the causes, or because the agents and suppliers will eventually run out of excuses.

POSTAL SERVICES FOR THE DIRECT MAILER

This is mainly for British readers. And notice the heading says 'for direct mailers' not direct marketers. That means that I'm going to give you an overview of the services that relate to direct mail not those, for example, to do with the mail order business—such as parcels.

Letter services

You'll need to know what's on offer for your outgoing direct mail. The main letter services are listed below.

FIRST-CLASS POST

In their own sponsored book—the Exley published *Direct Mail Handbook* (see Bibliography)—the Royal Mail bit its lip, crossed its fingers and agreed to leave in my comments about first-class mail. I said that if you use it, you've got to be one of three things: rich, late or crazy! And my view hasn't modified since. There is, however, a discounted equivalent to first-class post which you can read about under the heading 'Mailsort'.

The delivery standard is 'next day', and they aim for 90 per cent delivery within that time.

SECOND-CLASS POST

This is the 'norm' for small quantities and its discounted equivalent, again explained under 'Mailsort', is favourite for picking up time if there's a panic to maintain a landing date. All you have to do is upgrade from Mailsort 3 to Mailsort 2 and then argue about whether it is the client, the agency or the lettershop who pays the extra postage costs!

The delivery standard the Royal Mail looks to provide is 96 per cent on the third day after collection.

MAILSORT

This is a combined 'branding' for three Royal Mail discount services for large users. While the Royal Mail gives you discounts, it makes you earn them. However, with computerisation of lists and the onset of database marketing this is not such a problem. There is firstly a requirement to postcode your addresses, and although they will no longer do the whole job for you as they did in certain cases in the past, they will still offer some help in this direction. It will be worth enquiring, if you are mailing, or thinking about mailing, large quantities. You should enquire through the nearest main Royal Mail office or through one of the 'approved' computer bureaux, many of whom proudly advertise this status in the trade press.

Apart from requiring certain levels of postcoding (which is both understandable and sensible), there is also a requirement with Mailsort to pre-sort the mail into specified areas and 'prepare' the mail in a particular way. This is not the place to go into more detail, but you should note that the requirements are quite demanding.

It is structured in three layers and is available if you are mailing over 4000 letters or 1000 packets in one single dispatch.

- *Mailsort 1* provides first-class delivery standards at discounts currently up to 15 per cent, including the bonus for posting early in the day.
- *Mailsort 2* works to second-class mail delivery standards and offers discounts from 8 to 13 per cent.
- *Mailsort 3* has a delivery standard that is markedly longer—within seven *working* days after posting. So this time must be built in to your Reverse Timetable. However, the discounts are also much greater, offering between 15 and 32 per cent.

Despite its fairly inauspicious first appearance there is an element of rationalisation in the Mailsort scheme and certainly it is far more geared to the future than the schemes that preceded it.

OVERSEAS DIRECT MAIL

As well as paying the full normal tariff for air or surface mail to reach foreign parts, Royal Mail International offers a range of services for the direct marketer. However, those here of particular interest specifically for the direct mailer are *Airstream*, *Printflow* and the *International Business Reply* Service. The latter of which is actually to be found just a little further on under 'Business reply'.

- *Airstream* is a contract facility for those sending large volumes of business airmail. It is available for personalised or other mail.
- *Printflow* is for non-personalised mail, such as mailings, information packs, card-decks and so forth. It offers a choice of speeds and prices to suit your needs.

- Top of the range is *Printflow Air*, being the fastest offering 3 to 5 days for European destinations and 5 to 7 for the rest of the world.
- *Printflow Airsaver*, as its name suggests, is the economy version. It's not available for Europe, but covers 90 countries

elsewhere. Delivery is usually between 14 and 21 days from dispatch.

- *Printflow Surface Saver*, offers you low prices but at the cost of speed. However, for Europe delivery is still only 7 to 14 days. Beyond that, for the rest of the world, it takes up to 12 weeks, so watch those closing dates!

Other services

Now we turn to those all important services to handle the incoming responses. Let's start with the UK.

BUSINESS REPLY

Available as first or second class, the main difference between the two is the readers' perception—that is, their view of how highly you value them and their response. Plus, for you, speed and price.

I believe the perception element is important but in other respects it's a matter of choice; except that is, in lead generation, where the tendency for the first class replies to be delivered with the first class post and at least one day quicker can be very valuable.

Leads cool off from the day the enquiry is posted. Therefore, the faster you can get back to the responder the better. In fact, you can organise with your local Head Royal Mail Office, first delivery service for first and second class response pieces, for a quite moderate fee. Sample business reply designs can be seen in Fig. 9.2.

FREEPOST

Originally Freepost was invented to provide a free (or rather post paid!) service for responders and enquirers to those media where it was difficult (or impossible) to provide a business reply opportunity such as a card or envelope.

That use remains. But it has also been widened to provide an

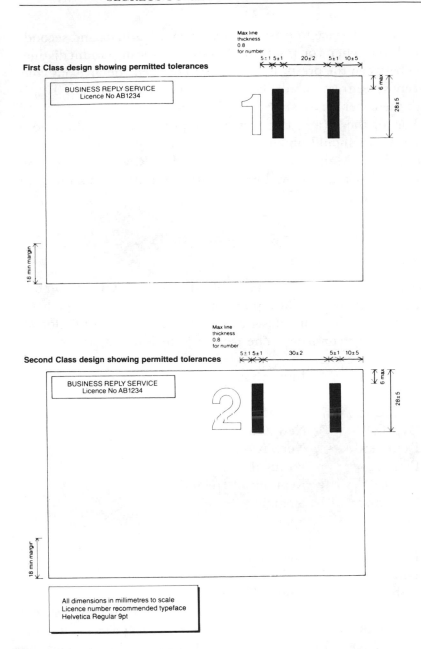

Figure 9.2   Sample Business Reply design (Courtesy of the Royal Mail)

alternative service to Business Reply; again at first- and second-class levels when you pre-print the design. One important distinction between the pre-printed service and when you give out your Freepost address on ads, coupons, labels or the radio or TV, is that the latter service is second class only.

For all these (and the overseas) reply services you'll need a licence and should obtain the design 'patterns' from your local Head Royal Mail Office (see Fig. 9.3). The Royal Mail will also need to check proofs. And watch out! You'll be given a different postal code!

OVERSEAS REPLY SERVICE

The service operates on very similar lines to the UK but on one class of service only. The replies come back to you by Airmail and you can use the same design (and therefore print run!) for all participating countries. The countries included at the time of going to press are:

Australia	Luxembourg
Belgium	Monaco
Bermuda	Netherlands
Cyprus	New Zealand
Denmark	Norway
Finland	Portugal
France	Republic of Ireland
Germany	Singapore
Greece	Spain
Hong Kong	Sweden
Iceland	Switzerland
Israel	United Arab Emirates
Italy	United States of America

It is worth noting that there are other international reply services available these days. TNT, for example, are fast carving a name for themselves with international mail handling for outgoing and response services.

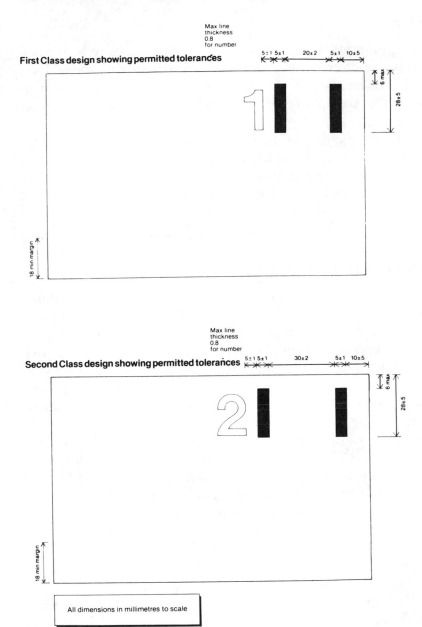

Figure 9.3   Sample Freepost design (Courtesy of the Royal Mail)

ADMAIL

Lastly, in terms of the major response services, there is Admail. This is a re-direction service enabling you to give a local address in advertising of any kind. The replies are re-addressed to you, or the address you specify. Admail can be combined very effectively with Freepost.

Interestingly, I have had some valuable experiences in this particular area, and can tell you that a number of *English* companies and charities have enjoyed substantially better responses in Northern Ireland, Scotland and Wales when a local—as opposed to English—address is used.

FRANK TALK ABOUT STAMPING

There's more choice to stamping a mailing than you might think. You have basically three choices: stamping it, franking it, or pre-printing it. As far as stamping is concerned, experiences vary. In the consumer and business-to-business field, it is often forgotten that while stamping may serve to add the benefit of making your mailing look as though it's not a mailing, it can make people feel that the letter is from a small, insubstantial business. This can be an advantage or a disadvantage.

You can frank your own mail or arrange for the Royal Mail office to do it. They also offer a pre-franking service for bulky items where the address labels or envelopes are franked before enclosing. If you frank your own mail, you can add a message in the space next to the franking mark.

Alternatively, there are a range of designs available. These are called PPIs—Printed Postage Impressions—and are for use with mailings in excess of 4000. There is a leaflet, available from the Royal Mail, which shows the designs, and they will also supply high-quality reproductions from which your studio can 'lift' the reference for artwork. PPI is another facility that requires a licence, and your licensed impression will have a unique serial number which your studio should add to the artwork.

If you are printing or over-printing your envelopes I heartily recommend the use of a **PPI** and, of preference, suggest that the nearer it looks like a classic franking or cancellation, the better.

One particular advantage of a **PPI** is that you will not get an angry letter from anyone whose stamp wasn't stuck on or whose envelope wasn't franked. No one likes to pay the postman for the dubious pleasure of buying something from you. This is particularly true of charity appeals.

. . . and lastly

To close this penultimate chapter, here are some general production wrinkles all wrapped up in the last giant Mailbox . . .

MAILBOX

- Be aware of forthcoming price increases on paper and envelopes. Sometimes it pays to buy early. If you have standard stationery or print items that you use all the year round, try to order them at the same time as ordering items for your direct mail campaign. Volume purchasing can cut costs dramatically.

- Try to make copy timeless. It's expensive to change artwork and printing plates every time you want to mail. Of course, dated material such as closing dates or special offers, etc., are used as a device to increase response, but you should try to use them in situations where they can be changed inexpensively from one mailing to the next—such as adhesive stickers, and letterpress over-prints. They should never appear reversed out of a four-colour process, as one simple date change could involve the cost of four new plates.

- Ensure that reply envelopes or cards meet the postal service requirements. Check that all printing on envelopes is within the Royal Mail regulations. The regulations are there for good reasons. The minimum weight and size ensure that your replies don't get trapped in other's mail or get mangled in franking machines!

- For personalisation the paper must be of the right weight—normally 80/90 g.s.m. Also, it must be delivered several days before it is required to allow time for it to acclimatise or 'cure' in the atmosphere in which it is to be printed.

- If your letter has more than one side, the reverse must be pre-printed unless you are duplex printing. Normally the laser bureau will typeset the reverse side for you to ensure a matched typeface with the personalised side.

- Perforations, gummed stamps and the like, all favourites with the big mailers, must be within certain areas and sizes for the laser process to work properly. These should be carefully checked.

- Because the cost of reel-fed computer printing is often calculated by the metre, length is important. Think about how you use this advice! Remember: the longer the run, the more economical printing becomes!

- If you're using personalisation on more than one piece that will become separated before or during enclosing, make sure that all pieces carry a code number that will enable a visual or mechanical match to be made. It's the only way to be absolutely certain they are twinned correctly in quality control checks or if something gets out of sequence. How can this be done mechanically? With OCR (Optical Character Recognition) equipment or bar codes. Such codes should be in a position that is discreet to the recipient but discernible for the production team.

- Deciding on a format can be a difficult task. Here is a simple routine that will help you decide on number, shape, and size of your components.

1   *What am I trying to achieve?*
   1.1   Why should they want to do it?
   1.2   What will convince them?
   1.3   What will make them do it now?

2   *How can I achieve it?*
   2.1   What is the logic to my sales story?
   2.2   What natural steps or stages does it fall into?
   2.3   How much space will I need?

3   *Are there any practical or functional aspects relevant to the format?*
   3.1   Do I need to get cash back or is the reply sensitive or confidential in any way?
   3.2   Is there any other reason for mailing . . . and, if so, what are the requirements (such as a bonus notice, statement, invoice, membership details, etc.) . . . and can they be used in any way to relate, enclose, or support my primary objective?
   3.3   Is there anything that requires, or is worthy of, particular highlighting or emphasis?
   3.4   Will the recipients need any help handling the documentation? If so, how and where should I give them that help and advice?

4   *Which of the options open to me . . .*
    4.1   will make the most sense if handled as I plan, but still work best if, dropped, misunderstood or mis-handled?
    4.2   will work hardest to dramatise the sales story and be interesting for the reader?
    4.3   will work out best from production, timing and budget points of view?

And then to review your decision . . .

5   *As a cohesive selling machine . . .*
    5.1   Does it work?
    5.2   Is it logical, clear, and simple to assimilate?

And, lastly . . .

6   Is there anything I can do to improve it, to make it more interesting, useful, or simple to handle and respond to?

Remember! It is quite possible that, in achieving many of the above you may fall upon a fairly basic format. There is nothing wrong with that. You can still use materials—paper, texture, and three-dimensional objects—to add an extra lift!

One last secret

And so we arrive at the last chapter! I hope you've enjoyed yourself and found everything you need here to get your mailing planned, created, prepared and finally produced and placed in the hands of the postal service with the very minimum of fuss and worry, and the maximum of effectiveness and success for you and your business.

Although I must confess I'm a little worried! I have a reputation for being thorough (probably often being quite boring about it too!). And, you see, I know there's a lot more I could have told you. But in all honesty, if you want to get a mailing together, I believe the information in this book should enable you to do it.

However, if you should want to know more about direct mail, how to integrate it more fully into your business, or how to master the whole spectrum of direct marketing and bring its remarkable powers into play for the marketing of your business, perhaps I can point out two further opportunities for you.

As you will have realised, this book is an edited version of the original book, *The Secrets of Effective Direct Mail*. The original unexpurgated version is somewhat wider in its scope and more explicit in certain aspects than has been possible here. However 'Secrets' is just one of a comprehensive series of direct marketing books published by McGraw-Hill as The John Fraser-Robinson Direct Marketing Series.

In the series I have pulled together the best talents in the direct marketing business and they have poured out all their knowledge and wisdom, creating, I have to say, some fine works and brilliantly inspiring and valuable books in the process. You'll find, by the time this extensive series is complete, that every facet of the direct marketing business has been examined, described and explained in a way that gives you access to a vast potential treasure chest. As well as direct mail, the subjects cover:

- Telephone marketing
- Direct response marketing
- Database marketing
- Insurance and financial services marketing

and finally,

- TV, radio and electronic media.

WAS THAT THE LAST SECRET?

No! The last secret is this. Before you do anything else, concentrate on getting your lists and other data into the best possible shape. Then and only then can you start to learn as much as possible about all those individuals who are out there. Don't miss out this step for it yields the potential answers to your questions of timing, the offer or proposition (or both) and, of course, the creative approach. And the last secret for you is that this is not only the best order in which to tackle things, but is also my favoured order of priorities as far as investment of time and money is concerned.

My secrets are yours! Use them well and enjoy your success.

Bibliography

Books

Advertiser's Desk Book, Business Publications Ltd, London, 1963

Andrews, Les (ed.), *The Royal Mail Direct Mail Handbook*, 2nd edn, Exley, Watford, 1988

Baier, Martin, *Elements of Direct Marketing*, McGraw-Hill, New York, 1983

Bayan, Richard, *Words That Sell: A Thesaurus to Help Promote Your Products, Services, and Ideas*, Asher-Gallant Press, New York, 1984

Bird, Drayton, *Commonsense Direct Marketing*, The Printed Shop, London, 1982

Brann, Christian, *Cost-effective Direct Marketing by Mail, Telephone and Direct Response Advertising*, Collectors' Books Ltd, Cirencester, 1984

Caples, John, *How to Make Your Advertising Make Money*, Prentice-Hall, New Jersey, 1983

Caples, John, *Tested Advertising Methods* Prentice-Hall, New Jersey, 1974

Cohen, William, *Building a Mail-Order Business*, John Wiley and Sons, New York, 1982

Corby, Michael and Robin Fairlie, *The Mail Users' Handbook, or How to Really Get the Most from your Post*, C. H. W. Roles & Associates Ltd, Kingston-upon-Thames, 1984

Crompton, Alastair, *The Craft of Copywriting*, Business Books Ltd, London, 1979

Davies, John, *The Essential Guide to Database Marketing*, McGraw-Hill, Maidenhead, 1992

Data Protection Act 1984, HMSO, London, 1984

Dillon, John, *Handbook of International Direct Marketing*, McGraw-Hill, Maidenhead, 1976

Dyer, Nigel and Roger Anderson (eds), *Marketing Insurance*, Kluwer, 1986

Effective Ways to Merchandise Advertising, Report no. 19, The Marketing Communications Research Centre, Princeton, 1968

Fairlie, Robin, *Direct Mail: Principles and Practice*, Kogan Page, 1979

Forrester, Martyn, *Everything you always suspected was true about advertising . . . but were too legal, decent and honest to ask*, Roger Houghton, London, 1987

Fraser-Robinson, John, *The Secrets of Effective Direct Mail*, McGraw-Hill, Maidenhead, 1989

Fraser-Robinson, John, *Total Quality Management*, Kogan Page, London, 1991

Goodwin, Leslie, *Direct Mail Databook*, Gower, Aldershot, 1984

Harper, Rose, *Mailing List Strategies: A Guide to Direct Mail Success*, McGraw-Hill, New York, 1986

Hill, Lawson Traphagen, *How to Build a Multi Million Dollar Catalogue Mail Order Business by Someone who Did*, Prentice-Hall, New Jersey, 1984

Hodgeson, Dick, *Direct Mail and Mail Order Handbook*, Dartnell Press, Chicago, 1980

Hoge Sr, Cecil C., *Mail Order Moonlighting*, Business Studies, Inc., New York, 1976

Hopkins, Claude, *Scientific Advertising: The Classic Book on the Fundamentals of Advertising*, MacGibbon & Kee, London, 1968

How to Co-ordinate Industrial Sales and Advertising, Industrial Advertising Research Institute, Princeton, 1958

How to Improve Results from Business Direct Mail. Report No. 14, Marketing Communications Research Centre, Princeton, 1973

Jenkins, Vin, *Direct Mail Advertising in Australia, A Handbook in 6 Volumes*, Australia Post HQ, Victoria, 1981

Jenkins, Vin, *The Concept of Direct Marketing*, Australia Post HQ, Victoria, 1984

Leiderman, Robert, *The Telephone Book*, McGraw-Hill, Maidenhead, 1990

Lewis, Herschell Gordon, *How to Make Your Advertising Twice as Effective at Half the Cost*, Prentice-Hall, New Jersey, 1986

Lewis, Herschell Gordon, *More than you ever wanted to know about Mail Order Advertising*, Prentice-Hall, New Jersey, 1983

Lewis, Herschell Gordon, *Direct Mail Copy that Sells*, Prentice-Hall, New Jersey, 1984

McIntosh, Dorothy and Alastair McIntosh, *Marketing: A Guide for Charities*, The Directory of Social Change, London, 1984

McLean, Ed, *The Business of Copy, A Monograph on Direct Marketing*, Ryan Gilmore, New York, 1977

McLean, Ed, *The Basics of Testing, A Monograph on Direct Marketing*, Ryan Gilmore, New York, 1978

Martin, Tony, *Financial Services Direct Marketing*, McGraw-Hill, Maidenhead, 1991

McCorkell, Graeme, *Advertising that pulls response*, McGraw-Hill, Maidenhead, 1990

Mitchell, Jeremy, *Marketing and the Consumer Movement*, McGraw-Hill, New York, 1978

Montague, Joy, *The A to Z of Shopping by Post*, Exley, Watford, 1979

Myers, James, *Marketing*, McGraw-Hill, New York, 1986

Nash, Edward, *Direct Marketing: Strategy, Planning, Execution*, McGraw-Hill, New York, 1982

Nash, Edward, *The Direct Marketing Handbook*, McGraw-Hill, New York, 1984.

Peacock, J., M. Barnard and C. Berill, *The Print and Production Manual*, Blueprint, London, 1987

Posch, Robert, *The Direct Marketer's Legal Adviser*, McGraw-Hill, New York, 1983

Raphel, Murray and Ken Erdman, *The Do-it-yourself Direct Mail Handbook*, The Marketers Bookshelf, Philadelphia, 1986

Raphel, Murray and Ray Considine, *The Great Brain Robbery*, Business Tips, Pasadena, 1981

Rapp, Stan and Tom Collins, *MaxiMarketing*, McGraw-Hill, New York, 1987

Ries, Al and Jack Trout, *Marketing Warfare*, McGraw-Hill, New York, 1986

Ries, Al and Jack Trout, *Positioning the Battle for your Mind*, McGraw-Hill, New York, 1986

Simon, Julian, *Getting into the Mail Order Business*, McGraw-Hill, New York, 1984

Simon, Julian, *How to Start and Operate a Mail-Order Business*, McGraw-Hill, New York, 1981

Sizer, Richard and Philip Newman, *The Data Protection Act: A practical guide*, Gower, Aldershot, 1984

Stanton, William and Charles Futrell, *Fundamentals of Marketing*, McGraw-Hill, New York, 1987

Stephenson, George, *Graphic Arts Encyclopedia*, McGraw-Hill, New York, 1979

Stone, Bob, *Successful Direct Marketing Methods*, Crain Books, Chicago, 1979

Booklets

31 Tips to Improve Your Order Form, Webcraft, 500 Chesham House, 150 Regent St, London W1R 5FA

Andrews, F., *Fundraising—Marketing for Human Needs* Direct Marketing Association Inc., New York, 1976

Benn's Direct Marketing Services: Industrial Lists Directory 1987, Benn's Business Information Services Ltd, PO Box 20, Sovereign Way, Tonbridge, Kent TN9 1RQ

The British Code of Advertising Practice, 1985, Code of Advertising Practice Committee, Brook House, 2–16 Torrington Place, London WC1E 7HN

The British Code of Sales Promotion Practice, 1986, Code of Advertising Practice Committee, Brook House, 2–16 Torrington Place, London WC1E 7HN

Business/Industrial Direct Marketing: Monograph Vol. 5, Direct Mail/ Marketing Assoc., New York, 1982

Changing the Advertising Budget?, Billet & Co., 55/57 Gt Marlborough St, London W1V 1DD

Code of Practice: covering the use of personal data for advertising and DM purposes, 1987. The Advertising Association, Abford House, 15 Wilton Road, London SW1V 1NJ

Consumer Credit, Report of the Committee (Chairman Lord Crowther), Cmnd 4596, HMSO, London, 1971

The Data Protection Act 1984, Infolink, Coombe Cross, 2–4 South End, Croydon CR9 1DL

The Data Protection Act 1984: Introduction and Guide to the Act, The Data Protection Registrar, Springfield House, Water Lane, Wilmslow, Cheshire SK9 5AX

Direct Marketing Industry Statistics, 1987, British Direct Marketing Assoc., 35 Grosvenor Gardens, London SW1W 0BS

Get Results from your Mailshot, IPCD Direct Mail Services, Quadrant House, The Quadrant, Surrey SM2 5AS

Guideline: Data Protection Act 1984, 1987, The Data Protection Registrar, Springfield House, Water Lane, Wilmslow, Cheshire SK9 5AX (Eight booklets: 1 The Data Protection Registrar; 2 The Definitions; 3 The Register and Registration; 4 The Data Protection Principles; 5 Individual Rights; 6 The Exemptions; 7 Enforcement and Appeals; 8 Summary for Computer Bureaux.)

Henley, Miles, *The Marketer's Guide to Computer Printing*, Christian Brann Ltd, Cirencester, 1985

How to Generate a More Cost Efficient Response from Direct Consumer Marketing, Billett & Co., 56/57 Gt Marlborough St, London W1V 1DD

How to Get your Sums Right: price strategy in direct marketing, British Direct Marketing Assoc., 35 Grosvenor Gardens, London SW1W 0BS

How to Select, Purchase and Use Advertising Premiums Successfully, Innovative Marketing International Ltd, 21 Dorset Sq., London NW1 6QG

How to Work with Mailing Lists, Direct Mail/Marketing Association, Inc., New York, 1976

How to Write Successful Direct Mail Letter Copy, Direct Marketing Association, New York, 1976

Introduction to Fulfilment Operations in Direct Marketing, Monograph Vol. 4, Direct Marketing Association, New York, 1981

The Mail Marketing File, 1982, Mail Marketing (Bristol) Ltd, Springfield House, Mill Ave, Queen Sq., Bristol BS1 4SA

Mail Order Marketing Checklist, 1975, Institute of Practitioners in Advertising, 44 Belgrave Sq., London SW1X 8QS

The Mail Preference Service 1984, Mailing Preference Service, 1 New Burlington St, London W1X 1FD

Mailing Lists: A Practical Guide, Monograph Vol. 8, Direct Marketing Association, New York, 1984

Making the Most of Direct Mail, British Direct Marketing Assoc., 35 Grosvenor Gdns, London SW1W 0BS

Measuring the Effectiveness of Industrial Direct Mail, IARI Report No. 14, 1965, Industrial Advertising Research Inst., 15 Chambers Street, Princeton, New Jersey, USA

The Planner's Guide to Direct Mail, 1984, The Direct Mail Sales Bureau, 12–13 Henrietta St, London WC2E 8BR

Precision Marketing, 1985, Direct Mail Sales Bureau, 14 Floral St, Covent Garden, London WC2E 9RR

Precision Marketing: The Media Perspective, Billet & Co., 55/57 Gt Marlborough St, London W1V 1DD

Pricing Survey 1985, Direct Mail Producers Assoc., 34 Grand Ave, London N10 3BP

Report of the Committee on Data Protection, Cmnd 7341, IIMSO, London, 1978

Sell More!: 101 hints for effective direct mail and higher sales, 1975, Scriptomatic S.A., 35 rue des Jennes, 1211 Geneva 26, Switzerland

The Systems of Control of Advertising Standards: Report of the Committee of Inquiry, 1987, The Advertising Assoc., Abford House, 15 Wilson Rd, London SW1V 1NJ

Typefaces, E. G. Willis & Sons, Willow Street, Chingford, Essex

What People Think about Direct Mail, Direct Mail Advertising
Assoc., 230 Park Ave, New York NY 10017, USA
Working for Customers, 1983, Confederation of British Industry,
Centre Point, 103 New Oxford St, London WC1A 1DU

Royal Mail publications
The following booklets are available, free of charge, from The
Customer Care Unit, Room 141, Post Office Headquarters, 33
Grosvenor Place, London SW1X 1PX

The Guide to Effective Direct Mail (1988)
The Mailsort User's Guide (1988)
The Postcode Portfolio (1988)

Index